FLESH AND BLOOD

FLESH AND BLOOD

A HISTORY OF MY FAMILY
IN SEVEN MALADIES

STEPHEN McGANN

**SIMON &
SCHUSTER**

London · New York · Sydney · Toronto · New Delhi

A CBS COMPANY

First published in Great Britain by Simon & Schuster UK Ltd, 2017
A CBS COMPANY

Copyright © 2017 by Stephen McGann

1 3 5 7 9 10 8 6 4 2

Simon & Schuster UK Ltd
1st Floor
222 Gray's Inn Road
London WC1X 8HB

www.simonandschuster.co.uk
www.simonandschuster.com.au
www.simonandschuster.co.in

Simon & Schuster Australia, Sydney
Simon & Schuster India, New Delhi

A CIP catalogue record for this book
is available from the British Library

Hardback ISBN: 978-1-4711-6079-0
Trade paperback ISBN: 978-1-4711-6397-5
eBook ISBN: 978-1-4711-6080-6

Typeset in the UK by M Rules
Printed and bound by CPI Group (UK) Ltd, Croydon, CR0 4YY

MIX
Paper from
responsible sources
FSC® C020471

Simon & Schuster UK Ltd are committed to sourcing paper
that is made from wood grown in sustainable forests and support the Forest
Stewardship Council, the leading international forest certification organisation.
Our books displaying the FSC logo are printed on FSC certified paper.

To Heidi

CONTENTS

INTRODUCTION

So who are we, finally? What does our little life mean when measured against the vast ocean swells of life and death that come before us, and roll on through the centuries after we're gone? In what ways are we bonded in time to those people who share our surname or our DNA – the people we call our family? Are we simply the sum of the individual properties that describe us, or do our actions and choices in response to life's events form a wider story of kinship and identity?

I think they do. I guess this book is my way of finding out if I'm right.

My name is Stephen McGann. That's what my birth certificate tells me. I was born the fourth son of Joseph McGann and Clare McGann in Liverpool, England, in 1963. I'm fifty-four years old and 180 centimetres tall. My passport photograph reveals dark hair and pale skin. I have a driver's licence listing minor traffic convictions. Classified forms residing on government databases record my religious agnosticism and my declared occupation. I'm an actor – someone whose name might be found in theatrical programme collections or dusty television archives. I married a woman called Heidi Thomas in a church in Liverpool in 1990. Heidi gave birth to our son Dominic in Cambridge in 1996, and my scrawled signature can be seen on his official registration document.

That's me as data. Facts. Knowledge items, preserved in text or image or on hard drive. Features of an individual, rather than an individual's character. It's an X-ray skeleton – essential structure, without the softening subtleties of muscle, vein and flesh. What would someone living 200 years from now be able to learn about me from those facts? Can those items ever coalesce into a recognisable personality – the beat of an embodied soul?

Flesh and Blood is a book about people in my family tree – some still alive, most of them long dead. It's also a book about me (alive, last time I checked). *Flesh and Blood* is a family history that begins at a key point in my family's past – the mid-nineteenth century – and then traces its conflicted progress through the subsequent century and a half to the present day.

It's also, I hope, more than a chronicle – more than simply a sequence of events. I don't believe history is ever just a record of something. I think it's also a drama. History is about how people responded to recorded events and how they were changed by them; how they grew, shrank, laughed, fought, or fell into despair. History isn't politics or power or the cold clash of steel in ancient quarrels. History is people. Through each human action and response to events we tell a mutating story of our mortal selves. And, through the loves and loyalties that bind us as a family, we tell our own small part in the shifting tale of immortal humanity.

I guess it's not difficult for me to reflect on mortality given my current place of residence. You see, I live in a graveyard. Well, not exactly *in* a graveyard, but surrounded by one. My home is a former chapel, and the grounds include the graves of the Victorian parishioners who helped fund and build it. To get to my front door, you take a small tree-dappled path past crooked gravestones, each bearing faded dedications to the people buried there. It's all very picturesque, but not to everyone's taste. The occasional parcel courier takes my signature with startled haste before scarpering back down the path like the fleeing victim in a horror movie. But I love it.

The gravestones are plain, in the nonconformist style. They display simple epitaphs like, 'Thy will be done' or, 'She is not dead but sleepeth'. There's modesty to them – the marking of a life lived but willingly surrendered; a family moved to express love, but not persuaded by the need for excessive detail. The people lying in the ground beneath my courier's fleeing feet seemed to be the recipients of a love that required no hyperbole to make it meaningful. What's left is the minimum testament to a life: the age of the deceased and the names of their remaining close family. Love as data.

Their modesty made me curious to know more about them. When I perused the original deeds to the chapel, I found that many of the same names on those graves were listed there. These people had funded the chapel between themselves although many were simple rural folk: the deed signed with a single 'x' denoting their illiteracy. They were buried together in its vicinity – snuggled in the soil like a single family. These were people who'd built a life out of the strength of a faith they shared, and were happy for their lives to be defined by it. They were also content to suffer their harsher moments with quiet restraint.

Mary Jane Bassett. Died in 1933, aged only three years.

Her tiny grave sits close to our door, warmed by the porch

light. A child's death is the oldest of those answerless questions – an ancient outrage longing for explanation. I wondered if little Mary's life was larger than the miniature plot that now swaddled her, if the unvisited silence of her grave had once been attended by the voices and hands of those who loved her.

Then, one day, a middle-aged lady called by our house. The previous owners had told us she might. Her mother was buried in our garden, and she had attended the chapel as a young girl. She asked if it was possible to continue her occasional visits to tend her mother's grave. We were very pleased to oblige. When the lady saw little Mary's plot, a memory returned. She recalled her mother speaking of this girl, and of her moving funeral. She said that the other children of the chapel had carried Mary's tiny coffin on their little shoulders to its final resting place.

I loved that. A single beautiful scene. History as drama. A child so loved and cherished she was carried to her grave by her fellow innocents. Mary's face had suddenly been summoned into the porch light of a narrated memory. She breathed again. She lived.

Who was Mary, finally? She was a story woven by those who still carried her memory through time. By hearing this story, and now relating it to you, I've taken my place as one of Mary's bearers. And so she lives on, carried by us all in this tiny story fragment. The lesson of little Mary is that we are only recorded data in the absence of a better insight. We are always more. Always more human. Always more meaningful than facts. Data is just the starting place. The beginning of the journey, not its end. We are a story, not a stone.

And so it is with my family in this book. *Flesh and Blood* is a book about relatives to whom things happened, but also not really a book about those things. It's more about the way those people responded to events that afflicted them, and how those responses came to define the people they were, and the lives of the family that succeeded them. To tell this story, I've combined three separate lifelong preoccupations. First is my interest in genealogy – the study of my family history through the public records. The second is my life spent as an actor portraying the mechanics of human motivation in drama. The third is my academic interest in the relationship between medical health and the complex society that it helps to sustain. This book is therefore a single family's story refracted into three primary colours of experience: health, family history and the drama of human testimony.

I first started tracing my family tree when I was seventeen – a gauche teenager on the cusp of an adulthood I didn't yet understand. My search for a wider context to my life made me curious about the people who'd come before me – the McGann family, the ones who'd given me my surname. Who were they? What did they do with their lives, and how did that end up with me? I knew nothing about them, and my father knew very little more than I did. His dad had died when he was just five years old, and the children who remained were left with only second-hand scraps of stories from their mother. McGann was an Irish name, and Liverpool, I knew, was a famous embarkation point for Irish emigration to the United States in the nineteenth century. I assumed they were Irish, but didn't know for sure. So one day I plucked up courage and ventured into my local records office in Liverpool to see if I could find out. I began, piece by piece, to build up a data skeleton of my ancestry from records held in our public archives. It was the beginning of a genealogical journey that has taken me my entire life, and is still a work in progress.

Like with those graveyard parishioners, I wanted to know more about the people I'd found as *people*. What did they think and feel? Why did they do the things that history recorded? To do that I had to turn the bare bones of history into a living narrative. I had to turn data into drama.

The famous drama theorist Konstantin Stanislavsky believed that there was a strong link between representations of human relationships in drama and the way that humans behaved in real life. Drama is an ancient way for us to understand who we are by projecting human experiences onto dramatic characters in a story. A good story isn't just defined by stuff that happens – illness, murder, flood, famine – but by the desires and emotions of the characters that initiate and respond to those things, and then make key choices based on those responses. Stanislavsky said: 'Real life, like life on the stage, is made up of continuously arising desires, aspirations, inner challenges to action and their consummation in internal and external actions.' Our real life is a constant state of responding to things that happen to us – to challenges we face or the wants we feel – and then taking actions. Events aren't drama; they're just the 'challenges to action' – the antagonist in a hero's journey. The drama is in what we do about it, and who we become as a result.

All genealogy is drama in disguise. Disguise, because human motivation doesn't show up amongst the X-ray bones of recorded facts. Drama, because history is the exploration of humanity in response to internal or external events. To bring a human's data to life we have to find those things that motivated their actions.

Yet in order to identify the source of their motivations, we also have to identify the antagonist that drove them to act.

Antagonist: one who opposes the hero in a story. An adversary. An enemy, but not always a person. Sometimes an affliction. Sometimes an emotion. Sometimes an enemy within, not without. So who was this adversary in the saga of my own family? Was there any single force that – more than any other – pushed and challenged and harried my ancestors to move and change their lives, to grow or shrink as people? I think there was. As I discovered more about my family over the years, I found the fingerprints of this particular felon all over the historical documents in my possession. I came to the conclusion that no story concerning my kin would be complete without reference to the constant villain that stalked them, and by whose challenges they were constantly tested and defined. That villain was not human, yet belonged totally to humanity. It was the shadow thrown by our mortality – the dark twin that we all carry through our lives on earth. Teaching us. Taunting us. The furnace in which we're incinerated, or from which we emerge newly forged. That antagonist is health.

Human health haunts all genealogy. It's there at the recorded birth with the ancient perils of labour and its resultant high mortality. It's there on every death certificate as medical terminology, coldly documenting the causes of expiry. It stalks a soldier's military record. It stares mute from every census form recording the hovels of a city and its inhabitants. It squats in the columns of Victorian newspapers and in the public records of local authorities. Poor health is the shadow that our ancestors cast onto the lives of their descendants – a lesson from history, and an indication of our progress: the wintry fever that drives our own green age but ultimately extinguishes it.

Health can't be untangled from the family that experiences it. An illness is never a singular medical event – never just the clawed breath in a single chest. It's the collective hope of the sanatorium ward, the enforced bonhomie of an anxious family at the bed of a patient, the tears of a lover for their ailing partner. Health is a human force: a motivator for wider human drama. It has the power to change our identities, mould our characters and the nature of our relationships.

In fact, so deep and complex is the relationship between humans and their health that the metaphors we use to describe our reality are peppered with references to healthiness, vitality or wellbeing – and their opposites: sickness, malady and death. We describe relationships as 'healthy', or love as 'sickness'; we describe an economy as 'in robust health', or a terrorist ideology as 'a cancer'. We give health a metaphorical altitude to correspond to human mood, like when we describe someone as being at the 'peak' of health, or 'laid low' by disease. Illness can assume metaphors far beyond the inanimate – as when cancer is 'the enemy', or when cold and fever become things we must 'feed' or 'starve'. In this way, health shows itself as sentient: a character in the drama of our lives. An antagonist, not just a diagnosis – as meaningful to our happiness as our own family.

As I looked back over my family tree, I started to see this character again and again, influencing every twist and turn of fate and choice that my forebears made on their way to the present day. Not simply in the terse death-certificate Latin of medical cause, but in the wider context of their social privations and their thwarted prosperity. I spied this character hiding in my family's embattled courage, in their religious consolation or their hard-bitten hopes. It was the antagonist that pushed, pressed and harried them into a constant restless action through time – an enforced growth that required them to bloom or perish. I realised that the story I wanted to tell was a family history of health – the story of my family's relationship with wellness and disease in the last 150 years, and how it had made us who we are now.

Health presents many faces to human experience – some physical, some metaphorical, but never simply medical. I felt another word was needed – a word that could give health a more motivational breadth. The word that suggested itself was 'malady'. A malady is more than just an illness. It suggests a wider disorder – one that can be ascribed to a situation as well as an individual. It can describe the spiritual distemper of nations, of families, or the self. It's a flaw of human character as well as of human physiology. A malady is a disturbance of the norm, a state that offers a narrative turning point and a crossroads on the road of life. The story of my family is a story of maladies: confronted, conquered, surrendered to.

This book is a history of my family in seven maladies – each malady a particular chapter in my family's story. These maladies are hunger, pestilence, exposure, trauma, breathlessness, heart trouble and necrosis – seven maladies for seven ages of growth that have taken my penniless clan from their blighted Irish potato fields to our relative comfort as British media professionals in the space of a century and a half. These maladies aren't confined to an explanation of medical illness, but embrace wider human emotions and endeavour, often more positive and motivational. They're the teachers, life companions and crossroads in a story. Each chapter has three interconnecting elements addressing each malady: a medical exploration of the disease or ailment, an account of a period in my family's history connected with it, and the personal testimony of people in my family that this malady influenced.

Although these seven maladies map broad periods of consecutive history, the testimony within them makes departures from strict chronology. Human experience has a natural resistance to being defined linearly. We edit our lives constantly – jumble the pieces round until they mean what we need them to. We order life by significance, not by date. We piece together what we know of our forebears and fuse it with what see of ourselves: what we need to feel or hear. We drop the incidental or the mundane, and select from the collage of oral rumour, faded images, scavenged text, terse documents, hidden feelings and unspoken pains. We search for sense, for a lesson in the love given or the blood spilt by those who went before us.

Humans live as long as the stories they tell about each other. A family history is the greatest and most intimate of these mythologies. It's the flesh and blood hanging on the lifeless skeleton of time. The immortal aspect of our mortal selves. A love poem to our own quiet creators, and a parting song to those who follow – those loving infants who will one day carry us to our graves.

1

HUNGER

Hunger n.

1. A very great need for food, or a severe lack of it.
2. A strong desire for something.

MEDICINE

The human body is a remarkable family of processes. Like any good family, it can unite in a crisis, organising itself with remarkable sophistication when faced with unexpected privation. Like the best families, it will sacrifice all it can to preserve the most valuable parts of itself. Yet there are limits to its ingenuity. Essential needs can't be deferred forever. A body and its mind must eventually be supplied with the things it can't do without. Starved of the essentials, even the most resilient family must eventually perish.

Human starvation is not a singular event, but a process – a ticking clock that begins only hours after the last morsel's been consumed. It's the body's management of a slowly mounting crisis, against which strategies are adopted and altered according to the length of time malnourished, and the changing priorities this entails. The body's response to hunger is to buy time by managing energy resources, trusting in the mind's ability to relieve the body's siege with new sustenance. It is, like humanity itself, fundamentally optimistic.

Food gives the human body two basic things: essential nutrients, like protein, vitamins and minerals, and energy, in the form of calories. Remove specific nutrients and we can quickly succumb to disease. Yet remove the energy to power our brains and bodies, and soon there won't be any system left to suffer. Preservation of energy is therefore the most pressing of our hungry body's needs.

In the first six hours after consuming food, everything is normal. The body digests what we've eaten and breaks down glycogen – molecules in the food that store energy – to make glucose. Glucose is our body's normal fuel supply. It's stored in the liver and muscles, and is used to power our cells and brain. In well-fed mode, the brain will consume a full quarter of our total energy requirements.

About six hours after eating, the supply of glucose in the liver becomes depleted, and we start to feel hungry. The body shifts into a new energy mode called ketosis. In ketosis, our body makes alternative fuel by breaking down spare fat to release energy. The brain gets priority on the remaining glucose, and supplements this with the products of ketosis. If no other food is forthcoming, the body can continue in this new mode for several weeks. After this point, however, all the glucose supplies are gone and the brain urgently needs more. The body shifts mode again – this time breaking down the protein in our muscles and tissue to make amino acids, which the liver then converts to glucose. So our brain gets its fuel back. Problem solved.

Except it isn't. This phase is called autophagy. A polite term for self-cannibalism. The body is now eating itself for fuel. Our metabolic system does this cleverly – identifying the body mass that can be consumed, and that which must be preserved at all costs so our bodies can find new food. Yet it's a temporary fix. Without food the body will eventually run out of things it can burn. In this state of serious starvation the immune system becomes compromised. The places where famine occurs are often those where tropical disease is rife and hygiene difficult to maintain, so hunger can quickly lead to deadly infection.

Dysentery is an intestinal infection with two causes – bacillary dysentery, which is bacterial, and amoebic dysentery, caused by a single-celled parasite. Both kinds are highly infectious, and spread by transmission of infected faeces on hands or in contaminated water due to insanitary conditions. Symptoms include vomiting, cramps and bloody diarrhoea – a painful inconvenience to a healthy westerner, but a disaster to a starving and dehydrated child with no access to medical aid.

Then there are diseases like beriberi, which spring directly from deficiencies in the famine victim's diet. Beriberi is a disease that results from a lack of vitamin B1 or thiamine. There are two kinds: there is wet beriberi, which affects the heart and lungs, and dry beriberi, which attacks the nervous system. The former can lead to heart failure, while the latter damages nerves, reduces sensation and muscle control, and induces paralysis. Interestingly, it can be more prevalent in cultures where diets are dominated by white rather than brown rice, as the white variety lacks the thiamine content of rice bran. This contributed to widespread incidences of beriberi amongst prisoners of the

Japanese in the Second World War, where meagre starvation diets consisted almost entirely of white rice.

Towards the end of sustained starvation, two diseases in particular come to the fore: kwashiorkor and marasmus.

Kwashiorkor is caused by a severe lack of protein, and its most infamous symptom is the swollen belly seen on many starving children during famine, caused by too much fluid in body tissue. Marasmus is a condition brought about by a desperate lack of calorific energy, and it most often occurs in the young. Marasmus is characterised by dizziness, diarrhoea, loss of bladder control, and a creeping lethargy that takes life like the fading of a torch battery. When death finally comes it's most often by cardiac failure – the depleted heart is no longer able to find the strength to beat.

Hunger is one of the oldest maladies to antagonise the human race. Unlike other ailments, its pathology is clearly understood, and the cure to it – adequate food – is in plentiful global supply. Yet hunger continues to ravage the planet. Just under 800 million people in the world today receive insufficient food to lead a healthy life. About one in every nine people on earth. As the earth warms due to climate change, accelerating drought is predicted to increase the prevalence of serious famine due to crop failure, threatening the lives of many millions more.

Yet a human's response to hunger, and the reasons for it, can be as individual as their humanity. An unforgettable image of my teenage years was Republican prisoners on the evening news in 1981 wasting away in Northern Ireland's Maze prison. Ten of these protestors survived for between forty-six and seventy-two days without food – two and a half months without a scrap to eat. In 1943, Mahatma Gandhi – stick-thin and in his seventies – successfully completed three weeks of fasting in one of many political hunger protests. However, when a patient in a persistent vegetative state is denied all sustenance, death usually occurs within just two weeks. Why the variation? The main factor is water. If a person can remain fully hydrated, it's possible to survive months of starvation. This can be stretched to years by even small amounts of food, as was demonstrated by survivors of prison camps in the Second World War. Greater body weight can help too, as fat reserves provide essential energy. Genetic factors also seem to play a part. A 2008 study found evidence that a population exposed to starvation could pass key genetic changes onto subsequent generations. Scientists examined babies born to mothers in the Netherlands during the war-induced famine of 1944. They discovered that the genes of these children were permanently changed by the famine their mothers had endured. They tended to be smaller in size, and more prone to diabetes. What's more, it appeared that their own children inherited these traits. Recent studies on nematode worms suggest that starvation can produce multi-generational effects on DNA. Less a case of 'the sins of the father' than the pangs of the mother.

Then there's individual psychology. Hunger is an assault on the mind as well as the body. How much does the *choice* to be hungry, as in the case of the hunger strikers, affect the ability to withstand its effects, as compared to those whom hunger attacks uninvited? And how much does our own personal will, past experience and character affect the ability of our bodies to survive?

The psychological dimensions of hunger are as subtle and

profound as those of the body. In 1950, the University of Minnesota published a famous study on the behavioural effects of starvation. The experiment took thirty-six young, healthy and psychologically sound men and observed what happened to them when they had their calorific input reduced to the point of semi-starvation for a period of six months. It's known in academic circles as 'the starvation study'.

The study saw profound effects on these subjects – not simply in physical decay, but in behaviour, attitude and virility. The men became preoccupied with food: how to get it, how to eat it, even how to prepare it. When they got it they would often binge on the little that was theirs, losing all self-control. The study also noticed wild mood swings in the subjects, and a 'deep dark depression'. There were emotional impacts. The more gregarious subjects became progressively more passive and isolated. Humour diminished, and any interest in sex disappeared. One subject stated bluntly, with an interesting side-reference to seafood, that he had 'no more sexual feeling than a sick oyster'. The study exposed a wicked truth concealed within the wider malady of hunger – that the physical want of our bodies echoes in the outlook of our minds.

There are delicate behavioural echoes to be found in even the mildest hungers. A 2013 study at Cornell University in the United States found that if a subject shopped for food when hungry, they were more likely to stock their trolley with high-calorie products. It seems pretty intuitive – if you're hungry you want more food. But the study went further than this. Hunger doesn't just make you want food: it can affect *what* food you want. It can change the way that you think – the choices you make.

Our free will is like a child in the company of ancient needs. We're not just hungry, we're hungry *for* something. It's a directed desire – a desire whose trajectory can be steered by the privations of the body.

A focused hunger.

HISTORY

The Arrivals: The McGann family, 1840–1871

A death certificate dated 5 March 1868. Address: 31 Sherwood Street in the sub-district of St Martin, Liverpool. A child, Teresa McGann, daughter of Owen McGann and Susan McGann. Pronounced dead. Mother present. Age, one year old. Recorded by Robert McLelland, Registrar. Cause of death: Marasmus. A condition of extreme malnutrition occurring chiefly in young children.

Starvation.

Outside, barely a minute's walk from the filthy hovel in which Susan McGann watches her infant waste away is the largest continuous stretch of dockland in the world. Through this vast commercial gateway flow the goods and wealth of a global empire. Food from five continents fills the great brick warehouses nearby, throwing their huge shadows across the teeming dockyards and the stinking slums beneath. Outrageous plenty. Close enough to touch, yet unimaginably distant for those in its filthy shade.

Teresa McGann. Death by starvation in a land of plenty. Present at death: Susan McGann. Her mother. My great-great-grandmother.

I stop for a moment to reflect on that human scene playing out beneath the facts of the document. A mother watches her own child starve to death in a filthy hovel. A child she'd baptised, with all the hope inherent in the act. The mother's helpless to keep her child from dying. She has older children who are likely present in the same tiny room, and equally malnourished. She's hungry herself. Hunger is ever-present. A constant lodger.

And yet she continues. Susan lived for many years after this terrible scene. How does she cope with what she witnesses? How does she rise the next day and go on, like the records tell me she did? I think about my own son – his Mediterranean diet, his fine physique and his good health. I imagine him starving in my arms while I look on helplessly. I expel the image from my mind.

In September of 1866, the same registrar had recorded

Teresa's birth at the same address. Mother Susan had signed the baby's birth certificate with a simple 'x'. She was illiterate in the language of her daughter's country, but fluent in the universal language of hope. A new child, a new future. Yet in 1865, just a year before Teresa's birth, I found another death certificate. Teresa's sister, Susan. Named after her mother. Dead at just nine months old. Cause: Marasmus. Starvation. This was the second daughter Susan McGann had lost to hunger in just fourteen months.

What did this hunger do to Susan, that she could keep placing one foot in front of the other? How did any of my family survive the year – let alone a century and a half? Where did these McGanns come from, and how did they end up in this Liverpool dockland slum? How did the hunger that now consumed them come to change the way they thought, the places they travelled, and the choices they made?

The answer to all of this begins a couple of decades before this child's premature death. And it turns on the fortunes of a single lowly vegetable.

* * *

Genealogy is a rather upside-down form of storytelling. You start with what's effectively the ending – the present day. That's the most complete chapter; one in which the main players are, helpfully, still alive to contribute. The task is then to work in reverse to flesh out the earlier chapters, generation by generation, digging backwards through the records like a miner with a pickaxe, searching for that crucial starting place: the defining rich seam for everything that followed. Chapter one. A family's creation myth.

Like mining, it's hard, slow work. And the problem is that it's hard to know when you've reached the end – or, in this case, the beginning. Any genealogist worth their salt will try to push back as far in time as they can – back and back through the generations until the available records peter out, and you're left with little more than intelligent guesswork and a few rough clues in some field name or ancient land taxation document. This means that the chronological beginning of any family's story is usually the most vaguely formed: hardly the most compelling way to begin a narrative. 'Once upon a time, I think there might have been some guy who may have lived here at some point . . .'

That said, it helps if you can at least start with a broad defining aim: a milestone in time that provides a focus for your family's history research. In the case of the McGann family, one presented itself to me quite quickly. The name McGann is of Irish origin – a variation of the old clan name Mac Cana, meaning 'son of the wolf'. Liverpool, the city where I was born and where my family had lived for generations, experienced a huge influx of Irish in the nineteenth century as part of their mass emigration to the New World. They brought their Roman Catholicism with them – a religion that had been part of my family for as far back as anyone could remember. It seemed likely that the McGanns were a part of this great Irish diaspora. It only remained for me to find the evidence.

Only? Bless my youth! I was just a spotty seventeen-year-old when I started, and prone to bouts of romantic optimism. A family historian begins by gathering all of the family stories they can from those who are still alive to give it: anecdotes, names, rumours, illnesses, births, deaths, joys, tragedies. Even though elderly human memory can be unreliable, the living accounts of those who remember places and faces from years ago are the richest source of genealogical information. The first task is to commit these to record before they're lost for good.

I immediately hit a snag with Dad's family. There were three surviving siblings in middle age: Mary, Jimmy and my father Joe. My paternal grandmother Lizzie had died when I was nine. Her husband, Owen Joseph, had died in 1929, when my dad was just five years old. There were no other surviving McGanns we knew of. No distant aunts or uncles – only vague scraps gleaned from when Dad's generation were young children. Also, there was no knowledge of Irish heritage in the family. Nothing at all. Scottish? Plenty. But that was from my gran's side of the family. They were textile weavers from Paisley who'd settled in Liverpool at the end of the nineteenth century. Yet not a thing from the Irish McGanns. Only that they'd lived up in the poor north end of Liverpool, in those narrow streets that nestled beside the docks.

Spotty and unbowed, I resolved to find proof of my family's Irish roots, and trace them back to the specific town or village in Ireland where they came from. My own origin story. I imagined myself pacing grandly into some windswept Irish village to announce my family's prodigal return, enfolded in the welcoming arms of raven-haired colleens. Unsurprisingly, reality was a little less accommodating. I spent most of the subsequent thirty-five years or so searching, without success. Then, just two years ago, I stumbled on it.

Tibohine. County Roscommon, Ireland.

* * *

The tiny settlement of Tibohine sits on the road between Ballaghaderreen and Frenchpark in the northwest of County Roscommon, near the border with Mayo and Sligo in Ireland's lake-strewn mid-west. It's a rural region of sparse, rugged beauty, bounded by the River Shannon to the north and over-looked by the ancient Fairymount Hill to the south: the tallest spot in Roscommon and site of a Neolithic hill fort. It's the kind of place where time stands still, unless provoked.

Unfortunately, such provocations are a periodic feature of Irish history. One of St Patrick's bishops had reputedly founded a religious settlement there in the Middle Ages, but it became the feudal property of the Protestant English De Fresne family after Cromwell's ravages. Following Catholic emancipation in 1829, a little parish church had been established in Tibohine – and into this poured the burgeoning mass of Catholic rural peasantry: to baptise their children, to sanctify their marriages, to lay their dead in the ground. It was the endless rhythm of life that had characterised this blameless corner of Ireland for centuries.

The parish register of births for Tibohine in 1859 is a veritable crowded room of a document – hurried ink mottled with blots on unlined paper. It takes a few moments for the eyes to settle, and for names to begin to crystallise in the chaotic cursive. But there, under the entries for baptisms on 3 June, is a child. Eugenius (Owen) McGann. Son of Owen McGann and Susan McCarthy. My great-grandfather Eugene. A witness too – Teresa McGann – after whom our poor child in the Liverpool slum was likely named. A single flash of history's camera.

I found the baby's father, Susan's husband Owen, in the baptism records for nearby Croghan for 7 March 1819: his father was James McGann, and his mother was Elizabeth Fitzpatrick. The lives of his parents stretched back into the late eighteenth century. This was a family that had likely inhabited the same landscape for generations. Yet it was a family now on the cusp of traumatic upheaval.

Successive conquests, land confiscations, rebellions and punitive laws had turned rural Ireland into a population flirting constantly with disaster. One of the most pernicious causes of this was the system of land ownership. During the 1700s, absentee English landlords leased large tracts of rural land to middlemen, who then sub-let as they pleased for profit. This encouraged widespread exploitation of the most vulnerable tenants, with land being split into ever smaller and less sustainable plots. Added to this were the draconian laws of tenancy. A tenant could be evicted on a whim, with no rights over the land they'd rented. Any improvements a tenant may have made to a plot or its dwelling would immediately belong to the landlord – so there was no incentive to improve one's life or situation. Land was often of poor quality – boggy and infertile – making it difficult for a tenant to grow the cereal crops common in England. Then there were the extortionate rents charged by the middlemen, leaving very little for a poor tenant after the crop had been harvested. But without any form of welfare apart from the dreaded workhouse, families were forced to accept these terms.

Most wicked of all perhaps was the common form of rent bondage known as the 'Hanging Gale' – the 'gale' being a regular rent due on the land. By 'hanging over' this rent in a constant state of arrears a tenant was trapped in rolling debt to the landlord without any security whatsoever. It was this perpetual condition of fear and insecurity that was to create one of the most destitute peasant classes in Europe – a class to which my Tibohine ancestors belonged. Infant mortality occurred in a fifth of all births, and only 34 per cent of the population was literate.

And yet they survived. Not only that, but Ireland's population was actually booming. In a mere fifty years, it had more than doubled. What was holding this rotten system together? How was the peasant population able to survive and thrive year after year under such impossible economic conditions?

The answer lay, surprisingly, with the humble potato.

The potato was introduced to Ireland in 1590, and quickly became a vital staple for the rural Irish. It was extremely easy to grow, requiring only a spade and some primitive digging. It could grow in extremely poor soil, and came packed with essential vitamins. Also, it provided an incredibly high yield; just an acre and a half of potatoes could feed a family of six for half a year, whereas grain for the same family would require six times as much land and need greater agricultural skill. A third of the potato crop could even be spared to feed a pig, which provided much-needed extra income. This was a true superfood.

Yet the reliance on this single vegetable for a nation's survival was precarious to say the least. The potato crop was prone to regular failure, which threatened starvation for those most reliant on it. There had been famines in 1816, 1822, 1826 and 1831, causing localised deaths and fever. Even in the good years, the months before an annual harvest were known as the 'summer hunger' – when last year's stock ran out, and a family were forced to beg for food until the new crop came in. This was a population only ever one step from starvation. Susan, who would later watch little Teresa die from hunger in Liverpool, had been weaned on malnutrition like mother's milk.

As the sub-divisions of peasant land became increasingly mean and unsustainable, a less nutritious but much hardier variety of animal-feed potato became the new staple. It was called the 'horse potato' or 'lumper'. This could grow in the very poorest soil – making it ideal for the rough terrain families were now forced to inhabit – and it was resistant to common diseases. Yet it had one fatal flaw. It was highly vulnerable to an as-yet little-known fungal disease from the Americas called *Phytophthora infestans*. Potato blight.

Potato blight is a fungal organism that spreads in spores carried on the wind, and it thrives during periods of damp, humid weather. It starts as small black spots on the leaves of the potato and then spreads into large brown lesions, some with a downy growth. These produce thousands of new airborne spores that spread the infection widely. As the plant shrivels and dies, the spores penetrate the ground and infect the tubers. The diseased potatoes then become a cankerous brown and collapse into indigestible rot. Worse still, the fungus hides over the winter in the seed potatoes that remain, waiting to strike again when the weather warms and new planting begins. Blight had spread to Europe in 1845, devastating potato crops and causing many deaths in Germany, France and the Netherlands. Yet these nations didn't depend entirely on the potato for their dietary survival . . .

In September of that year, blight finally arrived in Ireland from mainland Europe. What happened next was to be one of history's great humanitarian disasters: a famine so profound that it would drive a nation's people across every ocean in the world for the meagre chance of finding something more digestible than the hell they'd known. My family were amongst them.

* * *

The Great Famine in Ireland lasted from 1845 to 1852. It involved the catastrophic collapse of the nation's potato crop for consecutive seasons due to potato blight. It caused starvation, destitution and death on an enormous scale. It destroyed the economy, obliterated the population, and set the nation on an inevitable course towards rebellion and ultimate independence from Great Britain. It changed everything.

The McGann family survived, as that baptism in 1859 shows. But how many of them? The records don't reveal. Roscommon lost a third of its population – the highest proportion of any Irish county. In the first outbreak of famine in 1846, the north Roscommon area where the McGanns lived quickly began to suffer hardship. A Quaker from Liverpool called Joseph Crosfield passed through the area in December, and commented on the state of the people he saw:

> Many of them declare that they have not tasted food of any kind for forty-eight hours; and numbers of them have eaten nothing but cabbage or turnips for days and weeks.

Such scraps of food would soon be considered a luxury. As the famine worsened, the desperate would turn to nettles, berries, dandelions and plant roots. Dogs, cats and horses quickly disappeared, then wild animals such as foxes and badgers. Cattle would be bled for the nourishment that could be gained from a few pints of their blood. By 1847, the second year of famine, there would be nowhere left to turn.

Before the famine, 60,000 acres of potatoes were planted in Roscommon County. Yet as blight killed off the seed potatoes, there were fewer left to plant. By 1847 the acreage had reduced to 6,900. *The Nation*, a Dublin newspaper, reported: 'In Roscommon deaths by famine are so prevalent that whole families who retire at night are corpses in the morning.'

The owner of the land on which Tibohine church stood wrote to Westminster to report that the conditions were calamitous and food must be sent urgently. What would the British government do to ease their suffering?

Not enough. Though relief funds were substantial, a stumbling block in Westminster's approach to Irish famine relief resided in the mid-Victorian devotion to *laissez faire* economics. The free market was considered sacrosanct, and nothing should interrupt its invisible hand – not even mass starvation. This meant that the supply of any emergency aid mustn't be allowed to distort the local market price for produce. Under this doctrine, the Irish couldn't just be *given* help – they had to show that they were deserving of it. And, where possible, they had to earn it. This attitude was fed by a British suspicion regarding the Irish character. The Irish peasant was thought by many as feckless, deceitful, rebellious and ungrateful. The very model of the undeserving poor. So the authorities set up relief works: small-scale, publicly funded infrastructure projects that could employ the local destitute and provide them with the means to purchase emergency food aid. The starving peasants were put to work building roads and bridges in desolate corners of the country and in all weathers – work with little practical purpose but to provide employment. Some were so weak with hunger that they could barely lift a shovel.

Deadly fever would soon follow. Famine-ravaged Ireland was utterly unprepared for infectious disease. The area where the McGanns lived had a population of 30,000 spread over 135 square miles of rough country, and only one hospital. It's a fact of famine that the sufferer will be more likely to die from disease than starvation. The body's immune system is so compromised as to invite any infection. It was reckoned that ten times more people were dying of typhus and dysentery than from malnutrition. The hospitals and workhouse infirmaries of Roscommon were soon full to bursting, and new patients had to be turned away to die.

Under the terms of the Poor Law Act, the tax burden for these hordes of sick and destitute fell onto the local ratepayers. Yet few able ratepayers remained. In parts of Roscommon, just 4 per cent of the population were supporting all the rest. These ratepayers were the traditional landowners, many of whom had large estates containing hundreds of starving sub-tenants on tiny plots of over-divided land. A landowner was responsible for paying the rates of any tenant who paid less than four pounds in rent. Many of these cash-strapped landowners now decided on a draconian solution: they would evict those in debt, and then consolidate their tiny plots into larger, more valuable land. So, at the famine's darkest hour, the landowners called in their desperate tenants' hanging loans.

These 'clearances' became an infamous chapter in the story of the Great Famine. Between 1848 and 1854, nearly 50,000 families were evicted from their dwellings with nowhere to go. Gangs of bailiffs, army or police would tear down cottages and burn them to the ground to ensure that no shelter remained to encourage the occupiers to linger. Once they were evicted, families could find little shelter. Evicted wraiths would haunt their local communities, living like wild creatures in bog holes, until disease and hunger finally took them and their unburied bodies were discovered.

This was the hunger that Susan McGann and my kin had experienced. A pitiless horror that branded the mind of the sufferer with the urgent attainment of safety in a world of stark choices. A merciless motivational antagonist. Hunger can change the way you think – the choices you make. Not just hunger – hunger *for* something. Survival. The tyranny of hope. Escape.

Emigration was nothing new to the Irish. Since the beginning of the nineteenth century, there had been a steady increase in the tide of emigrants that left to seek a better life in North America and Australasia. A million and a half had already gone – usually through the port of Liverpool. What characterised these pre-famine travellers was their relative degree of youth and aspiration; 70 per cent were between sixteen and thirty-four. Many had friends and family already living overseas, who sent back passage money and tales of better prospects. Yet once the famine was under way, the tide of emigrants became a vast flood. More than a million left in just six years – but these were no longer young and fit aspirants. They were the old, the penniless, the fatally diseased and the starving. An exodus of the desperate.

The famine had tripped a switch in the collective psyche of a nation, and it wasn't something that could now be switched off by a change in agricultural fortunes. After the famine finally subsided in the early 1850s, the tide of emigration continued unabated – accounting for a massive four million souls over the next half-century. The people had seen enough. They wanted out, regardless of whether their potatoes grew or not. My family was amongst them.

* * *

The McGanns left Ireland for good sometime between 1859 – when Owen and Susan christened Eugene in Tibohine – and 1864, when they first turn up in the public records of the slums of Liverpool. Intriguingly, the McGanns seem to have gone to the United States first, but had then returned to Ireland. A census form records that eldest son James was born in 'Philadelphia, America' in 1857. By 1859 they were back in Tibohine for Eugene's birth. Five years after that, they had settled in Liverpool. This was a period of remarkable restlessness for a family that had never previously travelled beyond their immediate neighbourhood. It was as if their hunger possessed three motivating forces: an active retreat from the horror they knew, a love of home that drove them back into its arms, and a feverish hope that propelled them into the unknown despite all dangers and obstacles.

This was an age when the slow wooden sailing ships gave way to fast metal-hulled coal steamers – vessels that could carry greater numbers of passengers across the seas at much cheaper cost. These competing ships could also ferry passengers from Dublin to Liverpool much faster, and at a price even a pauper might afford. The McGanns therefore gathered what they had and walked the entire 170 kilometres from Tibohine to Dublin, where they caught a steam ship for Liverpool costing several shillings. This was a pretty wretched trip: embarkation was chaotic and crowded, the crossing was frequently hazardous, and the poorest passengers were crammed onto the open deck, exposed to the elements. In evidence to a Select Committee in 1854, a travelling eyewitness described conditions for these deck passengers:

> ... they were generally crowded around the funnel of the steamer or huddled together in a most disgraceful manner; and as they have not been used to sea voyages, they get sick, and perfectly helpless, and covered with the dirt and filth of each other.

Despite the cheap cost, such a trip would still leave many Irish families penniless when they arrived. The fortunate ones might have some extra put by for their onward passage across the Atlantic, but those less fortunate, like the McGanns, would be forced to remain in Liverpool, and hope that they could earn enough to emigrate later.

What would Owen, Susan and the children have been confronted by as they disembarked?

Liverpool docklands was a teeming, stinking, chaotic and disorientating place. Hungry passengers, bleary-eyed and freezing, spilled out onto an urban dockside where hustlers and thieves exploited the unwary, and noise and confusion reigned. The *Liverpool Mercury* newspaper reported on the scene:

> In the cold and gloom of a severe winter, thousands of hungry and half naked wretches are wandering about, not knowing how to obtain a sufficiency of the commonest food nor shelter from the piercing cold. The numbers of starving

Irish men, women and children—daily landed on our quays
is appalling; and the Parish of Liverpool has at present, the
painful and most costly task to encounter, of keeping them
alive, if possible . . .

Indeed, basic survival would be the most immediate priority
for my family. This meant procuring food and any kind of a roof
over their head. For people like Owen and Susan, the options
were few. Local Poor Law relief, the parish-based welfare system
that existed at the time, excluded immigrants with less than
five years' residency. There were some charitable foundations
that provided short-term meals, but nothing more. There was
begging, which was rife at that time, and essential for many. If
a family could put its children out to beg, they might scrape the
pennies together for basic shelter and sustenance.

Shelter would generally be sought in the Vauxhall district of
the city – the ghastly close-packed slum streets huddled up next
to the docks, running north from the city centre between Great
Howard Street and the River Mersey. These streets were dangerously overcrowded with Irish refugees, and lacked the most
basic sanitation. Deadly epidemic diseases were a persistent threat.
Most immigrants were forced to find accommodation in one of
the infamous lodging houses or cellars for a penny per person per
night. Local physician William Duncan described these places:

> At night the floor of these cellars are covered with straw and
> there the lodgers – all who can afford to pay a penny for
> the accommodation – arrange themselves as best they may,
> until scarcely a single available inch of space is left unoccu-
> pied. In this way as many as thirty human beings or more

are sometimes packed together underground, each inhaling the poison which his neighbour generates, and presenting a picture in miniature of the Black Hole of Calcutta.

The energy expended to get to Liverpool with bodies racked by hunger was to prove too much for some. Cases of starvation began to appear with shameful regularity in coroners' reports: Mary Mageney of Vauxhall Road, discovered dead in bed from starvation – she'd not eaten for four days. Young Patrick Curren, starved to death in a cellar in Ashby Street. These were the streets where the McGanns lived when they arrived, and where they were to remain for more than three decades. It was the place where little Teresa ended her short life.

And yet, those of my family who lived, lived on. Day after day. Year after year.

In the 1871 Census I found them crammed into a single room in nearby Clay Street. Owen, Susan and their surviving children – James, fourteen, Eugene, twelve, Sarah ten, Mary, eight. Still on the edge. Still desperate. But very much alive. I remembered the Minnesota study – how starvation left its victims with a consuming passivity and 'no more sexual feeling than a sick oyster'. But the frequency of baptism records in Owen and Susan's family suggested that the sexual feelings of these particular oysters were far from sickly. In that crowded, stinking room, full of their own sleeping children, Owen and Susan clearly found time for plenty of physical contact.

How? Why hadn't that constant hunger and misery simply consumed them with a passive despair? Why didn't they just lie down with their empty distended bellies and surrender?

I was missing something. There was clearly a motivating force beyond their medical condition that I couldn't see. I knew what hunger could do to my family in that room, but what could it make them capable of? Perhaps their desperate hunger became a focus for their minds – an embraced privation that sharpened their resolve, making them more determined to succeed. More determined to live. Stripping away the trivial and leaving only the naked love they felt for each other. A motivating force beyond passivity. Hunger as focus.

And yet – focus on what? Is it just love distilled by want that had my starving ancestors copulating amongst the rags and the rattled breathing of their nearby children? No. They weren't just hungry, they were hungry *for* something. It was a directed desire. Raw and soil-stained. A passion.

Focused hunger as a raw passion. What could such a hunger make someone in my family capable of?

TESTIMONY

William Routledge. Born June 1918 in Liverpool. Died May 1984.

My uncle Billy.

I can see Billy's face clearly in my mind's eye. It's 1943. I see those grim laughter lines around his eyes, blackened and bruised. The nicotine fingers and the gaunt, sunburned, deathly-sallow cheeks. The unforgiving sun. A cloud of flies and the vivid green of a palm against the sky. He's almost naked, but for a grimy loincloth. A handful of scrawny potatoes lie scattered at his feet in the yellow dirt. A Japanese voice can be heard, screaming in fury. Billy stares directly at me and opens his lips wide in a smile.

His mouth is scarlet with fresh blood. His front teeth have been reduced to a broken row of shattered shards by some violent force. He grins at me like a lurid skeleton from a child's nightmare.

Sarawak, Borneo.

William Routledge, or 'Billy Ruck' as he was known to all of us, was the husband of my mother's sister Mary. The Routledges were a part of that same Irish flotsam that had blown across the Irish Sea to Liverpool in the years following the Great Famine. Billy's grandfather Francis had been born in Dublin just a year before Eugene was christened in Tibohine. Billy grew up in the Edge Hill area of Liverpool – an urban warren just a stone's throw from my own inner-city streets. He was raw and hard and irreverent and funny – a lover of boxing, beer and football – but also reticent and thoughtful in company. A man of fewer words than you might suppose, and certainly fewer than you felt he knew.

Not that he wouldn't say a few choice words sometimes – mainly swear words for the benefit of the younger children who crowded into my auntie Rose's kitchen on our regular Sunday visits. All the kids loved Uncle Billy. What kid wouldn't? As my mum and her two sisters fussed and cleaned and brewed and gossiped, he'd sit at the kitchen table with us, rolling cigarettes from an old tin of tobacco, pulling funny faces and releasing profanities like stray bullets. We all howled with mischievous laughter as the women tutted. On other days it would be funny rhymes or nonsense fairytales – 'Little Hood Riding Red' and 'Who's Been Sleeping In My Porridge?'

The best thing was when he'd do his party trick. He'd take a daffodil or a tulip from the vase on the table as the women talked, and he'd slowly begin to eat it. The whole thing! We'd squeal with revolted fascination. First the petals, poker-faced as we giggled. Then the head – crunching on the bloom with bulging eyes. Our laughter would elicit patient shushes from Mum. Finally the stem. The women would roll their eyes, and Billy would grin triumphantly. Once it was a whole banana peel and one of the lads said he'd even eaten a fly, though I'd never seen it. To us he was a superhero with a special power. Was it just a magic trick? A sleight of hand and stomach he'd perfected for our amusement?

Apparently not.

'Billy can eat anything,' my mother said.

'But *how*, Mum?'

The answer was simple and brooked no further enquiry.

'The war,' she said.

The war. That great veil thrown across the generation that bore us. The verbal dustsheet that concealed and protected the furniture of their younger lives. Silences like holes in the fabric, through which we spied too little to determine the nature of the things their earlier lives had rested on.

My auntie Mary had met Billy in March 1946, in those heady days of peace that finally fell on an exhausted Britain following victory in Europe and the Far East. She was just a shy eighteen-year-old, enjoying the dances and parties that had resumed with the returning servicemen. These men were noticeably different from the callow boys who'd been her dance partners in the war years. A different breed. She'd first noticed Billy talking to her father about football in the bar. He'd seemed brash and loud – but Mary detected shyness behind the bravado. They started courting, and within a year they were married.

Billy had been repatriated to Britain at the end of 1945. He'd

been a sergeant in the Royal Signals Regiment stationed in Singapore, and Mary discovered that he'd spent three and a half years in a Japanese prisoner-of-war camp. Stories were already circulating about the horrors suffered by the troops imprisoned there, but Billy would say very little. There were nightmares that woke him – sweating and shaking – but no flesh on the skeleton that haunted him. In the party thrown to welcome Billy home, his family told Mary that Billy had spent the entire evening sitting in the kitchen with his mother, drinking in silence.

It's now the early seventies. I can't be more than nine years old. My brother Mark is less than two years older than me. We're both sitting with Uncle Billy in the café area of a leisure centre in North Wales. It's summer, and we're on a day out from Liverpool. The sun is blazing through the sheet glass and glaring off the white melamine surface of the cafeteria table. There are crisps and fizzy drinks, and Billy has his tobacco tin open – eyes down, his yellow fingers rolling the paper patiently and nodding as the women talk. My mum and Auntie Mary are standing over us, handbags over forearms. They won't be long, they say. Just a stroll around the shops. They leave, and it's just the boys. Nearby, children splash in the pool and the sun continues to shine.

Billy is relaxed in our company. More talkative than usual. We're loving it. We relish the chance to have our superhero to ourselves. Like all boys of this age, our minds are full of cartoon adventure stories of military derring-do played out in the war-time comic books we read, and in the black-and-white British war films that fill our television screen on rainy afternoons. Emboldened by Billy's calm contentment, and in the absence of our mother's restraint, I venture a bold question:

'How can you eat everything, Uncle Billy?'

His fingers stop rolling. He looks up at me for a moment, without tension or haste.

He considers before replying.

''Cause if you didn't, you died,' he says.

'In the prison camp?'

He nods.

'What was it like, Uncle Billy?' Mark asks.

A child's question. So wide and simplistic as to demand specifics, or else be dismissed with an ironic quip. Yet this time Billy doesn't. Maybe it's the peace, or the steady sunlight. Maybe it's because he's in the company of children, which he loved. Whatever it is, he decides to answer. Slow, steady voice, eyes down as he rolls cigarettes, or else staring off into the distance as he holds each chain-smoked fag in his rugged builder's fingers. Before the women return, he'd tell us what it was like in his awful war. Just once. From the beginning to the end.

* * *

The island of Singapore was a grievous loss to the British in 1942 – perhaps the worst military defeat the nation has suffered. Situated at the bottom end of the jungle-covered and suppos-edly impassable Malay Peninsula, Singapore was an essential strategic maritime gateway to the Far East for an empire facing the new threat of Japanese expansion. Britain had fortified Singapore heavily before war broke out: massive guns faced out to sea to repel all maritime incursions, and a garrison of 90,000 Commonwealth troops was stationed there. Yet no guns faced inland across the causeway to the peninsula, as it was thought impossible to mount an invasion through such inhospitable terrain. This was to prove a disastrous miscalculation. When the Japanese swept down through the peninsula at lightning speed, the British were undone by the ferocity of the attack, and were soon besieged on the tiny island. The fearful command of 'every man for himself' went out. The young Sergeant William Routledge joined a group of fourteen men who fled across the causeway to make their escape.

His unit met up with a band of Gurkhas and embarked on a remarkable four-week journey behind enemy lines to the peninsula coast and, after stealing a local fishing boat, to the island of Java and freedom. The injured and exhausted troops were briefly hailed as heroes, until the Japanese overran Java and rendered their escape futile. Billy was taken prisoner and sent to Batu Lintang POW camp in Sarawak, Borneo. He was to survive there until the end of the war, three and a half years later.

Batu Lintang was a former British barracks that housed both military prisoners and civilian internees in separate compounds. The treatment meted out to prisoners by their Japanese captors was appalling. There was torture, forced labour, cramped living conditions, insufficient clothing and inadequate medicine. However, most devastating to life and health was hunger – the withholding of adequate food. The basic diet of prisoners contained only 44g of protein and 1,600 calories, and was devoid of essential vitamins. The rice ration was further reduced as the war progressed, so that by the end each man received little more than 100g per day, on which he was expected to labour for long hours. Starvation and disease soon took those previously at the peak of health.

Hilda Bates, an internee at the camp and a former nurse, observed the deterioration of Billy and his comrades from a distance:

In the soldiers' camp . . . many of the men were just skeletons, crawling about, as few were able to stand upright. Even our toddlers received the same rations as these poor souls, and the children are still hungry, so what must have been the suffering of those men, many of whom are hardly more than boys?

Billy was just twenty-five years old. A skeleton from a child's nightmare. He was incarcerated with a couple of other Liverpudlians, and he told us that they stayed close – brothers from a distant town, looking out for each other and pooling their rations. There was another friend, Selby Sutcliffe, who lived just a few weeks until hunger and fever took him. Billy watched him die.

But Billy didn't die. He refused to. He focused his hunger into something else. A dark passion grew in his empty stomach.

The prisoners would eat anything they could find or catch. Snakes, snails, cats, dogs, rats. Insects. Flowers. Superheroes with a special power. Yet they still fell. To dysentery. To beri-beri. The camp hospital was its own death sentence – a waiting room for the makeshift cemetery they nicknamed 'boot hill', visible just outside the fence. The camp doctor refused all but the most basic medicine to inmates, and even denied the sick their rice ration.

The death rate in Billy's part of the camp rose to ten a day.

Anyone who could still walk was required to report for work – long hours of pitiless labour – and then, on their return, they had to dig graves to bury their dead. When this was done, there was one final humiliation: scavenging through the belongings of the deceased for any food scraps they might have left behind. Yet Billy worked, and he dug, and he scavenged, and he went on.

His clothes soon rotted away in the tropical humidity, and weren't replaced. The men were forced to wear makeshift loin-cloths while they toiled, skeletal and naked, in the baking sun. But Billy went on – feeding on his dark passion like a fungus.

There was a lifeline. A thin and dangerous one. Outside the hidden gaps in the large barbed wire perimeter, local Malay and ethnic Chinese civilians lived under an oppression of their own, and were sympathetic to these Allied captives. It was possible to slip out unseen, and to barter for scraps of food in exchange for old wedding rings, tobacco, or stolen camp equipment. Failing that, a desperate inmate reared on the tough streets of Liverpool might try to steal what food they could, before returning with their prize. Billy became an expert thief and scrounger. He and his fellow Scouser, Jack Osborne, would take it in turns to venture beyond the wire and bring back what they needed to survive.

Yet the price of capture was appalling. Guards were unspeakably brutal to even the mildest perceived wrongdoings. Punishments were vicious and ingenious in their cruelty. A favourite was to make offenders stand in the midday sun holding a heavy log of wood above their heads. If they weakened and lowered their arms, they would be kicked and punched senseless. More serious offenders would be handed over to the military police for torture or execution.

Suddenly, at the cafeteria table, Billy remembers something, and he starts to laugh. A deep, warm chuckle, squeezing the lines around his eyes and shaking his shoulders. The laugh is almost tender in its sincerity – and in jarring contrast to the awful account he is giving us. My young brother and I look at him, quizzical and unsettled.

'One of the funniest things I ever saw,' he says.

One day, the Japanese guards had devised a special punishment for their own amusement. They lined up British soldiers in pairs facing each other, and ordered them to fight their partner. If they didn't throw genuine punches at their comrades, the guards would do it for them with rifle butts, boots and fists. The starving, sick men would have to inflict real pain on their fellow sufferers, or else leave them to the cruelty of their jailors. So they did – punches pulled as much as it was possible. Yet there was a further twist. The guards removed a single soldier at one end of the line, so that the soldier remaining had no partner to fight. They then ordered this soldier to fight himself – to punch his own gaunt face and rib-poked body. If he didn't do this convincingly, he would be beaten to paralysis by his captors. So this man did so.

Billy watched this poor man between punches of his own and dissolved into hysterical laughter. The guards were furious, but Billy didn't care, he laughed and laughed. Even as he recalled the macabre sight, his old face was transfigured by a wicked smile. 'If you've never seen a man trying to beat himself up before, you've never lived!' he said.

Mark and I were caught between his laughter and the horror of the scene he'd recounted. We were still young. We didn't yet understand the purposes to which our native city could bend humour, and the dark passion that could fuel it. Liverpool is a city of comedians: of sharp wit and a resilient sense of the ridiculous. Its reputation is well deserved. In all my subsequent travels, it remains one of the funniest places I know. Yet its humour has claws. A native learns that there can be a difference between something that makes you laugh and something that's meant to be funny. Once, in junior school, I was beaten up by the class bully while a circle of kids watched me. This boy quipped constantly with the crowd as he kicked me. And he was hilarious! Genuinely laugh-out-loud funny. And not funny at all.

Sometimes laughter is decoupled from warmth, like the sound of crows chortling over discovered carrion. Sometimes it's the song our dark passion sings. A focused hunger. A grinning skeleton.

One day Billy was scrounging outside the wire, and he'd returned to camp with a few precious potatoes concealed inside the loincloth he wore. He tried to avoid any guards, in case they might require him to stop. In Batu Lintang, every prisoner had to bow low when in the presence of a guard. The punishment for failing to do so was severe. One internee had been paralysed for a week because his bow had not been considered deferential enough. Just then, Billy was spotted by a guard who called for him to stop. Billy knew that if he took his hands away from the potatoes he cradled in his loincloth he'd be discovered. He continued walking. The guard now screamed at him. Billy stopped. He bowed to the guard – and the potatoes fell out onto the yellow earth. The guard took his rifle butt and rammed it into Billy's face, breaking all of his front teeth. Scarlet blood on shards. A lurid skeleton from a child's nightmare. He beat Billy continuously about the head, neck and spine. These were injuries that kept him in an agony of back pain and neuralgia until his death. The potatoes were duly confiscated.

Yet Billy didn't die. He refused to. He focused his hunger into something else.

'How did you keep going, Uncle Billy?' we asked him.

Billy considered for a moment, before he settled, at last, on the simple truth. The grin was gone.

'Hate,' he replied.

That was it. That was the dark passion that sustained him. Hatred.

Billy Routledge hated all things Japanese until the day he died. He hated their cars, their television sets, their smiling faces on advertising hoardings – the very idea of Japan. It burned from him like toxic fumes. We all knew this and accepted it like the seepage of an old wound, without understanding its true pathology. In the crucible of his starvation he'd fed on the only thing that would guarantee his survival beyond despair. Hatred. He'd turned his skeletal body into an organism that fed off hate, that thrived like a fungus on the privations he saw and suffered. A superhero with a special power. Hunger as hatred. Hatred as defiance. Raw and soil-stained. A dark passion. A motivating force. A focused desire.

Was that it? Was that the croaking carrion song that Owen and Susan were singing in the dank darkness of a Clay Street slum, their hungry bodies and tongues fumbling and moaning? Was it hatred that fuelled my family's survival? Endless hunger and persistent loss turned into a dark, rutting passion? Laughter without humour? Sex without love? A grinning skeleton?

No. There was something deeper still. Something beneath the hunger and the hate.

News about Hiroshima seeped into Batu Lintang like rain through the hut roof. Allied planes began to fly sorties over the camp and the guards started to dispense food and medicine with a newfound largesse. Eventually the Australian Army arrived at the gate to liberate them. They discovered men lying in their own filth; naked, covered in ulcers, and in the advanced stages of starvation. Weakness from hunger had led to a lack of movement and circulation, which resulted in gangrene of the limbs and digits.

Billy was attending to his Liverpool friend Jack Osborne, his fellow scavenger and survivor. Jack had succumbed to spinal malaria. Three days after the liberation, Jack died. Billy was so traumatised by Jack's death that he couldn't go home – not yet. Billy volunteered to stay on at the camp, attending to the men still too sick to travel. He returned to Liverpool a few months later. Of the two thousand Allied troops held at Batu Lintang POW camp, only one in three would walk out of those gates again. My uncle Billy was one of them.

At the leisure centre, Mark and I sit motionless. Nearby, children splash in the pool. The seconds pass. Billy is looking for the words. A reason. An explanation.

'I'm a bastard,' he said, finally. 'I was born a bastard. I grew up on those streets with just my fists, and with nothing but shit to eat. I could take anything. Or nothing. But there were men in that camp who weren't bastards like me. They were good men. Brave, kind, clever men.' He searched for the words. 'Poets, musicians, artists.' He breathed the memory down in his lungs with the cigarette smoke. Exhaled. 'I watched them die.

Watched them fade away because they couldn't hate like I did. They couldn't live on nothing.'

Billy looks directly at us, his crow's-feet eyes devoid of their laughter. 'You know who walked out of that place? Not the poets or the musicians. Not the good ones or the gentle ones. The Scousers. The Glaswegian slum kids. The cockney thieves. The kids who'd known nothing but shit,' he said. 'Bastards like me.' He stubbed his fag out in the plastic ashtray.

'I hate them for that. I'll hate them for that till the day I die.'

And there it was. Beneath the hunger and the hate. The truth of it, stated as fact and not as bitterness. Not hatred as defiance, but hatred as a toxin that Billy couldn't flush from his system, starving him of life's nutrients. A curse, crippling him as surely as the back pain and the agonising neuralgia. The goodness he'd seen, but couldn't save. The lost poetry. The music that he couldn't play himself.

At that moment, Mum and Auntie Mary returned to our table from their excursion.

'Hello boys! Have you had a nice time?'

* * *

Mary and my mum were amazed that Billy had opened up to us the way he did that day. He never did again.

Billy remained wonderfully raw and hard and irreverent and funny till the day he died. I like to think that his only son, Ritchie, gave him some respite from the toxin he'd endured. Ritchie Routledge grew to be a successful singer and guitarist in a hit band called the Crying Shames – a member of that wonderful Merseybeat generation – a glorious, bright, brash

37

burst of Liverpool song that took the world by storm before the ships sailed away and the factories closed.

If Billy hadn't survived Batu Lintang then Ritchie's music would never have existed. His would be a beautiful sound we'd never know. So Billy's hunger and defiance were a gift to those who followed, and a tribute to those who didn't make it. His hatred was redeemed by sacrifice: a grim, grinning skeleton that endured so that the ones who followed might sing a gentler song. The tooth-smashed love song of 'bastards like us'.

* * *

I'm back in 1868. Back at Teresa McGann's sad, simple death certificate.

How did her mother cope with what she witnessed? How did she rise the next day and go on? How did she consummate her renewed hope and passion with Owen – time and time again, rolling on that filthy bed at night with the coughs of her children close at hand? What was the motivating force that sprang from the hungers of the family that bore me? Just then I see it. Next to Owen's name on the certificate. The father's occupation, hidden by the official's careless pencil mark.

'Musician.'

Owen was a musician! The first artist of any kind recorded on my family tree. Not a docker, not a labourer, not a tinker. A musician. Of the lowliest sort, I'm sure – a cheap fiddler or tin whistle beggar, playing for farthings on the street or in the bar. But a musician all the same. This meant that there was music in that hovel, not simply silence. Owen was a grinning, dancing skeleton, playing his joyous, raucous, toothless reels until the kind and clever ones that followed him could play a gentler song.

There was music in their bed at night – passion like a melody, despite the filth. His music was a motivating force beyond passivity. A sound like Billy's skeletal laughter. The sound of something beyond mute suffering. The sound of a feverish hope that propelled a family forward into the unknown, despite all dangers and obstacles. The sound of a directed desire.

The sound was love. The passion of being alive despite the horror. A defiant song for all those who'd come after. A redeeming sacrifice for his descendants. A focused hunger to succeed beyond starvation.

The love song of bastards like us.

2

PESTILENCE

Pestilence n.

1. An infectious epidemic disease that is virulent and devastating.
2. An entity that is morally destructive or pernicious.

MEDICINE

Epidemic infection has been ripping families and societies apart since the very earliest civilisations, and many of these ancient pestilences are still with us today. Infectious disease is a medical disorder caused by a microorganism – a bacterium, virus, parasite or fungus – entering the body and disrupting its normal function. The characteristic of these diseases is that they are transmitted from one person to another. As human civilisation first became established, people began to live together in larger, denser, more interconnected settlements. This enabled infectious disease to establish quickly through close contact, and then spread widely through trade or conflict with others.

These pestilences could sometimes be so terrifying to our

41

forebears that a dark sentience, divine provenance or moral cause was ascribed to them. Pestilence even appears as one of the Bible's Four Horsemen of the Apocalypse, those mythical harbingers of our final moral judgement. Pestilence wasn't simply an affliction to our ancestors; it could also be an indicator, a verdict or retribution for some greater malady within the character of the sufferer and their kin.

One such pestilence was leprosy. Leprosy is an acutely disfiguring bacterial infection with a long history of public fear and prejudice. In many societies, it was believed to be a punishment from God – a curse for the failings of the sufferer. Lepers were isolated in colonies, stoned and shunned by the healthy, and forced to differentiate themselves as an alien group. The Old Testament's Book of Leviticus gave specific directions for their treatment:

> Anyone with such a defiling disease must wear torn clothes, let their hair be unkempt, cover the lower part of their face and cry out, 'Unclean! Unclean!'

We can all be grateful that a trip to the doctor now involves a more useful approach to the treatment of infectious disease than instructions on hairstyle and a light stoning. Yet even recent history has shown that public fear of infection can fuse itself in language and attitude to the nature of the people who suffer from it. In a sense, the pathogen and the person become one – or, in the case of typhus fever, an infection can even grow to embody a whole race.

Typhus fever is spread through lice that have been infected by a bacterium called *Rickettsia prowazekii*. As these blood-sucking lice feed on a human host they excrete the bacteria onto the skin. If the human scratches this bite, then the infected faeces are rubbed into the microscopic wound, transmitting the typhus. The faeces can also dry to a dust and then be inhaled as an airborne pathogen. The onset of typhus fever is rapid: headaches, rash, delirium, muscle spasm. After five days, a livid rash appears on the chest and limbs. After a fortnight the death rate is between 25 and 40 per cent. Typhus fever is a disease of close confinement, grinding poverty and an inability to keep clean. It was a common feature of the Irish famine, and was carried with the emigrants to the slums of Liverpool, where it became known simply as 'the Irish fever'. A pathogen had become fused in language to a people.

Infectious diseases can be as distinctive as the populations they infect. Each has its own unique method of transmission, deadliness and rate of infection. Scientists have devised a scale for the infectiousness of a pathogen called its basic reproduction number – or R_0 (pronounced 'r naught'). This is an approximate measure of how many unprotected people are likely to become infected by contact with a single person carrying this disease. An airborne pathogen like measles is highly contagious, with an R_0 of 12–18 – meaning that a single infected schoolchild might infect eighteen of their unvaccinated classmates. Yet deaths from measles are relatively rare. A disease like Ebola, spread only by bodily fluids, has an R_0 of just 1.5–2.5, yet it will kill about half of those it infects. The danger from a pestilence is therefore greatest when a pathogen is both easily transmitted and highly deadly – as was the case with one of the most infamous of all the historical plagues: smallpox.

Smallpox is caused by the *variola* virus. Infection occurs when a person inhales droplets of the breath of a sufferer, or if their infected bodily fluids manage to find their way into healthy mouths and noses. With an R_0 of about 7, it's not the most contagious of infections – and contagion depends upon prolonged close contact with someone who has it. Yet if the conditions are right – cramped housing and dense urban populations – it can spread like a bushfire. Once infected, the incubation period is long – about a fortnight. At first there are flu-like symptoms and the body temperature rises. Then there's nausea and vomiting. A few days later, red spots appear in the mouth and throat and on the tongue. When these spots burst, the virus spreads on the infected saliva. Within another two days, a signature rash of spots or macules begins to develop on the skin of the forehead and face, spreading to the body and extremities over the following days. In the most common variant of the disease, the rash develops into deep-lying, hard pustules that cover the entire face and trunk, and leak a vile fluid. These pustules finally subside into scabs that, when they fall off, leave the sufferer horribly pockmarked, and possibly blind. That's if they live. The death rate for smallpox is at least 30 per cent and as much as 80 per cent amongst children.

Smallpox is an ancient scourge. Evidence of smallpox has been found on the mummified body of Pharaoh Ramesses V of Egypt, more than three thousand years old. Traders were believed to have brought the disease from India during the first millennium, BCE. From India it spread to China, and returning crusaders were thought to have carried smallpox to Europe in the eleventh and twelfth centuries.

Though deadly and feared, there was a defence against it. Smallpox enjoys the privilege of being the first disease to be treated with vaccination. Edward Jenner famously inoculated a small child by infecting him with the closely related but non-fatal cowpox in 1796. Yet evidence for smallpox vaccination goes back much further, to tenth-century China. The traditional method, called variolation, was a simple one: a patient's skin would be cut or scratched open and material from an active smallpox macule would be inserted into it. The patient developed mild symptoms of smallpox but recovered, and thereafter was immune. Yet it was risky: introducing active smallpox to a healthy body could prove fatal in a significant minority of cases, and also risk spreading the full-blown disease to others. Jenner's cowpox method was safer, as the introduced infection was not, in itself, a fatal one, yet would still inoculate against its deadly cousin.

Smallpox enjoys another unique distinction in the history of medicine. It's the first infectious disease that humans have ever managed to wipe from the planet. It was finally declared eradicated in 1980 following a global campaign by the World Health Organization. This amazing feat was achieved by a crucial alliance of medical science with wider human qualities of collective organisation, education and knowledge sharing.

Right up to the 1960s, smallpox had remained endemic in Africa and Asia. Mass vaccination programmes had been effective in many parts of the world, yet they were costly in time and resources, and not always efficient in targeting those people most in need. A new strategy of 'containment and surveillance' was devised, led by American epidemiologist Donald Henderson. Every time there was a smallpox outbreak, a medical team would travel to the scene, vaccinate and isolate all those who were ill, and then trace and vaccinate everyone who had come into contact with them. At the same time, they educated local populations in risk areas about how to spot the disease, and offered rewards for any confirmed sightings. In this way Henderson and his team turned the blunt instrument of mass vaccination into a kind of 'whack-a-mole', seeking and destroying smallpox wherever it reared its head. Eventually the disease was whacked into extinction. The last natural smallpox case was in Somalia in 1977 – a young hospital cook called Ali Maow Maalin.

The word 'natural' is important here. Although smallpox no longer exists 'in the wild', it endures as a dangerous pathogen in laboratories in the United States and Russia. These supplies have been retained for military purposes, as well as for research. This has led to isolated outbreaks due to accidental exposure, thankfully controlled thus far. Smallpox is even more dangerous to us now, as the population has ceased to be vaccinated against the disease. Despite periodic appeals to destroy these dangerous stocks for safety reasons, the two superpowers have so far refused to do so – each mistrusting the other, and fearing that the pathogen could be weaponised against them.

The smallpox pathogen has avoided complete eradication not by the failings of medicine, but by that same ancient fear of 'the other' which turns an infectious disease into mistrust of an alien tribe considered incurably pestilent. Significantly, just two years before Ali Maow Maalin contracted smallpox, the soon-to-be President of the United States, Ronald Reagan, compared Communism to a dangerous pathogen: 'Mankind has survived all manner of evil diseases and plagues – but can it survive Communism?'

Pestilence is therefore like a beast with two heads. The first is the physical infection that assaults our bodies – killing families, disfiguring flesh, decimating communities. The second is a malady of the collective mind – a ghetto into which a disease can cast the infected, encouraged by the biblical stones thrown by those in society who most fear it. A physical infection may be treatable with medical science or prevented by the sanitary improvements of social progress. Yet cultural pestilence is the more subtle and enduring pathogen; one more likely to persist according to prejudice and expediency than to vanish completely.

Pestilence isn't just something we can catch, but something we can become. A way for others to define us, and a means by which we may ultimately come to define ourselves.

History

The Survivors: The McGann family, 1871–1900

When I last left my McGann forebears, it was the evening of Sunday 2 April 1871. They were huddled in a tiny dwelling in Clay Street, Liverpool: pauper immigrants from Ireland who had subsisted in an overcrowded and insanitary dockland neighbourhood since their arrival from Roscommon nearly a decade before. Owen – forty-eight years old; his wife Susan, forty; their children, James, Eugene, Sarah and Mary. They'd already lost two children to hunger since they'd arrived. They were soon to lose another.

The reason I can be so specific about time, place and people is that the evidence comes from the United Kingdom census, the once-a-decade population survey that's existed in Britain since 1841, and whose careful preservation provides genealogists with unique insight into a specific British neighbourhood. There was an interesting detail to the McGanns' address on the 1871 census. They lived at '2 in 4ct' Clay Street, whereas a nearby neighbour simply resided at 4 Clay Street. Other families could be found at '5 in 4ct', '3 in 4ct', etc. What was going on with the street numbering?

The answer, I discovered, was socially significant. The abbreviation 'ct' stood for 'court'. Every few numbers along each street, the numbering would expand to embrace a particular court containing several sub-addresses, crammed with Irish families. These court dwellings were a feature of slum housing in Liverpool at the time and up to half of the city's population were housed in them by the middle of the nineteenth century. The McGanns were court dwellers.

A court was accessed from the main street by a low, unlit passageway, which opened out after a few metres into a narrow courtyard containing anything from four to a dozen or more houses that faced each other across the tiny space. Families were squeezed into single rooms or sub-let cellars in these houses, and most courts were 'blind' – meaning that the only entrance and exit was by way of the narrow passageway to the street. At one end of these courts was a single water tap; at the other end were the public toilets – foul closets that a hundred residents or more had to share. They were little better than open sewers. There were no conveniences, water or gas within the houses, and each dwelling backed directly onto the wall of the next court, so that the only access to light and ventilation was from the insanitary and foul-smelling courtyard.

In 1883, the *Liverpool Daily Post* newspaper set up a special commission to investigate these housing conditions. Its anonymous commissioners explored the very streets the McGanns were living in and reported on what they found:

> Here resides a population which is a people in itself, ceaselessly ravaged by fever, plagued by the blankest, most appalling poverty, cut off from every grace and comfort in life, born, living, and dying amid squalid surroundings, of which those who have seen them can form a very inadequate conception.

They called their report 'Squalid Liverpool' and descriptions of the courts featured widely in their account:

The passage entrance ... is strewn with refuse matter – animal and vegetable – so that one has to pick a careful way in order not to become bedaubed. In all this dirt and stench little children play about and roll over, perfectly regardless of the consequences.

They ventured into the court dwellings to describe the kind of single-room conditions that Owen's family were living in:

The room is perhaps eight or nine feet square. Into the boards is ground the dirt of years. The window does not open at all, and if the inhabitants desire to dilute the foul air of the room with a little of the foul air of the court they have to remove the sash bodily ... on the floor a few sacks of vile appearance and smell were arranged in the form of a bed.

And yet, in all of these houses, they found the people universally friendly, polite and approachable:

The house doors are nearly always open. You may go in if you like, no one will object. You will meet with nothing but civility. Your commissioners in all their visits never received a harsh word from young or old, men or women.

Filthy but polite. Squalid but friendly. Dens of sickness with their doors flung open in welcome. Owen playing his merry reels on a tin whistle while the lice crawl on his children's heads. As the commissioners' investigations continue, the impression gathers that the residents' relaxed disposition is regarded as a symptom and not a virtue. These were not only paupers by circumstance, but by social propensity. The commissioners remark upon the ease with which a householder will lie about most things, ignore personal hygiene, drink to excess, yet exude a passive contentment with their lot:

'Like all the rest, they inhabit filthy houses, and appear perfectly contented with their dirty surroundings.'

To the commissioners, these people were smiling incubators of infection, rolling over contentedly in their own dirt and stench like pigs in a sty. 'A people in itself'. An alien, infected tribe.

Certainly infected. If one wished to incubate a fatal disease, you couldn't imagine a more suitable environment than the crowded, filthy courts these commissioners described. Reports like 'Squalid Liverpool' were responses to the constant threat of epidemic facing the respectable citizens of prosperous Liverpool with regard to the Irish paupers in their midst. These slum dwellers were a breeding ground for pestilence, and had been for decades.

Sanitary conditions had been dire in Liverpool since before the Irish famine in the 1840s. Previous influxes of emigration had led to overcrowding and epidemic in the shabby backstreets of the docks. But now a new legion of the starving and diseased had arrived to swell the courts and cellars to bursting. So urgent was the problem that a law was passed in Parliament dedicated to the city's hygiene: the 1846 Liverpool Sanitary Act. I'm sure there are many who can claim that their ancestors were poor – but how many can say that the local nature of their family's poverty was so bad that it led to government legislation?

The Sanitary Act gave the local authority in Liverpool new powers to implement measures that prioritised public health, sanitation, disease control and housing policy. It led to the appointment of Britain's first ever Officer of Health – the campaigning local physician, Dr William Henry Duncan. Duncan had long campaigned for radical action to tackle what he called 'the most unhealthy town in England', and 'the hospital and cemetery of Ireland'. Duncan formed part of a new triumvirate of local health officers, along with the rather fragrantly named Thomas Fresh, who was appointed 'Inspector of Nuisances' (a forerunner of the Environmental Health Officer), and civil engineer James Newlands, who became Borough Engineer. Newlands would transform the state of Liverpool's dreadful sewer system, and such was his success that he was asked in 1854 to provide effective sewerage for the British Army at the Siege of Sevastopol, where more troops were dying of fever than of wounds. Florence Nightingale later wrote to thank Newlands, remarking: 'Truly I may say that to us sanitary salvation came from Liverpool.' These men were reforming Victorians in the finest tradition: scientific, methodical, patriotic, and of unimpeachable Protestant respectability. They now gazed down into an urban valley of pestilent humanity as alien to their sensibilities as the far Crimea.

Although Duncan didn't yet have our full medical knowledge of the way diseases such as typhus fever were spread, he drew a clear connection between population density, lack of basic sanitation and the prevalence of epidemics that plagued the town. By the time Duncan died in 1863, his campaigning legacy and influence were secure: Liverpool was on the road to cleaning up its act and getting healthier. Yet it was to be a long road – and Duncan had been unequivocal about the moral and social reasons for this:

... I am persuaded that so long as the native inhabitants are exposed to the inroads of numerous hordes of uneducated Irish, spreading physical and moral contamination around them, it will be in vain to expect that any sanitary code can cause fever to disappear from Liverpool.

A 'physical and *moral* contamination'. It seemed clear to Duncan that pestilence was a two-headed beast: not simply a pathogen, but bound to the morality of the people who suffered it. The first was increasingly understood, and could be cured with medicine, sanitation and slum clearance. The second was incurable, rooted as it was in a grim community whose moral corruption this physical malady must surely index, and to which those who carry it must belong in perpetuity. An alien nation.

Duncan was revolted by the Irish he encountered, and condemned their perceived 'innate indifference to filth', and their 'recklessness and peculiar habits'. By the time Owen McGann's family were sitting in that room in Clay Street in 1871, there was a clear connection established in the minds of the respectable citizenry of Liverpool between the diseases that plagued their streets and the moral character of the people believed to carry them. It wasn't simply hunger, poverty or their insanitary conditions. The immigrant Irish were an infected tribe.

Yet the McGanns survived with four of their children intact when the census enumerator visited in spring of 1871. Sadly, this state of affairs wasn't to last. Just a few weeks after that census was recorded, their daughter Sarah would die of a pestilence as old as the pharaohs, and during an epidemic that further stretched the resources and patience of the city they now called home.

* * *

28 April, 1871. 2 in 4 Ct, Clay Street. Sarah McGann, aged eleven. Certified dead. Cause: Variola.

Variola. Such a quaint word. Almost musical, like the name of an instrument, or the indication of a bright tempo. It swirls in confident cursive on her death certificate.

The truth is of a much harsher key. Variola is the medical term for smallpox.

Smallpox had been raging in Liverpool for a few months by the time of Sarah's death, yet many felt that the authorities had been slow to react with effective vaccination measures. In January 1871, the *Liverpool Mercury* newspaper aired its frustration:

> Now that the smallpox is carrying off scores of victims every week, the local authorities are beginning to do what they ought to have done long ago – put preventive measures into force ... As an illustration of the extent to which vaccination is neglected, Dr Trench, the medical officer, states that he recently requested the lodging house and nuisance inspectors to ascertain whether children coming under their observation had been vaccinated. He was astonished at the result, for in three days the inspectors, while merely performing their routine duties, came in contact with 133 people who had not been vaccinated. The necessity for enforcing vaccination in every possible instance has been over and over again urged by medical men, but it is only in cases of emergency that the authorities seem disposed to listen.

The best way of discovering if someone was vaccinated was to look for the telltale cicatrix, or small vaccination scar, on a person's arm. This mark, sadly, did not always denote foolproof protection. The efficacy of smallpox vaccination was observed to fade with time, and, in some cases, to fail altogether – either through imperfect application or through a person's failure to acquire immunity despite multiple applications. In a later review of the epidemic, the *Liverpool Daily Post* newspaper examined the death figures of those who'd been admitted to Liverpool workhouses with smallpox, and found that death could occur regardless of whether the patient had been vaccinated or not:

... Of those imperfectly vaccinated, one half died; of those who showed marks of from one to five cicatrices, one in eight died ...

What of little Sarah? Had Owen been a neglectful parent and left his daughter exposed to the infection without vaccination? I went back to her death certificate. There, beneath 'Variola' as the cause of death, was another single, sad word: 'Vaccinated'. Little Sarah *had* been inoculated. But she'd died all the same. Jenner's little miracle had not been able to protect her.

As the epidemic raged in Liverpool and mass vaccination proved inefficient as the sole solution, priorities shifted to measures for prevention and isolation. Yet those in positions of power and influence remained tardy in their efforts to eradicate infection and prevent its spread. On 16 February, there was frustration in the media with the landlords of slum properties where there had been smallpox outbreaks:

Yesterday, upwards of 20 owners and agents of property were summoned for neglecting to purify houses in which smallpox and fever had occurred, and in each case penalties had been imposed.

Safe disposal of bodies was also an issue. When local residents heard of a plan to set up a smallpox mortuary in the nearby Everton district of the city, there was:

... something akin to a panic in that neighbourhood, the belief being entertained that the bringing of bodies to the place would spread the contagion throughout the district. Dr Trench treats this apprehension as illusory ... if a place is well ventilated the contagion is not carried beyond half a yard from the patient ...

Even during the epidemic's most intense period, there was an all-too-recognisable 'not-in-my-back-yard' tendency that challenged the best scientific strategies. And yet even here, the stronger tendency was to blame the spread of the disease on the moral and cultural failings of the Irish immigrants who died. The Officer for Health, Dr Trench, reported that some Irish families were retaining diseased corpses of victims in their houses for days, in order to conduct a traditional funeral wake:

In Chisenhale-Street, a woman died of Smallpox on the 14th of February. The house was visited at 2 o'clock a.m. on the 17th, and more than a dozen persons were found in it, all intoxicated or under the influence of drink, holding a wake over the corpse. The assembly was broken up by the inspector, and two of the women were so drunk as to require to be carried from the house.

The wake runs deep in Irish culture. The body of the deceased relative is laid out in the room and family, friends and neighbours are invited to visit and pay their respects. Food and drink are consumed, and the spirit of the gathering is one of celebration rather than mourning. This practice endured in Liverpool until the 1970s.

Unfortunately, in the smallpox epidemic of 1871, an Irish wake was a real health hazard. An infected corpse coming into close contact with so many visitors presented an obvious danger of smallpox spreading rapidly throughout the district. Yet why did the Health Officer feel the need to detail the alcoholic inebriation he found at the wake? The drunken condition of women surely had no bearing on the transmission of smallpox? Unless, of course, the moral disposition of those at risk is considered indistinguishable from the infection itself. It was Duncan's legacy enduring in the minds of the Liverpool authorities. Dr Trench's words were implicit moral stones thrown to demarcate a tribe that was considered medically treatable but morally contaminated.

Looking back at my own McGann family at that time, I became curious to see if they displayed any signs of this 'moral contamination'. Was there any evidence that they lived morally dubious lives? The McGanns were certainly churchgoers, as the records of nearby St Augustine's church clearly showed. Every significant family event – birth, marriage and death – was recorded there. Was there anything to suggest that they were less than model citizens?

There was. Owen's occupation – when not listed as musician – was frequently cited as 'Emigration Agent' or 'Emigration Runner' on public documents. This rather grand title conjures images of an upstanding Victorian travel agent, dispensing tickets for New York to eager, smiling travellers. The truth was somewhat less glamorous. These runners were little more than disreputable ticket touts. They accosted emigrating families on the Liverpool dockside, falsely claiming to work for one of the many licensed shipping brokers, and then coerced them into parting with too much of their hard-earned savings for onward passage to the New World. In 1850, the *Morning Chronicle* newspaper called them 'man-catchers', and detailed their shady work:

The business of these people is, in common parlance, to 'fleece' the emigrant, and to draw from his pocket, by fair means or foul, as much of his cash as he can be persuaded, inveigled, or bullied into parting with. The first division of the man-catching fraternity are those who trade in commissions on the passage money, and call themselves the 'runners', or agents of passenger-brokers ... the passenger-brokers of Liverpool, in common with the unwary and unsuspecting emigrants, have suffered greatly from the malpractices of the 'runners' who pretend to be their agents. These man-catchers procure whatever sums they can from emigrants as passage money – perhaps £5 or £6 or even more – and pay as little as they can to the passenger-broker whose business they thus assume – often as little as £3.

Not only were these self-appointed middlemen exploiting the innocence and fear of the arriving emigrant, but most of their victims were also Irish – so an emigration runner like Owen was ingratiating himself as a friendly face to former countrymen and women in order to fleece them. Hardly churchgoing behaviour from my great-great-grandfather. Although there was no doubt of the prejudices stacked against them, Liverpool's Irish slum dwellers clearly did much to contribute to their own reputation for dishonesty. Perhaps Dr Trench had a point after all . . .

But what came first? Was it some innate immoral Irishness that turned Owen into a ruthless tout, or did the circumstances he'd lived through – starvation, exile, disease, death, prejudice – harden him to the reality of his family's need? Was he born bad, or did he have moral contamination thrust upon him?

One of the curious aspects of public prejudice against an alien tribe is that it flattens out the many delicate human distinctions existing within that group. In those Liverpool docks there would have been many different types of Irish character: good people and bad, the idle and the industrious, the pious and the godless, saints and touts, the quiet bright child and the aggressive dullard. All humanity – but compressed by the prejudice of others into a single pestilence. I often wonder what Owen's surviving children – James, Eugene and Mary – were like as individuals. Did they take their sister Sarah's death in their stride, or did they mourn her loss for many years? Were they thoughtful or boisterous children? Good or bad? We'll never know, and the social commentary at the time simply labels these children as Irish, pauper and pestilent. A single objectified target for stones.

Yet the Liverpool Irish endured, expanded in number, and slowly began to assert themselves. By the time of Sarah's death from smallpox, the Irish population of Liverpool had grown to over 76,000 – about 15 per cent of the city. Just as the outside had objectified them, so they began to self-identify, forming an insular community built around race, religion, and the work they now dominated in the nearby docks. Liverpool differed from other cities in the industrial north regarding the nature of the labour that dominated the workforce. It wasn't the fixed landscape of factories and mills, but an ever-shifting and opportunistic maritime economy of moving goods and people – casual work and transient incomes. Work was tough and clannish, whether you were a dockside tout like Owen or a stevedore unloading cargo. This was employment perfectly suited to the unskilled Irish labourers who lived nearby. George Smyth, a local businessman, commented on their dominance of the docks:

> The Irishmen in Liverpool perform nearly all the labour requiring great physical powers and endurance. Nine-tenths of the ships that arrive in this great port are discharged and loaded by them; and all the cargoes skilfully stowed.

Well, that was the cargo that didn't mysteriously disappear. Docks are famously porous places, where stolen goods can easily find their way into local hands. In the mid-nineteenth century there was a roaring trade in the theft of cotton and other goods from the Liverpool docklands by Irish criminal networks.

However, by the 1870s, the Irish workforce had also risen to occupy more legitimate positions, such as stevedore gang leader, master porter or warehouseman. These jobs were then passed down from father to son, so that by the end of the century the lifeblood of Liverpool's fortune – its port – was firmly in the rough hands of the Irish north-end labouring man.

And what of the women? Liverpool had none of those female-heavy textile mills of Lancashire, so the only work Susan or her surviving daughter Mary could do (apart from the immoral variety) was street trading, such as selling watercress, or chopped wood kindling in bundles of 'chips'. Gangs of Irish 'chip girls' were a common feature of the Victorian Liverpool streets.

The Irish were soon to extend their influence beyond the casual workplace and into the halls of power. The north-end had developed its own shopkeepers, small merchants and publicans to serve their insular community. These now represented a new Irish middle class: a constituency that could vote and represent others. A political movement developed in the north-end streets called the Irish National Party. It was an organisation founded culturally around the escalating issue of home rule for Ireland, but with a more practical local focus on the rights, interests and conditions of the Catholic immigrants. Soon INP councillors from the district were sitting in Liverpool town hall, lobbying for improvements to the health and welfare of their residents.

A huge breakthrough came with the parliamentary boundary changes of the mid-1880s, when north Liverpool was allowed for the first time to elect its own MP to Westminster. The election was won by the famous Irish nationalist politician T. P. O'Connor, who went on to serve the north end of Liverpool as an MP for nearly fifty years. North Liverpool remains the only constituency outside of the island of Ireland ever to return an Irish nationalist MP: a remarkable indication of the area's cultural history.

Sadly, Owen and Susan would not live to see these developments. Susan died in Clay Street in 1876 of paralysis, attended by Owen. Owen followed her four years later. His twenty-one-year-old son Eugene, my great-grandfather, signed Owen's death certificate with an 'x'. It is 1880; the first McGanns to arrive in England are now dead, and the future belongs to their children – anonymous members of a poor, diseased enclave of Irish exiles that still can't write their own surnames. In just a hundred years from this moment, their family's surname will be written on film posters and in numerous newspaper articles by the same nation that now glares at them suspiciously from over the ghetto wall. How did we ever get to here from there?

For Eugene, it started with a wedding. A few months after Owen's death, my great-granddad married a young woman called Mary Kelly in St Augustine's church. Mary was the daughter of an Irish dock labourer from the next street – the very definition of marrying your own kind. As for his older brother James, his trail goes quiet after 1871. I later find him as an able seaman, plying the oceans of the world. Sister Mary vanishes too, perhaps hiding behind a new husband's surname in the New World, or else languishing in some unrecorded grave in the old one. Eugene and Mary were now the last remaining McGanns in the north end. Would their lives be blighted by the same maladies that killed three of Eugene's siblings?

It doesn't start well. In January 1881, Mary gives birth to their first child, John Dennis, in a court dwelling in Carlton Street – one of the most infamous streets mentioned in 'Squalid Liverpool': 'That human beings should be permitted to live in such a place and under such conditions is a scandal and a disgrace.'

The commissioners weren't wrong. John Dennis McGann died of bronchitis at just seven months old. Something would have to change in those streets if the health of my family was ever going to improve.

* * *

Compulsory purchase legislation had been available to the Liverpool authorities since 1864 for the purpose of slum clearance, but very little had been done about the courts and cellars near the north docks. Cases became mired in vested interests, commercial compensation and local sectarian politics. Things finally began to move in 1883 with the formation of Liverpool's Insanitary Property Committee. This committee oversaw the destruction of insanitary housing, with new dock warehousing and railway development expanding into the spaces previously occupied by the courts. However, there were soon suspicions. Although the private enterprises involved had agreed to build replacement housing for the locals, the price of this new housing was way beyond the means of the poor Irish whose dwellings they'd demolished. The displaced labouring poor were therefore forced to leave the district and seek alternative slum housing in nearby boroughs like Everton – thereby simply transferring the problem of overcrowding and disease elsewhere. Meanwhile, the lucrative dockside district was cleansed of troublesome nationalist paupers.

Local INP politicians smelt a rat. They believed that the religious and political power-base of the Liverpool Irish was being gerrymandered by slum clearances in order to re-establish a Protestant control in north Liverpool. The INP demanded that all slum clearances be accompanied by healthy and affordable new housing for their tribe, close to their dockland place of work. It was an issue they were willing to fight for, and one that soon arrived at Eugene's own doorstep.

The death of Eugene and Mary McGann's eldest son was followed by the birth of two more children, James and Owen Joseph. This time, thankfully, their boys thrived. As the twentieth century dawned, Eugene, Mary and the now teenaged James and Owen Joseph were living in nearby Whitley Street. Yet this street had been earmarked for slum clearance, and Eugene's family were facing eviction. The INP stepped in and urged the tenants to refuse to leave unless they could be guaranteed cheap replacement housing – but to no avail. In August 1902, Eugene and his neighbours were forcibly smoked out of their dwellings. The next time I'd see them, they'd be living hand-to-mouth on the other side of the city. The McGanns' four-decade-long residence in the pestilence-ridden Irish ghetto of north Liverpool had come to an end.

Despite the loss of Whitley Street, the INP would eventually win its battle to balance slum clearances in the north end with cheap new housing for residents. Liverpool Corporation started to design and build local tenements: multi-storey municipal workers' dwellings that to our cosseted eyes might seem like a grim kind of gift. In fact, these tenements were by orders of magnitude more safe, clean and disease-free than the slums they'd replaced. There were windows for ventilation, a balcony for hanging washing and gas for cooking and heating water. And flushing toilets! Future generations of my family would call these tenements home. And they really were. It was real progress: a sword taken to the first head of the beast of pestilence – a humane, methodical approach to public health that married environmental policy with the aims of medicine to eradicate infectious disease. Hygiene, sanitation and public space: the potent new cicatrix scratched into the arm of civic life. By the start of the First World War, the city would be a noted international pioneer of social housing. Of the 22,000 court dwellings that had existed when Owen arrived in Liverpool, only 2,771 remained, and these too were scheduled for demolition. The grand epidemics that had plagued the city for nearly a century were at last on the run.

It may seem odd that the place that brought my family such misery and malady would be somewhere from which they'd finally have to be smoked out. But maybe it shouldn't. A family can stretch itself beyond the flesh and blood of the bodies that constitute it. It can grow by necessity to embrace those other families that live in the same fetid spaces; fused in the sweat of the dockyard or in shared eulogies over children's corpses. Those courts – however pestilential – were home to my forebears. For every tribe, even an infected one, needs a shared canvas on which to paint its identity.

The Liverpool Irish have always occupied a rather dowdy corner of the Irish emigration story. They were flotsam – washed up on a nearby shore while the rest travelled on to brighter lands across the oceans. As the twentieth century arrived, waves of Irish emigrants would continue to pass through Liverpool, yet these would quickly travel on to newer, more promising destinations. The Liverpool Irish were no longer replenished by people from the old country and as the first generation of arrivals died off, their children became increasingly detached from the culture that had defined them. They were left with the customs of a land they'd never seen, and a religion that offered joy in the next world but little in the way of social and economic redemption in this one. What would happen when the hovels of the north end were finally razed, and its people scattered throughout the city? Would the social pestilence that had characterised them in the eyes of others finally be consigned to the past?

The most poetic irony was that, as this ghetto tribe slowly dispersed, their culture and high birth rate eventually came to redefine what it meant to be a Liverpudlian in the eyes of the outside world. No longer was it the bourgeois Victorian seaport shaped by a south Lancastrian mercantile middle class; it would in future be known as an insular, working-class, essentially Irish-Catholic city. In a way, the worst fears of those genteel Victorian stone-throwers had been realised: the Irish slum dwellers had infected them all. Yet the infection was cultural rather than epidemiological. Half the population of modern Liverpool can now claim Irish ancestry. The north-end ghetto grew to embrace the image of the whole city.

Yet this view risks being just another form of cultural shorthand; a compressing of nuance that flattens out the many delicate human distinctions existing within the population. Liverpool has a proud Welsh heritage too – not to mention Protestant, Jewish, Chinese, Caribbean, Polish, African, Greek and a hundred other cultures that any cosmopolitan seaport can throw into the mix. All humanity is there, yet popular shorthand can easily compress this variety into a single convenient pen-sketched caricature, however benign.

* * *

The Irish of north Liverpool had always had a very particular relationship with the benign, in the shape of the Catholic faith they'd brought with them from Ireland. The Church's schools and parishes, with their associated sporting and social clubs, now became the glue that bonded the former Irish to their lost heritage. Attempts were made to import ethnic Irish games such as Gaelic football and hurling into the Liverpool Catholic sporting leagues to help retain some cultural link to the old country. Yet these attempts at cultural implantation were all in vain. The Liverpool Irish were now keener to test their tribal mettle across sectarian boundaries, partaking in the new English ball games enthusiastically adopted by the working classes of Britain. The greatest of these games was Association Football.

Liverpool's visceral love for the most popular sport on earth stretches back to the beginnings of the English Football League in 1888, when north Liverpool club Everton became one of the twelve founding members. Four years later, Everton would spawn another local club called Liverpool. These two teams grew to be giants of the nation's national game. Their vast commercial stadia now stare out over the cramped back-to-back terraced streets near where I grew up; a reminder of the clubs' humbler beginnings, and their previous close proximity to the supporters who followed them.

Liverpool's deep passion for football never divided along sectarian or social boundaries, making it distinct from other cities or regions with a religious or cultural divide. Whereas Glasgow had two clubs, Celtic and Rangers, that declared separate ethnic and sectarian affiliations, Liverpool's did not. A Catholic was just as likely to support Liverpool as Everton. Football was therefore a neutral space into which one could declare tribal allegiance without violent consequences. To the Irish of Liverpool, it was also a pastime as infectious as any pestilence. While the Catholic sporting leagues largely kept to themselves at amateur level, the urge to test footballing skills against the 'other lot' soon led to much greater cross-cultural cooperation. Football became a sporting lingua franca – common turf that helped to take the Irish Catholics of Liverpool beyond their ghetto walls and into wider British cultural life. Later, military service and its accompanying regimental sport would further cement a love of the beautiful game with a wider sense of British identity.

As the twentieth century got into its stride, the two-headed beast of pestilence seemed finally to be in retreat from my family. The first head, pestilence itself, had been cleaved by a marriage of medical science with enlightened social policy. Once the slums were flattened and government healthcare could organise widespread approaches to prevention in the form of vaccination and hygiene, the infectious scourges that had tortured my family for generations were finally eradicated.

But what of the second head? The pestilent people – those incurable carriers of Dr Duncan's 'moral contamination'? Did my family's dispersal from the ghetto, and the uniting cultural influences of workplace, barrack room and sports field, finally wash us clean of our ancient moral stigma?

Not entirely. A traumatic incident in my own life taught me that a cultural pestilence is a far more subtle and enduring pathogen, more likely to mutate according to expediency than to be entirely eradicated. Stones may be dropped, but they can remain forever near to hand.

The bitterest irony was that this lesson was communicated through the supposedly benign lingua franca of football.

Testimony

By their example and intercourse with others they are rapidly lowering the standard of comfort among their English neighbours, communicating their own vicious and apathetic habits, and fast extinguishing all sense of moral dignity, independence and self-respect.

Dr William Duncan, on the character of the Liverpool Irish in 'Local Reports on the Sanitary Condition of The Labouring Population of England', July 1842

Liverpool is a handsome city with a tribal sense of community. A combination of economic misfortune . . . and an excessive predilection for welfarism have created a peculiar, and deeply unattractive, psyche among many Liverpudlians. They see themselves whenever possible as victims, and resent their victim status; yet at the same time they wallow in it. Part of this flawed psychological state is that they cannot accept that they might have made any contribution to their misfortunes, but seek rather to blame someone else for it, thereby deepening their sense of shared tribal grievance against the rest of society.

Spectator, 16 October 2004

'Nobody dare say anything about [Liverpool] supporters for fear of being accused of insensitivity. But some of them were like animals. They were drunk and violent and their actions were vile.'

A senior police officer, speaking four days after the events that led to ninety-six Liverpool football supporters being unlawfully killed at Hillsborough Stadium, Sheffield.
Daily Mail, 19 April 1989

Mostly I remember the sound. Snatches of colour. The persistent low roar of human shock mixed with confusion. The red of football shirts on lifeless bodies. The gruesome crimson of a young man's face, dead from asphyxiation, his corpse lying on the pitch. The sound of my brother Paul crying next to me – something I'd never heard before. Twisted sobs that fought against their own release. A day of gasping breaths squeezed out against their will.

It's 15 April 1989. The kind of clear, clean spring day that promises are born in. Liverpool are playing Nottingham Forest in the semi-final of the FA Cup, and brother Paul and I have tickets to the game. The tie is taking place on neutral territory in Sheffield, in the faded grandeur of Hillsborough Stadium. There had been complaints from Liverpool supporters about the venue. Earlier matches had exposed organisational problems at the old ground – insufficient ticket allocations, ineffective crowd control. Yet these were small details. Complaints now gave way to the excitement of the moment, the celebration of a game that formed a common language for families displaced by geography, age or social class. Families like mine.

By 1989, our separate careers had propelled my family away from Liverpool, and, like all expanding universes, the galaxies of our individual lives had also accelerated us away from each other – geographically, emotionally, socially. Yet there was always football. That emotional and spiritual language which, for a brief time, enabled us to combine our disparate voices into a single oral history: a portable heritage that we carried with us throughout our new cosmos.

Support for Liverpool Football Club was rooted deep in my family's mythology. It even had its own creation myth. My father's older brother Jimmy began support for Liverpool in the early 1930s, when his uncle took him to a department store to buy a football kit. At the time, Liverpool was a small and unsuccessful club, dwarfed by the successes of their city rivals Everton. It was expected that young Jimmy would select the blue of Everton to wear. However, in an epiphany worthy of the saints, Jim saw the red kit of Liverpool covering a lowly shop dummy, and knew in an instant he could wear no other. His uncle pleaded, but to no avail. From then on Jimmy and Dad were lifelong reds and we inherited this tribe as children. When Liverpool later rose to dominance, the story was related as one of prophetic vision – the alignment of our family with a glorious future. Red was our talismanic colour: the irrepressible symbol of blood, passion and success.

Or so the story went. My brother Mark later made a wry observation about the mythical power of the colour our uncle had chosen. Jimmy, Mark said, suffered from a form of red-green colour blindness, which would have rendered the red he'd seen as a dull, muddy ochre. Like bird lime, or the cement between old bricks. Not quite so talismanic. But then that's what happens when medical reality meets a grand narrative: variations in human colour are secondary to wider imperatives.

A young girl's face, bleached white by savage experience, streaked with mute tears.

Paul and I had first noticed the pretty teenage volunteers of the St John's Ambulance charity walking down the touchline about ten minutes before the match started. Two girls smiling in the sunshine, flirting back at the young Liverpool supporters who threw grins and come-ons at them from the stand. They looked about seventeen, and had clearly modified their St John's

Ambulance uniforms to better suit their figures and youth: skirts raised a little, caps worn at an angle. Paul and I laughed. The timeless dance of it. The joy and novelty of spectacle. The endless blue skies of the young. Barely twenty minutes before the blackness descended.

The sun blazed down, and we had good seats near to the pitch in the North Stand, a little way from the old terraces allotted to the Liverpool supporters. We'd been lucky; ticket allocation had been down to chance, one's place in the ground depended entirely on the final digit of a serial number printed on your season ticket. We'd both fallen within the digits entitling us to seats. Other supporters had to stand in the Leppings Lane end of the ground. We looked over there; it was still strangely unoccupied a few minutes before kick-off, although the central area behind the goal seemed full. Crammed, even. We had no idea then just how lucky we'd been – how a single digit on a ticket could mean the difference between a harsh experience and extinction.

The football game started promptly at three o'clock, although few supporters standing in the Leppings Lane end had yet taken their places. The terrace was divided into five separate enclosures accessed from the rear. The front of these were caged off to prevent supporters invading the playing area. The areas to the sides were sparsely populated. The one directly behind the goal was now a writhing mass of red. We could see fans pressed tightly against the bars at the front, even as more supporters were arriving at the back.

A few minutes in, and I remember striker Peter Beardsley hitting a beautiful shot that rattled off the crossbar. It felt like a good sign.

Then everything went still. The Liverpool goalkeeper became distracted by events behind his goal. The referee waved for play to stop. There were minutes of confusion. We could see that supporters were struggling to climb over the fences in the central Leppings Lane area to reach the pitch. Rumours flew to compensate for a lack of announcement. It became obvious that something was wrong. If one looked carefully, one could spy supporters lying on the ground.

Soon all careful vision was unnecessary. We watched a Liverpool supporter walk off the pitch accompanied by police officers, and pass directly in front of our seats. He seemed perfectly alert – almost angry. As he passed, he raised his arm towards the crowd. There was a collective intake of breath. The bones in the man's arm had been crushed by some terrible force into the stepped shape of the staircase he'd been standing on. At the top of his misshapen arm his hand, like a grotesque puppet, wriggled freely. Even as I recall this, I find it hard to comprehend. My mind – like the public's mind in the disaster's aftermath – searches for a more accommodating explanation in the face of discomforting evidence. Yet sometimes comfort must give way to truth.

The minutes inched by. The pitch became filled with a roaring confusion of bodies and unfocused urgency. It was clear to anyone watching that we were witnessing an act of tragedy rather than violence. The opposition supporters stood, like we did, in their own enclosure, waiting for an announcement to explain the things we saw. After what seemed an age the police arrived, marching in long, close lines from the stadium entrance onto the pitch. To our disbelief, these close lines formed up next to our own immobile stand, and the terraces from which bodies were still being hauled – rather than going to assist the injured and the dead littering the field. The police turned towards Liverpool supporters in a defensive posture – as if to guard against a violent pitch invasion. We screamed in desperate objection. One could see the discomfort on the policemen's faces, yet they stood their ground. They were evidently under specific orders, which served a different narrative.

A few feet behind them, citizens lay dying – their faces discoloured by asphyxiation.

Looking back, it was the moment that the first uneasy hints of a further malady began to creep like vomit from the gut. The sense that we were witnessing not simply a terrible human tragedy, but the birth of something uniquely cruel – something perpetrated by the powerful that would transform the tragedy of innocents into an instrument of torture. However, hindsight is a tower, and we were still in the long grass, searching for a more accommodating explanation in the face of discomforting evidence.

I saw a father, shocked dumb, carrying his young child, the limbs hanging limply: a scarf-clad pietà. Denim-clad teenagers weaving in and out of the line of policemen tore the advertising hoardings from the walls for use as makeshift stretchers. The policemen, watching, hesitated. Should they arrest these delinquents for vandalism? The grim absurdity of their position began to insinuate itself into their ranks. First one broke. Then another. Humanity reasserted itself against obedience. The police began to help the dying and the dead. Yet the ambulances still did not come.

The bodies of suffocated victims were lined up in front of the North Stand, feet from where we stood. A row of corpses stretched along the turf – burgundy cheeks and hands like a grim smear on the vibrant green. Postmortem hypostasis is an intense purple-red discolouration of the superficial layers of the skin due to reduced haemoglobin in the blood. A garish ripening induced by oxygen starvation.

We saw the St John's Ambulance girls once more. They were standing on the edge of the pitch – pale and frozen with shock – clinging together for comfort as the horror danced around them. The young girl's face, bleached white by savage experience, streaked with mute tears. My brother began to cry. Twisted sobs that fought against their own release. I didn't cry then, although I would. Many times.

I mourn the loss of many kinds of innocence that day – my own and that of others. I often think of those young ambulance women, and where they might be now. Their youth bestowed a fundamental right to triviality that the grotesque events had stolen. Their expected treatment of minor cuts or mild heat exposure had turned into a forced attendance at a massacre. Despite the many larger acts of injustice perpetrated that day, I regard their lost innocence as a vicious theft.

It took hours before we were permitted to leave the ground. We were herded out of the twilit stadium in silence, and made our way towards the car. We needed to find a telephone. There had been no way to tell anyone we were safe. In an age before mobile phones, it was impossible to find a phone box within miles of the stadium that didn't have a huge queue of supporters waiting to ring their loved ones. Our family had to endure the purgatory of the bereaved until we were a sufficient distance from events. Yet we knew we were the lucky ones. For many good families, that night marked the beginning of a torture that our own family would never have to experience.

As Paul and I walked down a Sheffield backstreet, dazed by tragedy and wearing our scarves tight against the evening chill, we suddenly heard a shouted profanity above us, directed against supporters of Liverpool. Pieces of a paving stone were thrown from a high balcony in our direction. Shocked out of our daze, we ran for cover.

Stones for the pestilent. The first of many.

* * *

Four days later. I'm lying in my bedsit flat in Kilburn, London. The days since the disaster have been spent in a distracting anxiety. I can still hear that persistent low roar of human shock mixed with confusion like tinnitus in my ears. The world I knew the previous week has been subverted – the soft borders of my life whetted into a sharper kind of edge. Every day I walk to the newsagent's and purchase a pile of newspapers, scouring the reports on the aftermath for evidence of a deeper sense or purpose – an explanation that will clothe the horror I witnessed in the more merciful funeral garments of a shared human tragedy.

As I walk into the newsagent's that morning, the front page of the *Sun* screams at me from the newsstand.

THE TRUTH
Some fans picked pockets of victims
Some fans urinated on the brave cops
Some fans beat up PC giving kiss of life

It takes a few seconds for the enormity of the allegations to sink in. I pick up the newspaper.

In one shameful episode, a gang of Liverpool fans noticed the blouse of a girl trampled to death in the crush had risen above her breasts. As a policeman struggled in vain to revive her, they jeered: 'Throw her up here, we will **** her.'

The letters are coyly blanked out, but the meaning is clear. Fuck. 'We will fuck her.' Liverpool supporters are being accused of joking about having sex with a trampled corpse as the dead bodies of their own supporters and families lay all around them. It's a libel so grotesque it stops my breath. But so bold. So confident. On the front page of the biggest-selling newspaper in Britain. And directed, by association, at me, one of those 'shameful' Liverpool fans.

A year after this now-infamous front page, journalists Peter Chippindale and Chris Horrie described the events that led to its publication. They said that editor Kelvin MacKenzie had hesitated over the headline,* as he knew that to print such unsupported allegations beneath a claim of 'THE TRUTH' was a dangerous and provocative attack on part of his own readership – many of whom were currently burying their dead. Yet he went ahead.

More revealing, perhaps, was that they said he'd originally planned to use an even more provocative headline, but had been persuaded against it. The original headline read:

'YOU SCUM.'

'Scum' is one of the harshest insults in modern British urban

---

* Chris Horrie and Peter Chippindale, *Stick It Up Your Punter! The Rise and Fall of the* Sun (Heinemann, 1990).

slang. It's short for 'the scum of the earth', an expression defined by the *Cambridge English Dictionary* as referring to 'the worst type of people that can be imagined'. The word 'scum' itself references a filthy layer of dirt that forms on top of a liquid.

An insoluble, pestilential and disposable waste product.

* * *

The Hillsborough football disaster is a scar on Britain's public life. It was the worst disaster in British sport, with ninety-six fatalities – and it ultimately became one of its most protracted and painful scandals. This was due to a long-term institutional failure to establish the true cause and correct responsibility for those deaths. The cause of the tragedy was a catastrophic failure of crowd management by senior members of the South Yorkshire Police service who'd been responsible for safety that day. In order to deflect blame, officers had deliberately leaked misinformation to the press. They claimed that Liverpool fans had caused the tragedy by their own drunken behaviour and actions – even accusing these fans of urinating on police officers and picking the pockets of their own dead. The accusations were grotesquely false; not simply insulting to the lives and families of those killed, but also to the many Liverpool supporters who had helped security personnel to stretcher victims away and give first aid.

Yet the accusations resonated with the wider assumptions of the British public and media regarding the moral character of Liverpool fans. In contrast, the moral standing of those officers making the accusations seemed unimpeachable. The nation's press therefore gave enthusiastic prominence to those false stories over the following days and months, and a hasty libel settled into an assumed truth. One publication, the *London Evening Standard*, blamed the 'tribal passions' of Liverpool supporters for causing the tragedy.

Tribal passions. That incurable, pestilent tribe invoked again, more than a century later. Not simply a deadly event, but bound to the morality of the people who suffered it. Dr Duncan's disparaging moral voice echoing across time.

Despite an early report into the tragedy establishing that cause lay squarely with the police organisers, the libel continued and became established in the public mind. Politicians of all colours echoed this sentiment, rebuffing persistent calls for an independent inquiry. Despite the tireless campaigning of organisations like the Hillsborough Justice Campaign, the lies inflicted on the victims endured for an astonishing twenty-seven years. Eventually, in 2016, an exhaustive independent inquiry finally established the real truth: that the only pestilent tribe to infect the moral health of our nation that day had been the powerful tribe that lied to conceal its own failures.

Despite the many subsequent public apologies and reappraisals, there remains a small private scar in those events for me, scratched into my arm as a painful caution against future complacency. It's a lesson on the nature of pestilence.

One of the curious aspects of public prejudice against any tribe is that it flattens out the many delicate human distinctions existing within that group. Liverpool Football Club is a cosmopolitan and globally supported team. At that football match were many different types of character: good people and bad, idle and industrious, off-duty policemen, the unemployed, lawyers, single parents, rich businessmen. Actors like myself. All humanity – yet compressed by the prejudice of others into a single pestilence. The second head of the beast.

Hillsborough taught me that a stone can still be thrown down at my family from the higher balconies of the nation I love if those in positions of power have enough need of it. People like me can be slaughtered without adequate mercy, sympathy or redress. A libel can be freely perpetrated against those I love. This can be fuelled by the press, carried in the prejudices of the public, and sustained at the highest levels of public office.

Despite a century of medical advancement and social improvement, my family remains a pestilence of convenience to a nation in need of a more accommodating explanation.

3

EXPOSURE

Exposure n.

1. A medical condition caused by prolonged contact with extremes of temperature or climate. (cf. Hypothermia, Frostbite)
2. The introduction of an individual or group to new stimulus, insight or experience.

MEDICINE

Homo sapiens is an amazingly versatile species. We're able to live on every continent on earth and in a huge variety of conditions, from the freezing wastes of Greenland to the sweltering deserts of Africa. One biological reason for this is that humans are 'warm-blooded', or endothermic – able to regulate their body temperature regardless of external climate. This is known as thermoregulation, and it's controlled in an area of our brains called the hypothalamus. Our body maintains its core temperature at a remarkably narrow band of between 36.5 and 37.5 degrees Celsius. This ensures that vital enzymes in our system can carry out essential cell functions. Our body is a ship that sails through life's extremes with a portable boiler and a precision thermostat.

Warm-blooded humans have taken a different evolutionary path to cold-blooded creatures, which must get their energy from their surroundings. This gives humans specific advantages and challenges. We make our own heat from the food we consume, so our bodies stay active regardless of how cold it is. Lizards can be sluggish until warmed by the sun, so limiting the environments and hours they can thrive in. Yet self-heating means more of our food is used for energy, so we need to feed more often to keep the boiler stoked. Also, our body can only do so much itself to keep its precision thermostat balanced. If temperatures are too hot, we sweat to provide a primitive form of cooling by evaporation. In cold weather we shiver to generate a little warmth. Hardly high-tech stuff. Luckily, the human body outsources its key thermoregulation responsibilities to our sentient brains. As intelligent creatures, we've learned how to clothe ourselves in extremes of cold, or find shade in hot sun. Together, the mind and body make a great heat manager.

But what happens if extreme conditions mean we *can't* help our body maintain its essential temperature?

When core temperature becomes too hot – perhaps due to overexposure to hot sun – we enter a state of hyperthermia or heat exhaustion. This might only be a degree or so above normal, but already our body feels it; we can experience sweating, dizziness, fatigue and nausea. If it rises just another degree or two we reach heat stroke, and things get really dangerous. Our body's ability to regulate heat is overwhelmed. We become confused, blood pressure plummets, and if we don't get help soon our organs fail and we die.

Similarly, it only takes a drop of a few degrees to induce hypothermia due to excessive cold. At first we shiver uncontrollably and hyperventilate. A few degrees further and the shivers stop, but we become drowsy, slurred and confused. If our temperature descends to 28 degrees or lower we lose consciousness and, eventually, our life.

Hypothermia is accelerated if we become immersed in cold water. A sudden exposure to freezing water – for example, by jumping into an Arctic ocean from a sinking ship – may induce cold shock, a disorientating trauma state that compromises breathing and muscle control. After ten minutes in the water we are losing heat so fast that our body decreases the blood flow to our extremities in an effort to keep our core organs warm. Our limbs start to lose their feeling and movement – bad news if we're trying to stay afloat. Before long, hypothermia takes us to a watery grave.

Even if we manage to claw our way out of the water and onto something that floats, our exposure problems aren't over. Exposed flesh has its own susceptibility to freezing temperatures. This comes in the form of frostbite. Frostbite is damage caused to the flesh by prolonged exposure to extremes of cold, beginning at temperatures around freezing point. This can be exacerbated by wind-chill and damp. As with the limbs in the water, the circulation to the blood vessels in exposed areas becomes constricted to protect the vital organs. The first stage is called frostnip. Initially only the outer skin is affected. There are pins and needles and an aching of the digits, then a localised numbness. If warmth is found, the damage won't be permanent. If untreated, it progresses to hardness and blisters. Eventually the damage creeps deep into our bodies – to muscle, nerve and bone. Parts of our flesh begin to die. If rescue doesn't come soon, we're lost entirely.

Yet, what is affected most by the malady of exposure? Is it just a physical condition, or is there a freezing of the spirit that precedes the hardening of the flesh? Does exposure to the *experience* of our predicament chill us faster than the wind and water? Or might the psychological extremity of our condition provide the mental fuel we need to express our true nature in the quality of our subsequent actions?

Human beings are marked by exposure to significant events inside their brains as well as their bodies. At the front of our skull is an area called the prefrontal cortex. This is a significant area for what we commonly call our short-term memory – the place where we process our current lived experience as conscious thoughts. It's a vast but impermanent network of electrical connections, shifting and reforming as the seconds pass. When a stricken sailor jumps from that sinking ship into the freezing ocean, his prefrontal cortex is assaulted by an adrenaline-fuelled processing of inputs from the human senses: the gasping cold against the flesh, the lurch in the stomach from the icy plunge, the screaming of desperate humanity nearby, the hellish vision of iron and varnished timber plunging into the abyss. The adrenaline is an important element. Our sensory input at times like this is not merely physical, but highly chemical and emotional. We're in what we call our 'flight-or-fight' response – a primeval safety mechanism that heightens our focus, emotions and reactions in times of perceived threat. Events at these crucial times are given the highest priority by our brain.

Within a short while, the shifting clouds of our heightened short-term experiences are turned into more permanent form as memory. This involves a region deep in the brain called the hippocampus as well as the cortex. The brain contains billions of nerve cells called neurons. These are encoded with memories by forming complex physical connections with other neurons through synapses – electrical and chemical junctions where information is exchanged, and links between connected pieces of information in the memory are physically established. Our memory is defined by the nature of these synaptic links.

Not all memory is the same. There is implicit memory and explicit memory. Implicit memories include those subconscious manual skills we acquire, such as playing tennis or driving a car. Explicit memories can be simply semantic, like knowing the name of a town or the date of someone's birthday. But the most complex explicit memories are episodic – meaning a connected sequence of emotions and events, a narrative account of a particular time and place or the step-by-step visualisation of our way to a certain destination. When we 'remember' events in our life, this is usually what we mean.

Recent research suggests that episodic memories are stored in both the hippocampus and the cortex. Yet such memories don't just get filed away as a single item. Instead, they reside as networks of subtle or strongly associated images, emotions, thoughts, places and sounds. Recalling a single child's face from the sea disaster may later be enough to bring the whole awful event flooding back for that stricken mariner. These networks are *constructions* of our reality – they're not simply verbatim recordings of external events. We make our memories, we don't just observe them. They are built using the emotions and perspectives we already possess, and then go on to shape our perspectives and emotions in the future. In this way, an episodic memory becomes a unique contributor to our essential and evolving identity – that thing we call our 'life story' – a marker for our character and place in the world, and a reference point for future behaviour and growth. Our memories are the building blocks of what makes us into us.

So necessary is the exposure of our brain to new experience and its subsequent preservation that, without it, we can't retain a functioning personality. If a human is denied interaction and stimulus early in life, then the brain fails to learn and develop properly. In the United States in 1970, welfare authorities discovered a thirteen-year-old child known as 'Genie'. Genie had been profoundly abused by her father – locked up throughout her short life and deprived of all sensory stimulus. Despite subsequent efforts to rehabilitate her, Genie remained deficient in key cognitive abilities and language. Exposure is not simply a mark left on our bodies or brains by events, it's an essential tool – the means by which we can learn and speak and grow and know ourselves. If exposure to experience is blocked, then it can't help us to make memories, and we can't become ourselves.

Likewise, if we can't retain the memories we already have, we can lose the self we cherish. The heartbreaking effects of Alzheimer's disease are well known. Clumps of protein called plaques can form in the brain, destroying neurons and disrupting the storage and retrieval of memory by synapses. As our memories become lost, we slowly lose the anchor to our identity.

Yet even a healthy memory changes in time. Whenever a past event is recalled into our consciousness it is reconstructed, not simply fetched wholesale. Although we may think we're remembering the same thing each time, we're probably not.

With each revisit we unconsciously strengthen, embellish or prune those synaptic connections, delicately shifting the nature of the memory we've constructed. Our memories are not hard-wired, but, like our bodies and our life stories, shrink, alter and grow as we do.

Exposure therefore presents itself to us as both a statement and a question. There's the external event – a turn of fortune that acts outside of our human control to freeze or burn us. Then there comes the forming of our character's response to it. Our memory of it. Our answer to the question posed by fate. Will it make us shrink, alter or grow?

The answer lies in the application of our existing selves to the challenge of new experience, and the exposition of our evolving human nature shown in the subsequent response.

History

The Adventurers: James & Owen Joseph McGann, 1901–1920

Thirty-first of March 1901. A census form reveals Eugene McGann, 42, Mary, his wife, 40, and their two boys, James, 19, and Owen Joseph, 17, living in a court dwelling in Whitley Street, part of Liverpool's north-end Irish enclave. In another year, Whitley Street will be demolished, and they will be evicted. This family has only ever known the sub-let Irish potato plots of Roscommon or the pestilent Liverpool hovel. Their lives, despite occasional bursts of destitute flight, have kept to a familiar and narrow horizon.

Yet change is coming. The McGanns will soon undergo a

mental and physical exposure to world events. The force of this malady will threaten the lives and forge the characters of its two youngest members. Before the century is much older, the essential core of both brothers will be assaulted by the icy blast of cold experience. This chapter is their account.

Back in Whitley Street, things looked pretty much as they did when the McGanns first arrived in England in 1864. Yet a closer look at the census form reveals the first stirrings of the changes they were soon to be exposed to. In the column that records occupation, Eugene is listed as a 'Marine Fireman'. This strange new occupation belonged not to the docks, but to the dank belly of Britain's great fleet of merchant steamships; coal-powered vessels that plied their trade from the great port on the Mersey to every corner of the globe.

Eugene was a merchant seaman. The McGanns had begun to look further afield for work – away from the casual fortune of the dock gang and the emigration runner. In order to survive, they'd turned their attention to the oceans that fed their city and the world that lay beyond them. James and Owen Joseph would soon follow. The ghetto-bound McGann family had ventured out to sea. They would do so for three generations.

* * *

The British merchant fleet was the preeminent powerhouse of world trade in this era. By the middle of the nineteenth century, Britain controlled a third of all the world's shipping. The decline of sail and the rise of the great coal-powered steamships in the late Victorian decades further consolidated the United Kingdom's position, with a full 50 per cent of global steam-shipping flying the British flag by the time the McGanns were sitting in Whitley Street. Britain's steam fleet was the largest and most modern in the world.

So what kind of work did these seafaring McGanns do?

Metal steamships had first been developed as a replacement for wood in the early nineteenth century. With the advent of the Industrial Revolution, iron, and later steel, would come to offer a more capacious and less maintenance-heavy alternative. This coincided with a revolution in propulsion with the development of the steam engine. The first domestic steam-powered vessel appeared on a Scottish canal in 1801, and by 1845 Isambard Kingdom Brunel's giant steamship, the SS *Great Britain*, was making its maiden voyage across the Atlantic.

The early steamships used large paddle wheels on their port and starboard sides to propel them. However, strain would be placed on the engines if one wheel lifted out of the water and another was submerged by the action of rough seas. In the 1840s, they were replaced by steam-driven screw propellers placed at the stern. This was much more efficient, and the *Great Britain* would be the first of many screw-driven iron vessels to cross the ocean.

The introduction of metal and steam didn't spell the immediate end for sails. A stock of coal wouldn't take a ship very far, so if a journey involved weeks away from reliable supplies, then wind power could provide a free and limitless alternative. The decline of sail would really come after the invention of the triple expansion engine in the 1870s. It greatly increased fuel efficiency by allowing the steam from ships' boilers to be used three times for engine propulsion before being recycled for heating. A ship could now travel long distances without needing to replenish fuel stocks.

With the decline of sail, the lives of sailors would change profoundly. No longer were men required to labour with rope, pulley and canvas in the exposed elements. Steam propulsion now impelled them to toil away in the dim-lit, blazing hot cacophony of a ship's boiler room, stoking the furnaces with the coal necessary to boil the water that turned the screw. The close-knit team of men who undertook this grim task were known as the 'black gang' – a reference to the sweat-caked coaldust that covered every inch of their flesh. The McGanns were now members of this coal-black maritime family.

A black gang consisted of two main types of worker – a fireman and a trimmer. The fireman was in charge of stoking the coal-fired furnaces to produce steam and maintaining these fires over the long voyage. This was Eugene's job, and it would later be the principal occupation of both of his sons. This work involved far more than simply throwing coal into a furnace. Ships' boilers were huge and temperamental beasts. Each one consisted of multiple furnaces and their accompanying pressure gauges and ash pits. Once the fires had been fed, they had to be carefully maintained throughout a shift or watch so that they maintained steam with the hottest, cleanest flame and steady pressure. This was physically demanding work, requiring constant attention and skill in very hot conditions.

In order to keep the furnaces stoked, firemen needed a constant supply of coal. This was the responsibility of the trimmer. A trimmer worked in the coal bunkers and handled the loading, storage and distribution of coal to the firemen. They would use shovels and wheelbarrows to ferry coal around, ensuring that enough was always at a fireman's feet, and also making sure that the great stacks of coal were evenly distributed or 'trimmed' throughout the vessel so that the ship didn't list to one side with the uneven weight – hence their name. James and Owen Joseph were employed as both trimmer and fireman during their maritime careers, and recent work by maritime history author Richard de Kerbrech provides a fascinating insight into their lives.*

At sea, the black gang would be divided into three sub-gangs that worked the boilers in round-the-clock shifts to keep the engines running constantly. Each gang would do two stretches of four hours per day, with eight hours off between. It was a troglodyte existence. Passengers would very rarely see a fireman or trimmer, as they were confined to the depths of the ship close to

* Richard P. de Kerbrech, *Down Amongst the Black Gang* (The History Press, 2014).

their work. Temperatures in a boiler room could reach fifty degrees Celsius, and on the big liners the different boilers kept their work synchronised by use of a timing mechanism that blared out a shrill alarm every ten minutes or so to indicate when the stoking cycle had to be repeated. The time interval shortened if the ship had to go faster. It was the equivalent of the merciless drummer that beat out a rhythm for the slave oarsmen on a Roman galley. If a fireman needed to defecate during this busy shift, then often the only option was to do so on their coal shovel, and dispose of the waste in the furnace. Hygienic, if not exactly genteel . . .

To endure these conditions, the men drank gallons of honey water and oatmeal and ate like horses between shifts. A particular treat was known as 'black pan' – plates of food scraps left by the passengers upstairs, which might be plentiful in seasick weather. Yet despite these feasts, even the fittest would be close to collapse by the end of four hours. Charles Lightoller, officer and famous *Titanic* survivor, described the condition of the black gang at the end of a typical shift:

> It was no uncommon sight to see a man, sometimes two, three or even four in a watch, hoisted up the ash shoot with a bucket chain hooked roughly round under their arm-pits, to be dumped on deck unconscious. A few buckets of water over them and then they were left to recover.

It seemed that the life of my ancestors at sea offered no more respite from toil and squalor than the life they'd left. Yet it would be strangely familiar to them. This was because the black gangs of the global steam age were dominated and controlled by the Liverpool Irish. The great shipping lines insisted on employing these men because, although they could be hard to handle – with a reputation for being violent, militant, drunk and insular – they were equal to the immense physical and mental demands made of them. They did the job that others couldn't.

There was a certain poetic justice to this. The appalling social conditions that had weaned the men of my family were now a perfect qualification for the hellish demands of coal-fed maritime propulsion. The soot-black heart required to pump the mercantile blood of empire around the veins of its shipping lanes could only be regulated by a community long disparaged as a pestilential curse. The empire's lepers had become its hidden pacemaker.

Mind you, regulating the black gang itself wasn't so easy. Maritime historian John Maxtone-Graham described their difficult and often violent temperaments:

Hideous conditions nurtured a breed of ruthless men. On British ships, they were invariably Liverpool-Irish ... drunken stokers, sometimes wheeled in barrows back on board ship, used to embark upon fearful battles, going after each other with slice bars, tongs, shovels, anything that came to hand. Mates had a standing order when the black gang fought: close the hatches and stand clear.

Yet the black gang were immensely proud of their ability to keep a steady head of steam, no matter what. They were a rough brotherhood, forged in heat, dirt and common heritage.

Being a black-ganger meant embracing an itinerant and hand-to-mouth existence. Voyages could be months long, and between jobs a fireman or trimmer was rarely retained. This was the age before social welfare; so once ashore, a seaman had to get himself on another voyage quickly, especially if he had a wife and large family to support back in Liverpool. Black-gangers were paid off at the end of each job, but this could quickly be squandered. Southampton resident Alfred Fanstone observed firemen coming off a voyage in those days: 'They all came home like walking skeletons ... and they had one glorious booze up, which led to fighting, and then off they went again.'

As a precaution against their own natures, married men could opt to have part of their wages allotted to their families in advance. This system had been introduced because many crewmen would pawn their best clothes when going to sea in order for their families to feed themselves in their absence. They'd then reclaim the clothing when they were paid off.

This wasn't yet a concern for James or Owen Joseph. In the first decade of the twentieth century they were single men, and despite the rough conditions of their life, their world was expanding, exposing their minds to the bright light of new experience. James and Owen Joseph would routinely circumnavigate the planet in an age when others of their social class were confined to their immediate streets or fields. Once ashore, their exposure to the blazing Antipodes or the humid, fragrant tropics must have baptised their senses with a fresh synaptic burst of new memory. How would they respond? How would it influence their actions?

For Owen Joseph, the introduction to this new world was a baptism of fire. I first found him at sea in 1904, three years after the census in Whitley Street. He was employed as a young trimmer on the SS *Tropic*, making its maiden voyage from Liverpool to Australia. It was an eventful journey. When the ship finally reached Australia on 3 September, the *Adelaide Advertiser* described its ordeal: 'On August 13 a terrific west gale, with squalls of hurricane force and mountainous seas was encountered, lasting 48 hours.'

I try to imagine it. Mountainous seas, experienced deep in the fiery confines of a boiler room. Young Owen Joseph, his world rocked almost to vertical by the forces of the storm, struggling in the failing light as the coal spills and shifts, and the men shout curses and orders. He's unable to see the enemy that shakes him – adrenaline driving him onwards through the fear and the cries and the darkness. One imagines that the fitful attempts at sleep between the chaos of working in a storm for two solid days would torture the young mind even more than the work.

Was it here that Owen Joseph first developed a need to absent himself from the close confinement of others when his life required it?

When the voyage was over, Owen Joseph emerged into the bright light of New South Wales, newly paid off, his few possessions in his sack. Sydney's cramped dockside dwellings beckoned, as did the bars and brothels that offered to relieve him of his wages. If a black-ganger found himself paid off in a distant port, he'd look for a new ship to take him back to Liverpool, or else onwards around the world.

Before the First World War, both James and Owen Joseph were familiar lodgers in Sydney and the other Antipodean ports. In August 1909, James arrived in New South Wales as a trimmer on the SS *Afric*, via Cape Town and Melbourne. At the same time, his brother Owen Joseph was working a remarkable passage as a fireman on the SS *Oravia*, heading back to Liverpool from Callao in Peru, via Iquique, Antofagasta, Valparaiso, Port Stanley in the Falklands, Montevideo, Rio de Janeiro, St Vincent, Lisbon, Vigo, La Coruña and La Pallice. The brothers never worked together, but instead zigzagged across the oceans of the world, often at opposite ends of it. As the Edwardian age drew to a close, their bachelor lives were as rough and free as any McGann before them, and probably freer than most who came after. In their own shaky hand they began to sign their names on crew manifests, rather than the customary 'x'. They'd learned to read and write; new synaptic networks flourishing in young brains gorged on new experience. Although they were poor, they were masters of their own destiny and members of an adventurous fraternity. A new kind of family.

It would soon be the only family they had. In January 1910, their father Eugene died in Liverpool of phthisis pulmonalis – an antiquated term for tuberculosis. Just a year later their mother Mary would follow. The boys were now orphans.

They quickly returned to their new family. I found Owen Joseph in Sydney in early 1912, arriving on the steamer SS *Karori* from New Zealand. Meanwhile, James was leaving South Africa on the *Kinfauns Castle* bound for Southampton, arriving in the Hampshire port on 23 March. In spite of the recent death of Edward VII and the passing of their own parents, the world must have felt as rigid and secure as the maritime hierarchy they toiled under. Their lives were poor and tough, but they had their place. The twentieth century had so far shown no intention of disrupting the steady assumptions of the age that had preceded it.

So far.

A bittersweet privilege of historical hindsight is the ability to gaze back at lives lived in blissful ignorance of events about to unfold. It might be the Pompeiian citizen waking to hear Vesuvius rumbling; the American president waving from a Dallas car; or the Austrian archduke alighting in Sarajevo. We don't see history coming until it's pitched us into its icy water. As Owen

Joseph McGann arrived in Sydney, his world had just two years left before a colossal war would rip its assumptions to pieces.

* * *

As kids, we only had one picture of my paternal grandfather. But what a picture it was. He's posing in a photographer's studio in full army uniform, ready to go off to the Great War. Many

British families have a similar photo: the optimism of the new recruit, before slaughter took their bravado away. Yet there's a glaring anomaly in the image that marks it out from the standard Kitchener fare. Owen Joseph is wearing the wide-brimmed hat and khaki of the Australian infantry.

'He jumped ship in Australia, and signed up early in the war,' said Auntie Mary.

After that, he'd apparently been posted right back to a training camp near Liverpool, where the superior pay, easy discipline and healthy rations of the Aussies made him the envy of the British recruits from his old neighbourhood. 'They were so jealous, some of the lads thumped him for bragging!' said my uncle Jim.

I was curious. How did Owen Joseph end up in the Australian infantry? How did exposure to that awful war mark him? Where did he serve? Was it the gruesome cauldron of Gallipoli, or the churned mud of France? Would his exposure to that experience be as colourful as the uniform suggested?

Actually it would, although not in the way I'd imagined . . .

The earliest record of Owen Joseph's military service is the 'attestation paper' he signed on his enlistment into the Australian Imperial Force at Warwick Farm, New South Wales, on 15 September 1915. He'd been staying with his brother James in Kent Street, Sydney, down by the harbour. He's signed proudly as 'O. J. McGann'. The war has already been raging for a year, so it's not the hasty impulse of a fresh-faced recruit. He knows what awaits him. Did he jump ship to sign up like Mary said? It seems plausible. Both brothers plied their trade in Australian waters, and so Owen Joseph may simply have decided that enough was enough, and his country needed him back in Europe.

Whatever the reasons, Owen Joseph was now a private in the 2nd Battalion of the Australian infantry. He set sail on a troop ship to England and, just as Auntie Mary said, he was posted to a training camp in Warrington, near Liverpool. However, things soon took on a much less heroic tone. After just eighty-three days in the Aussie Army, Owen Joseph went walkabout: nine days absent without leave in early December. A disciplinary charge form reveals his docked pay as punishment.

Was this just an aberration? A pre-Christmas binge before they shipped him off to France? Unfortunately not. Owen Joseph did it again in early January – and this time the army issued a warrant for my grandfather's arrest for desertion. On the back of the warrant is a charming handwritten list of the kit items he's absconded with: 1 boots, 1 felt hat, 2 dungarees, 1 chin strap . . .

What the hell was he up to? Owen Joseph was nowhere near the front, so he wasn't deserting his post in battle. Was this behaviour unusual, or were his fellow soldiers up to the same tricks? Historian Roger Beckett observed that casual absentee-ism accounted for over half of all military offences in the Aussie Army. A memo to depot commanders in December 1915 illus-trated official concerns:

> It has come to notice that in several camps throughout the Commonwealth large numbers of men absent themselves without leave, some for short periods such as week-ends and others for long periods. That this offence should have become so general indicates a great lack of discipline in the camps concerned.

It seemed that those strapping volunteer Aussies didn't get the memo about a narrow conformity to British military discipline. Some would simply stroll out of the gates for a few days' sightseeing after square-bashing. So did Owen Joseph feel this offence to be a petty one – an optional excursion, rather than a desertion – or was it an indicator of something else in his character? A tendency to answer only to his own narrow disciplines when wider events impinged upon him?

Whether petty or serious, the fact remained that my grandfather was a fugitive for the next year and a half. Wanted notices went out across the Commonwealth for his arrest, as a listing in the February 1916 edition of the *New South Wales Police Gazette* illustrates:

McGann. O, Joseph. Private, 31 years of age, 5 feet 7 inches high, fresh complexion, brown hair, blue eyes, tattooed on both forearms; born England. Deserted 5 January 1916.

I love the biographical detail of my grandfather's diminutive size and tattooed arms – trademarks of a wiry, tough seaman – although I might have preferred the information to come through family anecdote, rather than through the British Empire's equivalent of *Crimewatch*. So where was he in 1916? I expect he went back to sea. Service in the vast mercantile marine might have provided temporary anonymity to a black-ganger who kept his head down. But surely not forever. How was he going to evade the long arm of military justice?

The answer, when I finally discovered it, made me laugh out loud. On 3 August 1917, Owen Joseph – now calling himself simply Joseph McGann – strolled into another army recruiting office in Western Australia and enlisted as a new recruit in the Australian Imperial Force infantry for a second time. A second attestation paper reveals that a 'fitter's labourer' called 'Joseph McGann' was recruited in Fremantle. Amusingly, when asked to list previous service, he states only that he'd been a member of the Royal Naval Reserve – wisely omitting to mention his more recent military adventures. The reborn recruit then undergoes a second bout of basic training at Blackboy Hill camp in the Perth hills, and is assigned to the 51st Battalion, leaving Fremantle on the troop ship *Canterra*, and arriving in Southampton on 30 January 1918.

Was my grandfather finally ready to embrace the discipline that an exposure to the Great War required of him?

Not quite. Upon arrival at a training camp in Wiltshire, the new Joe quickly returned to his old tricks. His service record reveals several fresh charges of absent without leave, complete with docked pay. A tendency for absenting himself in the face of unsuitable exposure clearly lay deeper in my granddad's character than any change of name could penetrate.

There was, thankfully, one event he did turn up for. In July 1918, Joe married my grandmother, Elizabeth Walls, a young laundress from Liverpool. Perhaps with the Western Front looming, he thought it time to put his life on a more respectable footing. Yet would Private McGann simply repeat his previous disappearing act, and vanish before his battalion departed for France?

To the eternal relief of this blushing descendant, Joseph McGann finally arrived at the Western Front in August 1918. The war was in its last violent stages; the German spring offensive had taken the battle out of the trenches, but had run aground. The Allied counterattack, known as the Hundred Days Offensive, was now underway. This would prove decisive – and the Australian 51st would play its full part. Joe would undergo a raw exposure to the statement and the question of experience.

The 51st was stationed near to Amiens and distinguished itself in battle during September in successful Allied attacks on the Hindenburg Line. I have no record of my grandfather's conduct in battle, except the knowledge that he was present. Yet I do know that he was plagued by persistent gastritis at this time, which led to numerous periods of disability and treatment in the military hospital.

Gastritis is a nasty condition caused by inflammation or erosion of the stomach lining. It can induce severe pain, nausea, vomiting and indigestion. It could well be stress-induced, or simply the result of the appalling conditions in which he fought. There was certainly nothing on his record to indicate malingering. Perhaps it was his body's answer to the things his mind had been exposed to – the heat and horror of battle burning like acid inside his stressed and overheated core.

Whatever its pathology, Joseph would survive exposure to it. Early in November 1918 the Germans surrendered. In the aftermath, Joseph McGann was diagnosed with chronic gastritis and shipped back to England. Just after this he was demobbed, completing his second term of service with a little more respectability than the first. Amusingly, he was now entitled to receive the Victory Medal – not bad for an active military fugitive! What's more, in January 1919 the warrant for his arrest was pardoned in a general amnesty, leaving our former deserter free to enjoy his new married life as a decorated veteran, and not a criminal. Joseph had survived his own potentially fatal exposure. Would it now make him grow as a result?

Not exactly. Despite his new life, Joseph's habit of wandering would endure. The final part of his military record concerns correspondence relating to the address to which Joe's war medal should be sent. The medal was dispatched to his family address in Liverpool, but returned by his wife Lizzie – who informs the authorities that her husband has run off to Australia, and can now be contacted at a harbour café address in Melbourne, care of a certain 'Mrs Ward'. Joseph had deserted again.

Family legend had it that a priest was dispatched to Melbourne to appeal to Joe's Catholic conscience and get him to return to his family. The appeal worked: Joe ended his life with Elizabeth and his three children in Liverpool. He was never known as Owen after the war, perhaps as a precaution against the exposure of his previous misdemeanours. Yet the wider exposure of the experience had not changed Joseph's core character. If anything, it seemed to consolidate the tendency he had to wander off when life made too many demands of him. Joseph's tendency to wander ultimately came to define him: as a seaman, a soldier, and a husband.

* * *

So what of Owen Joseph's brother James? What would he be exposed to in those tumultuous early years of the twentieth century – and would the experience make him shrink, alter or grow?

We last saw James McGann in 1912, leaving South Africa on the *Kinfauns Castle*, arriving in Southampton on 23 March. We take up his story from there.

James got paid off from the *Kinfauns Castle* in Southampton, but didn't go straight back to Liverpool. Instead, he found local lodgings near to the docks and looked for a new ship. There had been a major strike by coal workers, and the ocean-going ships were now low on the fuel they needed to travel. Work was therefore hard to find, but the great liners leaving Southampton for New York might still provide some quick employment for a capable fireman like himself.

There was a rumour that a gleaming new White Star liner had managed to secure the coal it needed and was looking for 250 black-gangers to stoke its pristine boilers for the maiden voyage to America. James landed a job as one of its seventy-three trimmers. He signed the crew agreement on 6 April 1912, and prepared to sail four days later.

The gleaming new ship was called the RMS *Titanic*.

TESTIMONY

It's the early eighties. I'm about eighteen. I'm sitting with my auntie Mary McGann, my dad's sister, in her tenement flat in Liverpool. I'm quizzing her about her father Owen Joseph and his family. It's the first week of my new preoccupation: a quest to find details of my McGann ancestors.

Mary's memory is a tease – capricious and enigmatic. Detailed one minute, vague the next. She'd remember something clearly on one occasion, only to forget it the next time I see her.

'Did your dad have any brothers and sisters, Mary?'

The question isn't trivial. Owen Joseph died when she was a kid, so information on unmet relatives is sketchy. Mary ponders.

I sip her strong, dark tea served with a compulsory overabundance of biscuits. She nods in sudden recollection.

'He had a brother. James. Worked on the ships like Dad did.' I note this down. She sips her tea and smiles.

'*Titanic* McGann,' she adds.

I look up over my cup.

'Sorry?'

'*Titanic* McGann, they called him. He survived the *Titanic*.'

I nearly spit out my tea. I'd been a genealogist for about a week. This revelation was equivalent to taking a bucket and spade to a quick beach holiday in Somerset and digging up King Arthur's grave.

'Are you sure?'

She seemed to be. Next day I rushed to the city's Record Office, unable to contain my excitement. This was pre-internet; newspapers from the time of the disaster were preserved on rattling reels of microfilm that had to be ordered and waited for. I checked survivor lists printed in the days following the sinking, scouring the names for James McGann. Nothing. There was a crewman called 'J Mc Cann' – but no McGann. Much later I'd find that this was a simple misprint. Disappointed, I returned to Mary.

'Can you tell me anything more about *Titanic* McGann, Mary?'

'Who?' she asked.

'James. Your uncle who survived the *Titanic*.'

Mary looked mystified. 'Don't know who you mean . . .'

She took a bite of her biscuit. I sighed quietly and put my pen down.

Mary never mentioned '*Titanic* McGann' again, and I never

pursued it further. A trick of the mind, I reasoned. A memory reconstructed falsely, synapses misaligned. A myth too grandiose to be true.

I was wrong. Mary's memory was a tease – but rarely false. On that occasion it had fired out a single bright truth like a maritime flare in the darkness, guiding me to a significant event. Being too young to embrace the improbable, I'd sailed right past it.

* * *

It's many years later. I'm newly married and living in a village in rural Essex. My wife Heidi arrives home from the bookshop and presents me with a gift – a reprinting of Colonel Archibald Gracie's famous eyewitness account of his survival as a *Titanic* passenger. I thank her. Heidi stands her ground.

'Turn to page ninety-seven,' she says. I do. Near the bottom of the page, Gracie had written the following:

> 'James McGann, a fireman, interviewed by the *New York Tribune*, on April 20th, was one of the thirty of us, mostly firemen, clinging to [the lifeboat] as she left the ship. As to the suffering endured that night he says: 'All our legs were frostbitten and we were all in hospital for a day at least.'

James. Not simply there, but speaking directly to me – his voice captured in time. The first voice of any McGann recorded in public.

* * *

The sinking of the *Titanic* has transcended the facts of its own tragedy to become an iconic myth depicted in multiple film dramas, and written about in many histories and memoirs. It's something of a cultural fetish, with websites poring over every detail of its construction, engineering, voyage and personnel, as well as details of the fateful night. But long before Winslet and DiCaprio cavorted on its bow, the sinking of the *Titanic* had established itself as a key historical event – a moral tale of hubris, lost-world grandeur, class, courage, cowardice, and the equality of all humanity when exposed to mortal experience. There have been bigger maritime losses and many greater tragedies. Yet little has ever managed to match the sinking of that one liner for sheer narrative potency. It sits in the pages of our cultural history like a first-class passenger at one of its plush dining tables: suitably attired and demanding our full attention.

The bare facts are these. RMS *Titanic* was the largest and most modern passenger ship of its day, considered by many to be 'unsinkable'. She set sail on her maiden voyage to New York from Southampton on 10 April 1912 with over 2,200 passengers and crew, including many members of the British and American Establishment. At twenty minutes to midnight on 14 April, the ship struck an iceberg about 600 kilometres south of Newfoundland. The pressure of the iceberg caused the steel plates down her forward starboard side to buckle, breaking the rivet seals. Seawater flowed through the gaps, filling five of the sixteen watertight safety compartments in her hull and making her loss inevitable. Passengers were evacuated into an inefficient supply of lifeboats, many of which were launched below their maximum capacity. The *Titanic* sank two hours and forty minutes after the collision, with the loss of more than 1,500 lives. Seven hundred and five survivors endured a freezing night in the lifeboats before being rescued by RMS *Carpathia* and taken to New York. Subsequent public inquiries in Britain and the United States led to major improvements in maritime safety. Many, such as the monitoring of Atlantic sea ice by the International Ice Patrol, continue to this day.

There have been many accounts of the gilded passengers who died that night; many discussions of the judgements and conduct of the captain and officers, the priority given to women and children, and of the treatment of steerage passengers. However, accounts from the men who worked in the boiler rooms are sparse. Once I'd heard James's brief, frostbitten voice in Gracie's book, I wanted to know more about his personal exposure to the tragedy: to piece together his private malady. I didn't care if his survival had been ignominious, or if his involvement had been far from the actions of the leading players. Genealogy has never been about status or pedigree for me (thankfully!). It's always been about my family's life as drama – the character of ordinary people expressed through lived experience and their reactions to it. So I set out to scavenge whatever details I could.

It's 2012. I'm searching online newspaper records for the *New York Tribune* article that Gracie had quoted from, which had featured James. I'm having no luck. I decide to follow another hunch. I figure that the interview the *New York Tribune* captured may have been part of a larger press gathering, and syndicated to other news outlets around the world. So I start searching more widely . . .

And there it is. The *Yorkshire Post*, 23 April 1912. So much more than I hoped for. Genealogical gold. King Arthur's grave. Not simply scavenged details, but an account of that night's events from the mouth of my great-uncle. I'm unable to breathe. When I finish reading it, I cry. For the first time in history, one of my ancestors is speaking publicly of their exposure to life, and for once the world is listening.

* * *

The maiden voyage began without much incident. The *Titanic* was a huge floating factory of propulsion. Twenty-nine boilers were divided into six separate boiler rooms that could be sealed off with a watertight door in an emergency. The black gang were split into three mighty shifts working around the clock in four-hour watches. Each watch had twenty-four trimmers, fifty-three firemen, and four leading firemen on duty. Each boiler room had four trimmers – some to fetch the coal, others to feed it to the firemen stoking the furnaces. When a shift was done, they'd shuffle back exhausted along the 'fireman's passage' at the bottom of the vessel and up a spiral staircase to their cramped accommodation in the lower decks of the ship's bow.

The collision with the iceberg happened on the evening of Saturday the fourteenth, four days into the five-day journey. It's impossible to know which shift James was on, so I don't know exactly where he was when the fatal collision took place. He could have been in his bunk, or working one of the six boiler rooms when the iceberg hit. Regardless of location, the entire black gang would soon be in the thick of it.

Fireman George Kemish was on duty in boiler room number two and recalled the moment it happened:

I had just sent a trimmer up to call the 12 to 4 watch – it was around 11.25pm 14th April when there was a heavy thud and grinding tearing sound. The telegraph in each section signalled down 'Stop'. We had a full head of steam and were doing about twenty three knots ... well the trimmer came back from calling the 12 to 4 watch and he said, 'Blimey we've struck an iceberg'.

The iceberg made several separate breaches in the front starboard hull along a ninety-metre stretch. Water flooded into the front-most boiler room, number six, through a hole about two feet above where the firemen stood. Number five had also been breached, though it was a smaller hole. The watertight doors connecting all boiler rooms were sealed by a signal from the bridge. All engines were stopped.

Stopping the ship abruptly from 'full steam ahead' created its own problems for the firemen. The boilers were liable to overheat, causing danger of explosion. The black gang were therefore tasked with damping the coal and making the boilers safe. Within fifteen minutes, boiler room six was flooded and abandoned. The men began the task of manually opening the boiler-room doors of safe sections to speed their work. Just then, the lights went out. Firemen were dispatched to fetch lamps, and when they gathered above they saw crowds of steerage passengers in lifebelts, heading towards the ship's stern. But the black gang still had work to do.

The firemen and trimmers who'd been off-duty were called from their quarters to help put out the boiler fires. Emergency power was started. Over the next hour, as the frightened passengers gathered above them, the black gang succeeded in making the boilers safe, and were attempting to pump out the incoming water. Suddenly, at five past one in the morning, the water pressure in boiler room six caused the watertight door to give way, flooding into room number five. The men scrambled out. In another ten minutes, the gang in boiler room number four were up to their knees in water.

The game was up. *Titanic* was doomed. At twenty past one, the following order was given to the black gang by Senior Second Engineer William Farquharson: 'All hands on deck. Put your life-preservers on.' The ship would sink in one hour. James McGann was at the very bottom of the listing craft, under a flooding labyrinth of passages, stairs and ladders. There were 2,000 desperate souls already in front of him.

The evidence I have for the next hours in James's life comes from his own testimony, as well as the accounts of some famous characters in the *Titanic* story: Colonel Archibald Gracie, a wealthy American passenger and author of a key book on the disaster; Charles Lightoller, second officer, lifeboat hero and star of many filmed dramas of the incident; and Marconi wireless officer Harold Bride. These men shared their next hours in the close company of my great-uncle.

By the time James made it into the fresh air, things were already well advanced. The last lifeboats were being launched containing the women and children, and directed by Officer Lightoller. The ship was sinking bow-first into the Atlantic. By two in the morning the bow itself had disappeared, and water was rising fast towards the bridge. There were still 1,500 people on board. James went straight to the bridge deck. This was a raised area to the front of the first funnel, and a place that was now threatened with imminent submersion. There remained a slim hope, however. Fastened to the top of the officers' quarters were two Engelhardt collapsible lifeboats for use of the crew.

These boats had a wooden hull with canvas sides that could be compressed for storage. There were four on the *Titanic*, but two had already been launched. The two remaining boats were known as Collapsible A and B. James jumped up onto the officers' quarters and began to help try to free Collapsible B for launching on the port side. Gracie was nearby on the deck, and Lightoller was assisting James with the lifeboat. The collapsible proved difficult to dislodge. Gracie describes the crew's struggle: 'Some of the crew on the roof where it was, sang out, "has any passenger a knife?" I took mine out of my pocket and tossed it to him.'

At that point, wireless operator Harold Bride arrived on the deck: 'I saw a collapsible boat near to a funnel, and went over to it. Twelve men were trying to boost it down to the boat deck. They were having an awful time. It was the last boat left . . .'

Time was short. The water was almost upon them. At last, the boat came free. They rigged up oars with which to slide it down onto the deck, but the heavy hull landed upside down, smashing several oars in the process. Before James and the others had a chance to turn the lifeboat over, the boat deck was suddenly overwhelmed by a large wave that swept a number of people, including Gracie and Bride, straight into the freezing ocean. The collapsible lifeboat floated off into the sea, upside down.

It was now or never. The remaining men on the bridge climbed up onto the sinking deck rail and prepared to follow the boat into the water. James now found himself alongside none other than *Titanic*'s captain, Edward John Smith. The fate of the captain in these crucial minutes has long been a subject of debate. Many believed that Captain Smith had taken his life on the bridge before the sinking – but James McGann strongly refuted this, insisting that he was there on the bridge deck till the very end. This is how James described his last moments with the captain to the *Yorkshire Post*:

'I was on the bridge deck' said the fireman, whose name is James McGann, Liverpool. 'I was helping to get off a collapsible boat. The last one was launched when the water was about to break over the bridge on which Captain Smith stood ... the water reached Captain Smith's knees ... the last boat was at least twenty feet from the ship. I was standing beside him. He gave one look all around, his face firm, and his lips hard set. He looked as if he might be trying to keep back the tears, as he thought of the doomed ship. I felt mightily like crying myself as I looked at him.

'Suddenly he shouted, "Well boys, you've done your duty, and done it well. I ask no more of you. I release you. You know the rule of the sea. It's every man for himself now, and God bless you." Then he took one of the two little children who were on the bridge beside him. They were both crying. He held the child, I think it was a little girl, under his right arm, and jumped into the sea. All of us jumped. I jumped right after the captain, but I grabbed the remaining child before I did so. When I struck water the cold was so great I had to let go my hold of the kiddie.'

The poor child. My poor great-uncle. The terror of it. The ruthless malady of exposure. The stricken sailor, jumping from the sinking ship into the black vastness of a freezing ocean. The prefrontal cortex assaulted by an adrenaline-fuelled processing of inputs from the human senses. The sudden blast of cold shock as he hit the water, forcing him to release his grip on the child. When asked about the final moments of the captain, James described those first chaotic seconds in the ocean:

> I think when he struck the water the cold made him let go his hold of the child, and he must have been swept away from the boats. Anyway, I don't think he wanted to live after seeing how things were. Dead bodies were all around, floating in the water when he jumped, and I think it broke his heart. I wasn't keen on living myself.

'I wasn't keen on living myself'. Such a simple comment. The enormity of the experience – actions, deeds and outlook bound synaptically to new memory. The application of his existing self to the challenge of new experience, and the dignity of his response to it.

Just then, as *Titanic* increased its steep angle before sinking, the huge front funnel beside the bridge deck came loose and fell into the water, crushing many of those who'd just jumped, and washing the overturned lifeboat and other swimmers further away from the ship. James was swept away with the resulting wave, and found himself beside the upturned collapsible: 'The next thing I knew I was swept toward the last collapsible boat which had been launched – the overturned one. I clambered aboard.'

The overturned hull had an air pocket trapped inside it that helped retain just enough buoyancy to hold the weight of anyone who could scramble on. But how many would it hold? And for how long? James joined an increasing number of freezing survivors who were balanced precariously on the lifeboat's hull – many of them black-gangers like himself. They were soon joined by Colonel Gracie, Harold Bride and Charles Lightoller. Oars had been lost, and some of the men were improvising with scraps of wreckage, trying to paddle the craft away from the *Titanic*, and the suction that could drag them down with it when it sank.

They watched as *Titanic*'s great stern finally rose vertically, black against the stars, before descending into the Atlantic with an unearthly gulp of sucked air and seawater. They were now adrift in a vast wilderness of water.

Then a new horror. The water around them was filled with desperate, freezing life – souls crying and wailing and drowning in the pitiless ocean. Gracie later described the grisly spectacle:

> There arose to the sky the most horrible sounds ever heard by mortal man except by those of us who survived this terrible tragedy. The agonizing cries of death from over a thousand throats, the wails and groans of the suffering, the shrieks of the terror-stricken and the awful gaspings for breath of those in the last throes of drowning ... which floated to us over the surface of the dark waters continuously for the next hour, but as time went on, growing weaker and weaker until they died out entirely.

What made the horror worse was that their collapsible boat now had thirty men on it, and could clearly take no more. It was dangerously low in the water. If it unbalanced and capsized, the trapped air would be released, and they would all be thrown off to die. The men on the hull had to discourage desperate survivors in the water from trying to scramble on board – sometimes by force. For the fortunate to live, the unfortunate had to die. This was exposure as both cruel statement of fortune and the harshest of questions. What will you do to live? Will the exposure to your true self in this extremity freeze you to your core? The Liverpool black-gangers on the boat made their feelings clear to Gracie, and I like to think James shared in their compassionate Scouse profanities:

> It was at this juncture that expressions were used by some of the uncouth members of the ship's crew, which grated upon my sensibilities. The hearts of these men, as I presently discovered, were all right and they were far from meaning any offence when they adopted their usual slang, sounding harsh to my ears, and referred to our less fortunate shipwrecked companions as 'the blokes in the water'.

Those 'blokes in the water' would likely have included James's own workmates.

Eventually they steered their collapsible away from the immediate vicinity of the dying swimmers to protect their slim advantage.

Then the waiting began. Hours in the darkness, cast adrift. Crouched and soaked on a crammed, unsteady hull in the bitter cold of a North Atlantic night. The air temperature was nearly minus three Celsius without wind-chill. Exposed flesh began to blacken with frostbite. Core temperatures plummeted. Uncontrolled shivering took over their bodies. Some men fell into the sea with exhaustion, or else were discovered dead of hypothermia on the craft. The well-heeled Gracie began to covet the warm cap worn by a nearby seaman:

He seemed so dry and comfortable while I felt so damp in my waterlogged clothing, my teeth chattering and my hair wet with the icy water, that I ventured to request the loan of his dry cap to warm my head for a short while. 'And what wad oi do?' was his curt reply ... Poor chap, it would seem that all his possessions were lost when his kit went down with the ship ...

This recollection gives me a wry smile, despite the grim setting. That unmistakable Liverpool twang in the reply from the black-ganger, letting the wealthy Gracie know that the social deference he expected lay at the bottom of the ocean with their ship. Just like their core temperatures, the world they now inhabited had shifted by small but significant degrees.

The ocean became more choppy as dawn approached. The collapsible was gradually losing its precious pocket of air and sinking lower. Lightoller organised the men to stand in two parallel rows on either side so they could sway in unison to counteract the ocean swell. Limbs and minds were numb. Time was running out. At last, a ship appeared on the horizon. The *Carpathia* was steaming to their rescue. Lightoller whistled to another of the *Titanic* lifeboats not far off, and James and the others carefully transferred to this other craft to wait for the steamer's arrival. At twelve minutes past eight on the morning of 15 April, James McGann climbed a rope ladder onto the *Carpathia* from the last lifeboat recovered. He was saved.

Of the 250 black-gangers who set sail on the *Titanic*, just forty-four firemen and nineteen trimmers survived. My great-uncle was one of them.

The *Carpathia* sailed for New York, arriving on the eighteenth. James was taken by ambulance to St Vincent's Hospital in Greenwich Village, where he was treated for frostbite to his legs. He made a good recovery. The United States was quick to organise an official inquiry into the disaster while the main players were still under their jurisdiction, and so they subpoenaed key survivors to remain. Gracie, Lightoller and Bride did so – but James was not considered sufficiently important. He and most of his colleagues were released to travel back to Britain on the SS *Lapland* on 20 April – and it was there on the New York dockside that James gave his priceless account to the world's newspapers.

Although his voice would never be heard in any official inquiry, James had ensured that I'd hear him one day, and that I'd feel that same biting cold in my own fingers. Two members of the same family had joined synapses across a century of time to bind a significant experience into their collective long-term memory. A family story is more than just an exposure to events. It's what the exposing makes of us all – the names we give to the things that come to define us. James was now '*Titanic* McGann'. A man exposed to awful things, but not frozen by them. A man who could find goodness in horror, pity in the fear of a child, and dignity in the actions of the doomed. A man whose character had found its core temperature.

After his return to England, James was paid off for his work on the *Titanic* – the princely sum of five pounds and ten shillings – and then went straight back to sea. In the two years following the *Titanic*'s loss he worked in the far Pacific, plying an exotic route between Australia and San Francisco, stopping off at Tahiti and Hawaii on the way. Tropical warmth to heal the chill of the Atlantic.

Yet there was a discernible change in him. Soon after, James got married to a Liverpool woman from his own streets called Kate McMeal. It was a happy bond. A year later they had a son – Joseph. A kiddie of his own that James could hold tight to in any disaster and, this time, never let go. It was a steady new warmth to heal his frostbitten memory. An answer to the question posed by the malady of exposure.

Just three years after that, James died of pneumonia. He was only thirty-six years old. Although his death was tragic, there was a small victory to it. He died at home in Liverpool, and not alone at sea. He was in the warm company of his wife and son, and not in the biting cold of an open ocean. Exposure had made him grow, not shrink, and love had made him unsinkable to the end.

Two brothers. Two exposures to extreme experience. Two separate responses that show the unique paths our characters take in the face of challenge. Exposure isn't the same dark mark left on all bodies or brains by events. It's unique to us; a private antagonist against which we learn and grow and know ourselves, or else a pitiless self-truth from which we shrink or hide.

4

TRAUMA

Trauma n.

1. A serious physical injury or wound to the
   body from an external source requiring
   urgent medical attention.
2. A negative emotional or psychological
   response to a stressful experience or
   event.

MEDICINE

The maladies mentioned so far have largely been the result of
social forces in the world beyond our bodies. Malnutrition,
filthy living conditions or the consequence of wider human
failings. These afflictions waited beyond the boundary of our
flesh until invited in by destitution, cruelty or ill fortune. The
diseased louse in a crowded Liverpool slum, thriving on deprivation; the beriberi flourishing in a prisoner's mistreated feet;
the biting cold inflicted on a stricken seaman's limbs through
hubris and human error. These adversaries attacked a body
already weakened by the maladies of others.

123

Trauma is a more uncouth foe – a devotee of the surprise attack, rather than the patient siege. It's an enemy that doesn't wait to be invited, but tears human flesh without warning, regardless of wider circumstances. It might be the terrible traffic accident that strikes a loved one down, or the gaping wounds torn into a healthy soldier by a grenade, severing limbs and scarring torso. It's a blitzkrieg on the human body that shocks our immune response, poisoning our blood and driving filthy infection deep into our bodies.

Physical trauma is a malady older than medicine – the cause of 9 per cent of all the world's deaths each year, according to the World Health Organization.* It occurs when the human body is assaulted by an outside force that lacerates, breaks or concusses it. This can be a penetrating trauma – the invasion of the body by foreign objects. A blast from a hand grenade, for instance. Fragments of shrapnel from a grenade penetrate the flesh in multiple places, often staying lodged deep in the body. They cause open wounds, septic shock, critical blood loss and, if not removed, fatal infection. Such is the lethality of this form of trauma that grenades are specifically designed to induce it. Shrapnel consists of many fragments of filthy metal that enter the human body at high speed. The resulting wound is multiple and complex.

The first thing the wounded soldier experiences is the body's shock response – an immediate diversion of blood flow from cell tissue to the vital organs like the heart and brain. There's fever-like confusion, a high heart rate, chills and shivering. Then there's the massive immune and inflammatory

* http://www.who.int/topics/injuries/en/

responses from the body, which is an attempt to repair multiple wounds and fight the many microscopic foreign bodies that have invaded the system and threaten it with infection. The body now floods with white blood cells, or leukocytes, to kill the invaders, but in doing so can place the injured system in even more toxic stress, overwhelming the functioning of vital organs in a condition called multiple organ dysfunction syndrome, or MODS. A chief contributor to MODS is the onset of multiple bacterial infections at the shrapnel wound sites, and, if the blood has become infected, system-wide. This is the dreaded sepsis or blood poisoning – a wounded soldier's killer since the days of Troy. If wounds can't be cleaned and the infection fought then the soldier's organs will fail and he'll die.

Battlefield amputation was the main weapon against wound infection right up until the mid-nineteenth century. However, by the beginning of the twentieth, science had begun to understand its microbial nature, and soldiers started to carry antiseptic in first-aid packs to treat wounds. The First World War brought many advances: rapid evacuation of the injured away from filthy trenches, blood transfusions for critical cases, a wider recognition of the various bacteria involved in gangrene. Medical scientists like Alexander Fleming identified key pathogens like streptococci that were wreaking havoc in a soldier's wounds. Yet once infected, there were still few ways to fight it. Things began to change with the advent of sulphonamide drugs in the thirties – an early version of antibiotics. But it was the accidental discovery by Fleming previous to this that would eventually lead to a much more potent ally. The antibiotic miracle drug penicillin.

In 1928, Fleming discovered that a food mould called *Penicillium notatum* – the mould you might see on old bread – had a powerful ability to kill bacteria. Fleming shelved further study as the substance was hard to produce in large enough quantities, but a team of scientists in Oxford led by Howard Florey later picked up his work. Florey set about trying to grow enough of the mould to be useful in treatment. Early tests showed remarkable results on infected animals, yet producing enough to treat humans remained elusive. The Second World War was raging, and industrial resources in Britain were prioritised for military production, so Florey asked the United States for help. Working in secret, the US pharmaceutical firm Pfizer used a process called deep-tank fermentation to industrialise the production of penicillin at its plant in Brooklyn, New York. The first batch was completed in early 1944, and was deployed exclusively to treat servicemen fighting in the D-Day landings in Normandy: a battle expected to produce mass casualties. Precious phials of the Brooklyn penicillin were shipped across the Atlantic just in time for the battle in early June. Its successful use on D-Day would usher the antibiotic age that we take for granted today.

The age in which my mother and father lived was a time of unprecedented progress and modernity. An age of miracles. Not simply an advance in medicine and science, but a wider transformation in social welfare and mass education. The contribution of these changes to the subsequent fortunes of the McGann family was crucial. The end of the Second World War heralded a new social contract that led to the National Health Service in 1948. New weapons like penicillin were vanquishing many of the ancient medical maladies. And it wasn't just the returning soldiers who benefited. Medical prospects were also improved for the women who'd stayed at home. When my family stalked the slums of north Liverpool in 1900, mothers were losing seventeen babies in childbirth for every one hundred born. By the start of the NHS, the figure had dropped to under four in a hundred.

Yet progress was still too slow for some mothers. Polyhydramnios is a condition where a pregnant woman's body produces too much amniotic fluid surrounding the foetus. It occurs in about 1 per cent of pregnancies, and can have various causes – foetal malformation, diabetes or perhaps an undetected twin. If polyhydramnios remained undetected it might lead to early separation of the placenta, premature labour and subsequent foetal death. Nowadays, however, polyhydramnios is rarely dangerous. Mothers are carefully monitored with ultrasound and, if severe, the fluid can be reduced. Yet back in the fifties, ultrasound in all maternity units was a distant dream.

So we have two contrasting traumas. One an assault of the body in the terror of battle. The other the loss of children to an unseen obstetric enemy. Interestingly, both of these traumas can ultimately be defined by their psychological, rather than their physical, dimensions. Scars on the mind; not simply wounds on the body.

Trauma as a psychological malady occurs when the effects of an emotionally severe or life-threatening experience damage the normal functioning of our minds. The traumatic experience can change the emotional assumptions on which we've built our world and personalities. It leaves us in a state of great confusion, stress or depression. We may relive the pain of it either consciously or through repressed thoughts and emotions. If untreated this can induce personality and behaviour change; depression, anxiety, emotional detachment. A well-known manifestation is post-traumatic stress disorder. PTSD is estimated to affect one in every three people who experience severe physical trauma.

Trauma can also exacerbate latent psychological conditions that were present before the incident occurred. Undiagnosed anxiety disorders may be brought to the surface by events, producing a crisis of confusion and stress that persists long after the ordeal. One such condition is anxiety neurosis – now referred to as generalised anxiety disorder. GAD is a constant state of distress or anxiety that overtakes a person's normal functioning. It can be genetically inherited, and has been linked to disrupted functioning in an area of our brain called the amygdala, which governs primal fear and panic responses. GAD can make us disproportionately anxious about everyday situations such as money, work, relationship or health issues. We may also manifest physical symptoms such as stomach trouble, insomnia or heart palpitations. When someone with a genetic predisposition to GAD experiences the profound stress of battle, then long-term anxieties may take root. If hidden or untreated, these anxieties may persist throughout life, blighting the sufferer's happiness, behaviour and relationships.

Similarly, a mother who experiences neonatal death can feel a catastrophic destruction of her hopes, as well as guilt, confusion and profound depression. In our enlightened age we recognise this as a form of grief: the complex human reaction to loss that manifests in complex behaviours and symptoms. Central to the healing of grief is an acknowledgement of the bereavement leading to emotional catharsis. If this is denied, then a condition known as unresolved grief can occur. An unrelated event years later may trigger the full force of the original trauma, leaving the bereaved mother deeply distressed, guilty or angry.

Great progress has been made in the treatment of psychological trauma in recent years, both therapeutically and pharmacologically. Sadly, this remained well beyond the reach of my parents in the years following the Second World War. Social taboos surrounding issues of mental health were still widespread. Postwar Britain was a society of stiff upper lips and problems brushed under carpets. As a result, both my parents would endure psychological malady following physical trauma, and their lives and relationship would be shaped by their separate responses to it.

History

War & Peace: My parents Joseph McGann & Clare Green, 1925–1960

As the McGanns progressed into the twentieth century things were slowly improving. No longer were they confined to the grim hovels of north Liverpool as illiterate labourers and court-dwelling paupers; they were now steeped in the experience of global travel, and soon to be the beneficiaries of social welfare and education.

James and Owen Joseph McGann had experienced momentous changes, both personal and in their wider world. A world war had rocked the old order and a maritime disaster had sunk all their comfortable assumptions. Yet as the empire in which they laboured started to fade, my family began its unassuming rise. It's a truth of my family's history that our social progress had an inverse relationship with the global aspirations and self-image of the nation we inhabited. When Britain ruled the waves, we slaved away in its grim belly or subsisted in its filthy slums. Yet as

Britain's pomp slowly seeped away, social equity was increased, and windows of opportunity presented themselves to us. A free NHS saved our lives, our children were educated to new standards, our families were housed in council dwellings with requisite hygiene and adequate space. Britain's decline was in global power, not in social cohesion. In the latter respect the golden age was yet to come – and the McGanns would be its grateful beneficiaries.

This chapter concerns my parents, Joseph – Joe – and Clare. Two quiet, bright, bookish children constrained by their social circumstances and rocked by personal trauma. One would cling to old certainties. The other would seek new solutions for old wrongs. Their separate paths came to define their lives and characters, and expressed the conflicted values of the progressive century in which they lived. The century that changed everything for us.

* * *

Upper Frederick Street lies to the south of central Liverpool. It is a long, narrow thoroughfare that runs down from the great Anglican cathedral towards Liverpool's oldest docks. In the early part of the twentieth century it was a street of tight, soot-black houses interspersed with drinking dens and Victorian tenement dwellings. This was the street that brothers James and Owen Joseph McGann would call home after abandoning their north-end Irish ghetto, and where their children would begin their lives.

It was love that brought the boys south. When James married Kate McMeal in 1914, he followed her home to Frederick Street, and it was there that his brother Owen Joseph met his future spouse, Elizabeth Walls, living next door with her family.

Lizzie was one of thirteen children. Her father Edward Walls was a man of inflexible Victorian attitudes and fearsome moral rectitude. He'd once banged on the door of the local cinema and publicly berated the cinema's manager for daring to screen a film of the scantily clad Ziegfeld Follies. His demands of the women in his own life were no less exacting. Lizzie was the eldest girl, and so when her mother died in 1906 she was ordered to keep house for her father and any brothers who'd not yet found suitably pliant wives. Lizzie did so until her father's death. This antiquated exemplar of a woman's servile place in the world of men would have a formative influence on Lizzie's children – most significantly on my father Joe.

By the time Lizzie met Owen Joseph in 1917 she was already in her early thirties – an age by which a woman was considered condemned to spinsterhood. The arrival of the erstwhile Aussie infantryman must have felt like a burst of sunlight breaking through the clouds. Lizzie married Owen Joseph on 13 July 1918, after which they both moved into her father's house so that Lizzie could continue her servile duty to the other men in her life. Their first son, Jimmy, was born just nine months later – by which time Owen Joseph had scarpered off to Melbourne and had to be persuaded to return to his new family. He did so, and by 1924, between Owen Joseph's maritime absences, Lizzie also managed to have my auntie Mary and then my father Joe. The Walls house in Upper Frederick Street was now home to a new generation of McGanns.

My dad's first five years of life were poor, cramped, but filled with bustle and familiar faces. Their rented house was on three narrow storeys that included attic rooms, parlour, front room and two damp cellars. Outside, the back yard contained the privy, and was permanently draped with billowing washing. There was no electricity or gas – a kettle of hot water was a permanent fixture on the fire – and there was a large tin bath for ablutions. The house was shared by the three children, Lizzie, her father Edward, brothers Charlie and Frank, and her husband Owen Joseph. Lizzie worked as a laundress in nearby Dexter Street washhouse – a Victorian civic innovation to encourage godly cleanliness amongst the city's deserving poor. When times were tough, Lizzie would also take in washing from the neighbours. As Lizzie slaved away, it fell to her daughter Mary to assume the woman's duties at home – serve the men, run the messages and ensure that little Joe was attended to. My father witnessed the lowly assumption of a woman's place passed from mother to daughter before he'd even learned to speak.

The return of their dad from a long sea voyage was a highlight of the children's year. Owen Joseph would appear, freshly paid off from a ship and bearing gifts – Turkish delight for his 'little girl' and a pair of boxing gloves for his eldest son. Uncle Jim recalled the subsequent sparring sessions with his dad between the hanging bedsheets in the back yard: 'One time I hit him a right belter – must have been too hard, because he hit me back with a real clout, and I ended up sliding down the back yard door onto my bum!'

The tough love wasn't to last. In October 1929, when my dad was just five years old, Owen Joseph arrived home sick from a voyage. He took to his bed with pneumonia. As Christmas approached, the kids prepared for the festive season at school, and Jimmy was delighted to receive a prize for his good attendance: a live goose for their Christmas table. The family were thrilled. When Lizzie told her bed-bound husband the good news, Owen Joseph remarked, 'You'll have a live goose and a dead man.'

He was right. Owen Joseph McGann died on Christmas Day.

Jimmy remembered his uncles chasing the goose around the yard to wring its neck as the curtains were being drawn in mourning. The funeral was four days later. The ice was so thick on the ground that the horse-drawn funeral carriage skittered on the cobbles as it made its slow way up the hill. The ground was so hard the gravediggers were still complaining when they arrived. Four fellow seamen from the Pacific Steam Navigation Company carried the coffin to the grave, slipping and sliding as they went. Then it was done. Lizzie was now a widow with three young mouths to feed, in an age before the welfare state offered any kind of safety net for plummeting fortunes. It was 1929. Wall Street had just crashed. The world had spun into depression. Dad's family were thrust into straitened times without a father's hand to guide them or the financial means to ride out the trouble.

Lizzie did what she could, and what she had to. She took on a crippling amount of laundry work and used the pawnbroker for short-term loans when the money ran low. The trick was to pawn any items of value in the lean days before being paid, and then reclaim them afterwards. Her brothers would discover their best suits missing, only to reappear like magic the next week. Or not. Lizzie lost many items to the pawn shop, including her own wedding ring.

She had other tricks, though. One was to dress her children in the oldest shoes she could find, and then send them to play on the floor of the room where her father always sat. The normally thrifty Edward, seeing the holes in his grandchildren's soles and concerned for his family's reputation, would provide

Lizzie with the money to purchase new footwear. Lizzie would then pocket the much-needed cash, and recover her children's real shoes from the hidden box under her bed.

At some point in those years my dad contracted rheumatic fever following a streptococcal throat infection. This condition causes fever, rash and painful inflammation. If left untreated it can develop into rheumatic heart disease, where the inflammation attacks the heart valves. The damaged valves may eventually fail many years later. Nowadays, we treat this with antibiotics. Yet the penicillin that could treat my father's rheumatic fever had yet to be developed. He would meet it later in life-saving circumstances, but too late to prevent this childhood malady from damaging his heart. A time bomb in my father's chest had begun ticking.

Dad began school, and proved to be diligent and bright. His siblings remembered him as a studious and intense child.

'He always seemed to have a book in his hands,' said Jimmy.

'You'd always find our Joe in a corner of the cellar reading,' agreed Mary.

At eleven years old my dad won a scholarship to St Francis Xavier, a prestigious Catholic grammar school. Yet his joy was short-lived. Attendance was out of the question. Lizzie wanted her kids out of school and bringing in a wage. The Education Act of 1918 allowed children to leave school at fourteen to work, while attendance at grammar school, even with a scholarship, would require the purchase of books, uniform, kit and bus fare – things the widowed Lizzie could never afford. Uncle Charlie offered to help with the expense, but Lizzie refused. The reason was cultural as well as practical. In the days before the welfare state, the working classes of those streets expected their children to make a direct financial contribution to the wealth of the household, and provide financial security for the older generation. To have one's children survive to working adulthood was considered a reward for years of backbreaking struggle.

My father was therefore denied his chance of further education. It was a sore point for the rest of his life – a source of deep frustration that fostered feelings of inferiority and coloured all of his later virtues and achievements. It helped to turn the optimistic intensity of that bright child's mind into an inflexible adult neurosis.

Uncle Charlie found him a job as a porter on the railway. His sister was already working, while his brother Jimmy had signed up as a regular in the Royal Air Force – sending a portion of his wages home to their mother. It was now 1938. Across the continent, armies of annexation were on the move. Within another year, Dad's constrained world would be shaken by the trauma of war.

* * *

The city of Liverpool represented a key strategic asset for the Allies during the Second World War. Its vast docks provided a vital gateway for essential supplies from America and the empire. As a result, its citizens endured the terror of the Blitz as well as the losses of its sailors in torpedoed ships. My dad was underage when war broke out, and so he volunteered to help the ARP wardens who patrolled the city during air raids. In spite of life's frustrations, my father always possessed an enormous sense of personal duty and service. When he was finally called up, he chose the navy. He was posted to the North Sea in 1943, and worked on the convoys that sent vital supplies to Stalin in the Arctic Circle. He became a talented telegraphist, or 'sparks', beating out encrypted Morse code messages to friendly ships in rapid-fire staccato bursts. One of my favourite games as a child was to throw a random sentence at him, and watch as he tapped out my words on the tabletop with his betting-slip pencil in a furious flurry of dots and dashes.

Back home, Liverpool was taking a pounding. Being close to the docks, the area where the McGanns lived bore the brunt of bombing raids, including an unexploded bomb that led to the family's temporary evacuation. Yet the McGanns managed to do their bit and keep their heads down. Jimmy, a hard-bitten regular, knew how best to ensure that you didn't end up in the firing line. There was one golden rule that he repeatedly impressed upon his conscripted younger brother: 'For God's sake *don't volunteer for anything!*' If you volunteered, the services took it as a generalised enthusiasm for danger, so you might end up somewhere you later regretted. Jim knew his little brother's keen nature, and so didn't want him doing anything stupid. With a bit of luck, Joe would see out the war in the radio room of a destroyer in safe waters.

Dad laughed drily at the memory – and his brother's furious reaction when Dad finally told him what he'd done. 'I fancied being a submariner,' Dad had said. 'So I went to my command-ing officer to ask about a transfer. Before I knew where I was, I was drafted into the RN Commandos and sent to Scotland.'

My father was recruited into the signal section of the Royal Naval 'Beachhead' Commandos, a specialised amphibious assault unit that formed part of Britain's multi-service Combined Operations force. This elite unit had the job of landing on an enemy beach at the start of a battle and securing the beachhead to ensure that the main forces and equipment which followed could land and move off quickly without becoming bogged down. They were the first in. The front line. They'd performed with distinction at the landings in Sicily and Anzio, and were now focused on the biggest task of them all: the forthcoming invasion of France.

Dad was sent to Troon in Ayrshire in late 1943 for training. The gruelling assault course seemed to energise him. He performed brilliantly, despite the undiagnosed damage to his heart. I suspect it was the happiest my dad ever was. We have a photograph of him taken with his unit. He's sitting dead centre, grinning and muscular. He'd been acknowledged as special and not found wanting. He shared the intense camaraderie of warriors engaged in a fearsome endeavour. He had a role that spoke to the intense sense of duty that guided him – but he had yet to be thrown into the cauldron that this role entailed.

By spring of 1944 they'd learned the full gravity of their task. My father's unit was to take part in Operation Overlord – the D-Day invasion of Normandy. Their mission was to land near the village of Arromanches-les-Bains and set up a beach radio signal station that could coordinate the naval shelling of enemy positions on the shore before the main army arrived. It wasn't a seaside stroll; the Germans had placed formidable obstructions on the sand and were dug in to repel any assault. They would have to fight to hold the beach at any cost. Dad's commanding officer told them it was a suicide mission. Their lives were dispensable. I remember my father's gallows grin and the shake of the head as he recalled this curious motivational speech.

Was it here that it began? That sleepless knot of neurosis in his stomach that fed the officer's words into a restless sense of injustice? I can't imagine the courage it takes to continue with one's duty in the knowledge of impending extinction. He had just turned twenty, and was a devout Catholic. Did he find solace in his sacrifice? A belief in a better life elsewhere? Or did that fear congeal to spite against the world he now inhabited; a world that rewarded intelligence, duty and enthusiasm with dispensable suffering? He'd served life with diligent obedience. Was life ever going to return the favour?

He'd soon find out. In the final days before the invasion he was moved to a camp in Hampshire for embarkation at Southampton – the very port his uncle James had departed from on his *Titanic* trauma thirty-two years before. They embarked on 5 June to cross the Channel. The weather was filthy, and the poor soldiers on the ships had seasickness to contend with as well as nerves. Eventually it was time. They were lowered into the crowded landing craft and set out for the coast of France. My father described the shells from the huge naval guns screaming overhead to bombard the Normandy coast, which now loomed dark before them.

Finally the ramp went down, and twenty-year-old Joe McGann was thrust into hell.

My dad's landing craft had beached too far out. The commandos jumped off the ramp into ten feet of bullet-pierced water with full packs on. Dad watched his friends drown. He scrambled to the shore and crouched for dear life behind a German beach obstacle. It was pandemonium. I once watched him recall the horror of the slaughter he witnessed. He paused. He breathed heavily. Then again. Eventually he said, 'War is a terrible thing, son. A terrible, terrible thing.'

He was just a boy. When I was the age he was then, I could hardly tie my shoelaces. Who would blame Joe McGann if he'd simply stayed there, crouching for dear life behind that obstacle? How could I say that I wouldn't do just that in his position?

Joe McGann didn't. He took his courage in his hands, got to his feet and zigzagged his way up that beach – firing and dodging and doing his duty. He reached the safety of the sea wall. His radio was shot to pieces, so his primary task was redundant. He joined some other men who were clearing a German defensive position of enemy troops. Things progressed well. He even bagged a fine souvenir to show the folks back home – some German field binoculars.

Then the stick grenade. Thrown over the wall by a defending German soldier. The troops scattered. My father saw it late. He instinctively turned his body away from the impending blast and the grenade exploded. Shrapnel pierced my father's flesh in fifty places – left arm, left leg, right thigh, abdomen. He fell to the sand critically wounded. Physical trauma.

The following hours were understandably hazy. He shivered on the sand with the shock and the loss of blood. Hours went by. He remembered lying semi-conscious on the famous Mulberry harbour, waiting to be evacuated – planes and bombs and bullets whizzing by.

Then he woke in Leicester Infirmary in England. He was in a ward full of D-Day casualties. He was alive.

How had the filthy shrapnel wounds not poisoned him? He looked for his precious binoculars beside his bed but they were gone. Damn. Someone had pinched them. Yet he'd been given a gift far more rare and valuable. Every few hours a nurse was injecting him with a new drug. Fleming's miracle, fresh from Brooklyn. Penicillin. In the ward, amazed servicemen gathered around each other's beds to show off their rapidly healing wounds. Their generation had never seen its like before. A medical wonder. An antibiotic. They were the first warriors in history to have their wounded bodies cleansed of internal infection by this new medicine. He never forgot the gift. He'd later scoff at the complacency of his children, who'd pop antibiotics for every tiny cough or cut. 'You don't know you're born,' he'd say. He was right. Dad was born in an age when a cut from a rose thorn could grow septic and kill – or when a simple streptococcal infection could silently eat the heart. Now physical trauma had a new foe, and it attended to my father's needs like his mother had tended to the men in her life – with unquestioning service.

After the euphoria of survival my father's duty was done. He went back to his base and was demobbed on 5 July 1946.

But something had happened during that time at base or in the hospital that made the medical staff take note. I don't know if it was one inciting moment of stress, or the gradual awareness of an older distemper that had been given wings in the heat of battle. Whatever it was, the military doctors wrote a two-word diagnosis on his medical record that my father regarded as a hidden badge of shame. Something that he felt had tarnished the brave service he gave and the medals he received. Something he could never talk about with his family. Something that his wife would stumble upon years later.

'Anxiety Neurosis.'

Trauma had lodged in my father's mind, eating away at his peace. A terrible cloud gathered over his emotional outlook. He'd survived, but remained wounded. Had the world he now inhabited been worth all the courage and the horror? His child-hood sense of injustice began to reassert itself – and so Dad did what he always did when humiliated by unjust wounds that his mind couldn't wash clean. He hid them deep beneath the rigid Victorian codes of the men who'd reared him. He buried his anxiety in an unmarked grave and moved on.

After being demobbed, Joe returned to his life in Liverpool. His family had moved from the bomb-shattered privations of Upper Frederick Street and were now housed in a tenement flat in Sydney Gardens – part of a bright new vision for Liverpool's working classes: internal bathrooms, gas, electricity, hot and cold running water. These estates would later become synony-mous with urban decay, but at the time they were built, and for the McGanns, they represented true progress.

Dad's siblings were all still living together with their mother – no one yet married. It was an insular atmosphere that my father found increasingly claustrophobic. The knot in the stomach that haunted him made him ever more anxious about the imagined taunts of neighbours who might scoff at his eccentric home life. Joe became desperate to move out. Start his own family. But where to – and with whom? As the austerity of the forties gave way to the fifties, Dad saw his twenties turn into his thirties. He was still a bachelor – still without a wife and family who might provide him with the public esteem and private service his hidden vulnerability craved.

Joe was drawn like a moth to those families who radiated the demonstrative love and warmth that his own home life lacked. One of those families was the Greens. In the smoke-filled parlour of the local public house, the Bay Horse Hotel, Dad struck up a warm friendship with Abraham Green, a devout pillar of the community who was the loving father of a family of seven in the next tenement estate. One of these was Abraham's pretty and extrovert daughter Rose Green, who immediately caught my dad's eye. Sitting next to Rose, eleven years younger than Joe and easy to overlook, was Rose's quiet, clever, but introverted younger sister, Clare Green.

My mother.

* * *

The Greens hailed from Lamport Street, just a mile south of Upper Frederick Street in Liverpool's densely packed Toxteth district. In the infinite gradations of urban working-class respectability, the Greens belonged firmly to the upper tier. The family was of West Midlands Protestant stock. Abraham, my granddad, had even spent his young life as a lay preacher. Yet despite his Protestant roots, Abe fell in love with and married a local Catholic woman called Mary Barratt, a move that caused raised eyebrows in his family. It was a love match that lasted until their deaths in the early 1980s. Abraham eventually converted to Catholicism, and the Greens went on to have eight children: Mary, Billy, Rose, my mum Clare, Winnie, Betty, Tony and John. Sadly, only seven would survive to adulthood. Little Betty was lost as an infant; the impact of seeing her laid out provided my four-year-old mother with her earliest memory.

The Greens soon had other things to think about. Within a month of Betty's death the Second World War was declared. The family moved to the bottom-floor flat of an old Victorian tenement in nearby Northumberland Street and went on as best they could. Shy little Clare started school in 1940, complete with gas mask and regular adjournments to the air-raid shelter. She immediately showed promise: 'I always loved learning. But I was just so introverted. Quiet. That's what Dad called me. Rose was the one with the sunny disposition.'

Things soon became decidedly less sunny for the Greens. One morning, during Liverpool's infamous May Blitz, six-year-old Clare woke to a bed covered in window glass and brick dust. The door lay on its side. 'We've been bombed,' said her brother Bill. 'We'd better get up.' The children scrambled through the rubble of the flat until they were rescued by the police and taken to the station. Being on the ground floor had saved their lives; above them several neighbours had been killed. One by one, a desperate Abraham Green recovered his pregnant wife and children – miraculously all alive, but now without worldly goods. The family had to walk through the city to catch a bus to a relative's house in the suburbs, wearing the same dust-caked nightclothes they'd been bombed in. Sympathetic strangers in the queue moved aside, seeing their misfortune. It was an age before the phrase 'all in it together' wore an ironic smirk.

Mum was sent to live with an aunt for three months, which she hated – shrinking further into herself and longing for the safety of her family: 'I just wasn't outgoing enough – I missed them too much.' After what seemed like an age, the family were rehoused in Myrtle Gardens, a large tenement estate that they'd remain in till the sixties, and which would bring them into eventual contact with the McGann family. My mum was finally able to resume school – and she thrived. The teachers moved her up two classes because of her abilities. While my father was enduring his physical trauma on a beach in France, my young mother was nurturing dreams of study in one of Liverpool's great Catholic grammar schools. But, unlike Dad, it was a dream my mother would fulfil. After the war was over, Mum passed her scholarship to Notre Dame Grammar School – a genteel centre of learning for the daughters of the burgeoning Liverpool Catholic middle class.

Since my dad's schooldays, the provision of selective education for working-class pupils of ability had begun to improve. The proportion of free places at grammar schools had increased to almost half. Yet when poorer children were offered these places, many parents still had to turn them down owing to the extra costs of clothing and equipment.

Mum's fees were paid for her, and her parents received a small grant towards the uniform, but that only stretched to the price of her coat. The rest of her uniform would later have to be cobbled together from meagre savings. My mother started school inadequately clothed, and sticking out like a sore thumb.

Despite these sartorial shortcomings, Clare was thrilled to enter a world of higher learning for the first time. There were new subjects – German, French, Latin, English literature – and Mum thrived on them. My mother was to stay at Notre Dame Grammar School for four years. Yet as she grew older, she began to feel increasingly isolated in her class – the target of an incipient social condescension from pupils and staff: 'Some of the teachers were a bit snobbish towards me. Back then they hadn't started taking a lot of working-class kids. Most of the girls who went there were daughters of doctors or businessmen. My dad was a docker! At ten, you don't really see the problem. At fourteen, you do.'

By the fourth year she'd had enough of it. She asked her father if she could leave, as education law still permitted pupils to leave school at fifteen. He was reluctant, but she insisted. She walked out of Notre Dame school without any of the qualifications another year would have given her. Yet she never forgot her time there. The condescension shown towards her academic ambitions, and her determination to carry the lessons of it forward, would later be the driving force behind the grammar school education of her children and her own subsequent education as a schoolteacher.

Clare's first job on leaving Notre Dame in the late forties didn't exactly tax her bright mind. It was in a factory making nylon stockings, and she absolutely hated it. Luckily she'd heard of a vacancy at Littlewoods Football Pools – an office environment that valued intelligence, numeracy and literacy, paid well, and gave a young unmarried woman like Clare a little independence before she was expected to marry. My mum got the job, and was quickly promoted. She spent eight happy years there.

With money in her pocket and the school books put away, it was a time for shy young Clare to go dancing. Her sister Rose would accompany her to the dance palaces of Liverpool – the Rialto, the Grafton, the Locarno – and Clare would watch as men gravitated towards her attractive and outgoing sister. She and Rose were lifelong friends and companions; sisters who shared a deep love and understanding. In those days, the introverted Clare was happy to hide in Rose's shadow. Beneath her newfound independence lay a timidity about life, a hidden terror of the world of men and their needs, and what these needs led to: 'I was afraid of the world back then. Afraid of sex. Terrified of having babies! I had no preparation for it. Mam never told me anything about that side of life.'

'That side of life'. Knowledge of sex was something that women of her faith and upbringing were expected to absorb by osmosis. There was no provision in school, church or home for Clare to acquire the knowledge about sexual desire that she might soon need. A shy girl was left alone to negotiate the confusion of her own desires, and the fears of where they might lead her. Not that there weren't plenty of men willing to help my mum negotiate them. She enjoyed many suitors in those teenage years – along with all the trips to the movies, the flowers and the many gifts – yet there was always a limit to how far Mum was willing to commit: 'The minute guys got too serious, I stopped it. I had a fear of getting too . . . intimate.'

It was at this time that my fifteen-year-old mum first met my father, Joe McGann, her sister Rose's new boyfriend. She immediately liked him. He was much older than her – part of the war generation. He was fatherly, respectable and a worldly presence in their home. Every weekend he'd come to the house to do the football pools with her dad, and they'd chat together. Clare found that Joe shared her love of learning – and when he found out that she'd gone to a grammar school, he was very keen to hear all about it. Clare felt comfortable in Joe's company – safe. When Rose announced her engagement to him, Clare was delighted. 'I started calling him "brother-in-law" straight away!'

Then, suddenly, things changed. Rose announced that she was going into the army. Their father, mindful of Rose's engagement, refused to allow it, but Rose, now eighteen and wilful as ever, defied him. Off she went, leaving Joe McGann stranded at home, and her sister Clare without her closest friend and protector. My mother was bereft.

In the months that followed, Mum, now sixteen, withdrew into her shell, while Joe – in romantic limbo – still visited the house to see her father. One night Joe called to find Clare alone. They chatted for a while, then my dad asked if she'd like to go to the pictures. Mum can still remember the film: Rita Hayworth in *Tonight and Every Night*. They had a great time. 'He was very easy for me to talk to – I never felt threatened by him.' At the end of their platonic evening he walked her back to the pub, and as they reached the top of the hill, young Clare challenged the fatherly Joe to a silly dare: 'I said to him, "I bet you wouldn't skip all the way down that hill."' To her absolute astonishment, he did! All the way down. It was totally out of character. They both ended up laughing breathlessly at the bottom. Mum never forgot that moment, and would often relate it to her children as evidence of an internal lightness that their father could so rarely display: 'I saw him differently from then on. He wasn't the "fuddy-duddy" I thought he was.

Of course, I didn't *really* know anything about him ... about his war.'

Life carried on. Rose eventually wrote to Joe from her base in Germany to announce that their engagement was off. Yet my father continued to visit their house.

Two years passed. Rose had left the army and married someone else. Clare had entered her twenties, still employed at Littlewoods, and content with the sheltered life she had. Then one night, out of the blue, Joe McGann asked her out. Rose, now pregnant, had no objections. Clare accepted. 'I wasn't looking for anything. I was twenty. He was a man I knew, someone I liked and respected. I felt there was a lot of good in him.'

Yet Joe clearly *was* looking for something. There was a new urgency to him – an anxiety that began to insist itself on Clare from the moment they started seeing each other. He was now thirty-one, and he wanted desperately to get married. Although Clare was not yet twenty-one and keen to wait, Joe kept insisting. In the end she gave in and accepted his proposal.

Her parents were delighted. My mum didn't receive an engagement ring because of my father's previous engagement to her sister. He didn't think it seemly; part of an anxiety about public appearances that she'd later know too well. As the wedding day approached in September 1956, Clare became more hesitant and wanted to put it off for a while. Dad wouldn't. The wedding dress had been borrowed, and the bridesmaids' dresses had already been embellished by her sister Mary for the occasion.

My mum and dad were married on 29 September 1956 at St

Anne's church in Overbury Street, a short walk from the tenements where they lived. The service was at ten-thirty in the morning, which made for a long day. There was an afternoon reception back at the flat in Myrtle Gardens – then back to the Bay Horse Hotel for the evening revelries. Songs and pints and celebration.

Then the wedding night.

Testimony

It's the present day. I'm sitting in Mum's cosy apartment in the beautiful city of Salisbury, nestling in the shadow of its glorious cathedral. My mother is now eighty-one years old; as fit and sharp as I'd ever wish to be at her age. In my own middle age I've grown to see the woman behind the mother who raised me – the forces that drove a quiet young girl to become the woman she was to all of her children. The traumas that shaped her. Clare Green is my friend, my inspiration, and the thread that holds my family to its past and present.

I ask her about the wedding night. My mum pauses. She takes a breath, searching for the right word to describe it:

> It was . . . fraught. I didn't know anything. I was expecting him to show me the ropes. He was an older man. A man of the world. But he didn't have any technique – any way of being tender, or of making you feel loved. It wasn't enjoyable.

My parents' wedding night was a disaster. My father, for all of his years, service and bravery, was a virgin. He was a virgin racked by an anxiety that made physical affection difficult, and a mindset that couldn't admit to the vulnerability it gave him. 'He put his arm around me – but there were no words of reassurance. He probably felt pretty terrible himself. It was hard for both of us.'

It would be three weeks before my mother and father were able to consummate their marriage. Sex quickly became a trauma that buried shame like shrapnel deep into my father's psyche. He suppressed the neurosis that it engendered beneath a carapace of outward propriety – retreating, wounded, into those rigid codes of gender that informed his undemonstrative childhood:

Sex became just a physical need for him. It wasn't enjoyable. There was no real tenderness – no romance. When I expressed a need for more closeness he just said, 'You've seen too many movies.'

Yet what my father lacked in tenderness and technique, he made up for in biological fertility. My mum became pregnant almost immediately. The newly-weds were living at Abraham and Mary's flat at the time – and so my mum felt insulated from the full force of her new married life with Joe. The early pregnancy had an air of unreality about it:

When I missed my period I went to the doctor. He confirmed it, and then told me to come back at six months. No scans, no checks, nothing. Looking back, I should've been seen properly before then, but I didn't know any better. It might have changed things.

As her pregnancy progressed through its early months, her bump grew unusually large. Her mother noticed it too, but there seemed little reason for alarm. By the end of the fifth month, her belly had grown so much that she could no longer sleep at night:

> I couldn't lie down because it was too uncomfortable. So I had to sit up in bed – and it got that way that I was disturbing your father's sleep. So I started sleeping in an armchair at night.

After six nights in the chair, sleep deprivation began to take its toll. My mum was slurring words and barely conscious. The doctor was called. He felt her abdomen – it was now tight as a drum. She was sent to the maternity hospital with her mother.

When she arrived, she was referred for an X-ray, but before it could even be carried out, her waters broke in a huge torrent of amniotic fluid that soaked the bed. Mum's eyes brim with compassion for the child she still was. 'I was so naive. I actually turned to my mum at that point and said, "Does this mean I can go home now?"'

She couldn't. An X-ray confirmed twins, and she had now gone into labour. She was only twenty-six weeks pregnant.

The unexpected labour meant that she had to spend a seventh night without sleep, and accompanied by two nurses who still make her bristle with their coldness and indifference:

> I hadn't slept for a week. I was exhausted and scared. Every time I cried out or asked for help, they just tutted. They weren't . . . compassionate. When the pains came I asked for pain relief. They refused, saying they didn't want me to fall

asleep. So I ended up with nothing for the pain. Instead, I'd count the tiles on the ceiling in the delivery room to take my mind off it . . . I'd see how many I could count before the next contraction . . .

When the babies finally came, the nurses called the doctor to cut her. The babies were small – just three pounds each – and she waited in the silence for their cries.

But the cries didn't come.

I watch Mum's face – the pain of it as fresh and raw today as it ever was: 'I saw one of them. I saw his little leg moving in the incubator. It must have been John.'

The baby's movement soon stopped. After an eternity, the nurse turned to her. She was brief and direct. 'I'm sorry. Your babies died. They were too small.'

Two boys. One stillborn, the other hanging on for a few brief minutes. The little corpses were quickly whisked away. My mum never saw them again. 'That was it. I didn't touch them. I never got to hold them. I never even got to see their faces.'

Mum stared at the ceiling. The doctor stitched her up in silence. Then the nurse said: 'Right. We're going to take you to the post-natal ward to recover.' It was a ward full of happy mothers and their newborn children. 'I said, "No! Don't put me with the babies! Please!" I must have made a hell of a fuss, because they put me back in pre-natal instead.'

The next day the doctor saw my mother and father in the ward. 'These things happen,' he said, briskly. 'Just try again and come back next year.' With that, he was gone. Mum and Dad were left alone to cope with it.

My mother spent the next ten days in hospital. It had been just eight months since her wedding day. In that short time all her hopes for future joy represented by her marriage and the new life inside of her had arrived stillborn, while the past certainties she'd known had been rudely whisked away without any opportunity to grieve. For the first few days she simply slept off her exhaustion. But then came the wound – the deep psychological trauma of it – spreading like sepsis inside her.

It must have been an awful time for my dad, too. While Mum was in hospital, he had to arrange the burial of his firstborn sons. In those days there were no special places in the graveyard for infants. There were no specific services in church. There was no counselling – even if he'd been the type of man to request it. He had to ask for permission to place his dead children in the coffin of someone recently deceased. His boys would be lodgers in death. The twins were sent to a public grave in Anfield Cemetery, and my dad cleared their flat of baby clothes.

We'd never know what it was truly like for him, because he never spoke of it. Ever. He never told my mother where the twins were buried, or what he'd arranged while she was in hospital. It wasn't done as cruelty, but in the sincere belief that to address such pain was counterproductive weakness. He was doing what he'd always done. Burying pain and love and sensitivity beneath a straight-backed, stiff-lipped carapace. By the time Mum got home, everything was tidied away. There were sad 'chin-up' smiles, but the expectation was that she should now put it behind her. She was numb: 'I wasn't in floods of tears. I didn't cry. I was . . . bewildered.'

At some level, Dad knew she wasn't right. He took Mum on a week's holiday to the Isle of Man. A change of scene. Mum still has the black-and-white photographs. Smiling stoutly in the wind-blown sunshine, my young parents were united in a way they rarely were in future. She remembers it with fondness: 'He was kind. Things were calmer. It was coming from a good place. Less fraught. Perhaps he needed to do it himself.'

However, when they got back from the holiday my dad made it clear that she had to move on. She was his wife and, pain or not, there were duties to fulfil. He found a rented flat for them nearby, so that she would now be removed from the childhood security of her family. She returned to her work at Littlewoods but Dad became more insistent that she give up work to look after him. My mum remembers the arguments – her nascent feminism seeded in the raw injustice of it:

I said, 'Joe, before we got married you and I were the same – both working, both loving the same things – books, learning. But since then your life has stayed exactly the same and my life has changed completely! I had a life of my own but now you just want me to step into your mother's shoes!' And he replied, 'Well, you're married now. You're my wife.'

As the summer progressed, the friction between them increased. My father's anxiety and agitation became clearer to her once he was removed from the need to maintain a public calm in front of her parents. Sex remained 'fraught'. By September, my mother could take no more. She went to see her doctor for a routine visit and burst into tears before she could even speak. Once started, the tears wouldn't stop. The doctor was alarmed at her condition, and immediately called a psychiatrist colleague in a nearby hospital. The psychiatrist came to see my mother at ten o'clock that night while my father worked a late shift at the factory. He was concerned at what he found:

> I was broken. So much had happened. I was trapped – I felt that nobody understood or cared. I didn't know what to do with my life, I didn't know which way to turn. I couldn't even tell my mum and dad, because they wouldn't have understood. I was trapped in this flat with a man who shut his mind down – retreated into doing his job, doing his duty, while I was supposed to get on with doing mine. I didn't know what to do ...

The psychiatrist's response to the complexity of her pain was astonishingly blunt: 'He said I was severely depressed. He told me that if I didn't improve in three months, they would have to consider electric shock therapy.'

Electric shock therapy. In just a year my mother had been transformed from a healthy, intelligent young woman into a profoundly traumatised wife through a desperate lack of medical sensitivity and the emotional constipation of those nearest to her. Yet the only solution offered to this complex trauma was to fix electrodes to her head and throw the switch in the hope of improvement.

Electroconvulsive therapy is a procedure in which small electric currents are passed through the brain, intentionally triggering a seizure. How it works is still a mystery, but it can be very effective in certain cases. My anger lies not with its existence as a treatment, but in the idea that my mother was offered no defence against her life's external antagonists beyond an induced seizure. The world's traumas had left her in shock, but its only solution was to shock her further.

Yet she never did receive electroconvulsive therapy. I ask her why. Mum turns to me with a thin smile, 'I got pregnant a month later.'

She became pregnant with my eldest brother Joe. An event, but not an answer. How did her depression lift? How did she manage to go on? 'I just did what everyone wanted me to do. I got on with it.'

My mother gave in. She packed up her job at Littlewoods and stayed at home. She became a dutiful housewife. As my brother Joe grew inside her, she prepared her husband's meals and washed his shirts. She took her trauma deep inside and kept it there. If she had to feel this alone, then she would do what she needed to in order to survive it. The person she'd been, and that woman she'd wanted to be, were now dead.

Except she wasn't. Not by a long way. When my brother Joe was finally born, something wonderful happened. Something totally unexpected. My mum finally got to hold her own child in her arms and the effect on her was utterly life-changing. She still can't speak of it without a burst of joy transforming her expression: 'I became a mother. It was ... amazing!'

She was totally surprised by her response to motherhood. My mum had never been particularly maternal – never longed to hold or tend to other people's children. Yet as she stared into the clear blue of my big brother's eyes, the clouds in her life were suddenly obliterated by sunlight – a reciprocated love that burned like fire in her veins. Everything became possible. Clare McGann embraced motherhood not simply with passion, but with a mission: 'I wanted to be the best mother I could possibly be. I went straight out and I bought Dr Spock's new book on childcare. I wanted to know everything about it!'

The months following Joe's birth were probably the happiest in my parents' marriage. The conformity my father required of his life in order to ease the anxieties he suppressed seemed finally to be in place. He was the Victorian patriarch with his own son and a wife who now conformed to her designated role as a stay-at-home mother. He was finally in control. The sounds of the beach were temporarily quelled.

Yet what my father took to be my mother's compliance was simply unfinished business. My mum burned with a new purpose. Her children. She would go on to pour all of her love and fire into them, and in doing so would rekindle a desire for self-improvement and education that would ultimately take her beyond her husband's control. Clare would ensure that her children's characters were forged not in the dour frigidity of their dad's upbringing but in the flexible courage of her own sensitivity. They would be a family of McGanns, but moulded in the image of Clare Green.

The happy days didn't last. Eventually my father's brooding depression and restless anxiety returned. He endlessly criticised my mum, finding fault with the smallest things. As Mum began to raise her new family, she learned to negotiate his black moods for the benefit of the children.

On one occasion, while visiting the family doctor, she decided to open up about it – and the doctor listened. At last, she found a physician who was sensitive to the psychological nuances she described. The doctor rooted out the medical file on her husband and showed it to her. It was there that Clare first saw the navy notepaper clipped into Joe's file, and heard the term 'anxiety neurosis' for the first time:

The doctor said, 'Your husband suffers from anxiety neurosis. This behaviour is due to his past experiences. He's putting you down because it makes him feel better – more in control. In reality, your husband feels the pressure and responsibility of married life very heavily.'

This was a revelation to her. An answer at last. Her husband was suffering, damaged, kicking out like a wounded animal against the trauma and the pain he'd felt. He'd had a visit to a psychiatrist just after the war but had never told her, despite her own later depression. He'd kept everything hidden.

Clare was suddenly overwhelmed with compassion for her husband. She raced home to my dad and told him what the doctor had said. She offered suggestions for how she might help lift some of the stresses of his life from his shoulders, so that they could work together to fix it. My mother smiles and shakes her head at her naivety. 'Of course he hit the roof. He was absolutely furious that the doctor had dared to reveal what was on his record. We never talked about it after that. Not ever.'

From that moment my mother and father followed divergent paths; together for many years to come, but increasingly estranged by their separate responses to their suffering. My mother learned to grow from the pains she endured. My father never could. Many years later and on his deathbed, my father took my mother by the hand and offered her the single acknowledgement that she'd spent a lifetime waiting to hear.

'I'm sorry,' he said.

'It's all right, Joe,' she replied.

But it wasn't. Not quite. Not yet. There was still something she had to do.

y mother Clare in 1953. A sheltered ghteen-year-old.

My dad Joseph at eighteen in 1942. He entered the war as a navy conscript, and served as a ship's telegraphist before joining the Royal Naval Commandos for the D-Day invasion in June 1944.

um and Dad on their wedding day in 1956. She was just turned twenty-one. He was even years older. 'I was expecting him to show me the ropes.'

1963: my first summer as a bonny baby, on a family outing. The Beatles are topping the UK charts for the first time. Dad holds me in his arms, with brother Paul on our left.

The four boys on the front wall of the house in Birstall Road, 1965. From left: Paul, me, Joe and Mark. I'm the blond with the ice lolly.

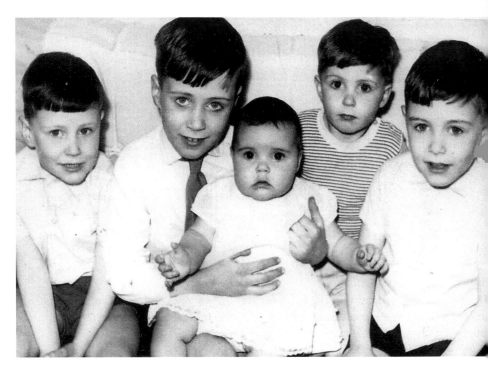

Birstall Road, 1966. The earliest photograph we have of all five siblings. From left: Mark, Joe, Clare, me, Paul.

atlin's holiday camp, Minehead, 1972. The McGanns are plucky runners-up in the appy Families' competition. Back, from left: Dad, Joe, Mum; front: Paul, Clare, me d Mark. The consolation prize was a year's supply of pickled chutney. I still can't eat a oughman's lunch without a lingering sense of thwarted ambition.

My first year as a grammar school pupil in 1974. Before life got complicated.

Newly arrived in London, 1982. I'm nineteen years old, and about as brave and scared as I'll ever be.

The siblings singing together in an aunt's house in the late seventies. Clockwise from bottom left: Paul, Joe, me in the background, sister Clare and Mark on guitar. Our harmonies were always there when other forms of unity eluded us.

he Four Musketeers: the McGann brothers on the opening night of *Yakety Yak* at the
alf Moon Theatre, London, 1982. From left: Paul, Mark, me and Joe as an irreverent
verend.

he last time my family were photographed all together. A newspaper shoot in Hyde
irk, 1983. I'm far left, Dad is kneeling in front, Mum is centre and my sister Clare is
hind her. It was my first year as an actor, and my father's last year of life.

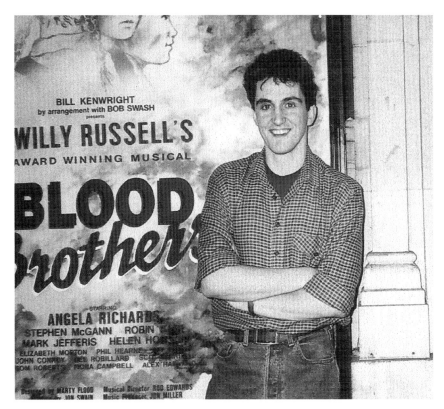

In between performances of *Blood Brothers* at the Albery Theatre, London, 1989. Exhausted but in love. I'd drive up to Liverpool every weekend after the show to be with Heidi.

Full circle: Owen McGann's descendants – Mark, me, Paul, Joe – starring in the Irish famine drama *The Hanging Gale* in Donegal, Ireland, 1994.

eidi and me on our wedding day – August 1990. The sun shone, outside and in.

eidi, just after the birth of our son Dominic in 1996. Bruises, joy and exhaustion.

Christmas 2016. The McGann and Thomas clans gather to celebrate at our home. David's candlesticks have pride of place at the centre of the table.

* * *

Following my dad's death, my mum, now in her fifties, decided to become a bereavement counsellor. It was typical of her – turning her loss into a useful benefit for others. The training involved an induction course on various aspects of bereavement. On one particular night, the subject was neonatal death. 'I was sitting listening to the counsellor talking about coping with the loss of an infant, when suddenly I began to cry uncontrollably. I just couldn't stop.'

The counsellor took her to one side, and Mum tried to explain herself between sobs.

The twins. Her lost twins, all those years ago. With the mention of neonatal death, the pain of it had suddenly roared back into her mind like a blow to the head. She was overwhelmed by the force of it – the unresolved grief suddenly released from its long suppression by her husband's death. '"You've never grieved for them," said the counsellor. "Nobody told me I could," I replied.'

That night she couldn't get the twins out of her mind. They were out there somewhere, huddled in an unknown grave. Lost. By morning she knew what she had to do. She had to find them. Call them by their names. Make them hers again.

Over the next weeks my mother did a remarkable thing. She set about finding her lost children. My father had told her nothing about the circumstances of their burial, so she had to rely on guesswork. She got lucky. She found the funeral directors my dad had most likely used back in the fifties. A friendly member of its staff took up her case and was able to confirm the stranger's coffin that the twins had been placed into.

Weeks later, on a cold day in Liverpool's Anfield Cemetery, my mother was taken by a grave attendant to the unmarked grave where her twins lay. They permitted her to place a small plaque of stone beside it. The plaque is inscribed with a simple quotation from the Book of Isaiah, chapter forty-two. It reads: 'Know that I have never abandoned you; I have called you by your name; you are mine.'

Joseph and John were the McGann brothers nobody would ever know. Their names would never appear in theatre lights or film credits. Yet they were the first. The eldest. The lost boys. Now found.

To my mother, those infants were so much more. They held in their little twin ribs all of the hopes she'd once harboured for her own young life – a life that had been snatched away before she'd even had a chance to grieve for it. She'd been thrust into a marriage lacking in the warmth and respect her love deserved, and had been denied the chance to cradle her dreams in a way that might be cherished by her husband.

Yet now, at last, she was free. Free to mourn her past, and free to know the peace that comes from the respectful commemoration of a life's passing. My dad had never managed to suppress my mum's quiet, steely spirit. And now he was gone, she'd returned to the place where he'd buried her lost innocence. She'd returned to where her lonely pain lay soil-stained and forgotten. She exhumed it. She took that brave young woman in her old, wise arms and cradled her with all the love she'd been denied. She called that young woman's courage by its name. Made it hers again.

There are wounds we can see, and wounds we can't – traumas that we treat, and traumas we prefer to conceal. But all of these maladies must be attended to with equal care if the resulting infection is not to destroy our life and health.

5

BREATHLESSNESS

Breathlessness n.

1. A constraint to normal respiratory
   function caused by insufficient quantities
   of oxygen in the circulating blood.
2. Emotionally induced suspension of regular
   breathing due to excitement, anticipation,
   fear or tension.

MEDICINE

Breath is the first evidence of life gasping from the womb, and
the final proof of our expiry. It is so central to the experience
and sustenance of life that we describe it in language ranging
from the most detailed medical physiology to the highest human
aesthetics. The functions of breathing aid the most fundamental
chemical processes in the human body, while the mastery and
control of breathing communicate the most profound expres-
sions of human culture through the operatic and dramatic arts.
The human voice – the words, tones and articulated emotions
that form a bridge between our internal experience of life and

the collective family of human society – can't function without the flow and regulation of human breath through our vocal chords. If we are what we say, then human breathing is the essential rhythmic beat of our projected selves.

Medically, the action of breathing with our lungs – known as pulmonary ventilation – is a key part of our respiratory system. This is a collection of biological and chemical processes that deliver oxygen to our cells to help provide energy for essential functions and remove unwanted carbon dioxide. Pulmonary ventilation consists of an inhalation and exhalation phase, and is mainly controlled by an internal dome-shaped muscle sitting just below the lungs and above the abdomen called the diaphragm. When we breathe in, our diaphragm contracts downwards, spreading out our ribs and creating a cavity in our lungs into which air rushes via the mouth and nasal passages. The air progresses down past our larynx, through the windpipe or trachea, before branching off into each lung via the bronchus tubes of the bronchial tree – so-called because the incoming air is diverted down ever-tinier branches in the lungs until it reaches the alveoli – millions of microscopic junction points where oxygen in the air is transferred to our bloodstream for carrying to our cells. As the oxygen passes one way, waste carbon dioxide from our bodies passes back to our lungs. When we exhale, our diaphragm relaxes, the ribs spring back to their previous position and this gas is expelled. In all, about a sixth of the air capacity in our lungs is exchanged with each breath. In normal, relaxed circumstances we perform this cycle entirely unconsciously, up to twenty times every minute.

But, of course, not everything we experience in life is

normal, relaxed or unconscious. During heavy exercise, other torso muscles aid the diaphragm to expand lung capacity and suck in much-needed oxygen to cope with increased demand. At high altitudes, our breathing rate can increase to compensate for the paucity of oxygen in the air. And it's not only unconscious processes that affect breathing. The automatic chemical exchanges that govern respiration can be overridden by conscious and emotion-based human behaviours. If someone to whom we're attracted walks into the room, we might experience an increase in the rapidity of our breathing. If we then wished to speak to them – or were even inspired to burst into romantic song – we could override control of exhalation to make our lungs funnel air pressure to the larynx and induce sound vibration in our vocal chords. This would combine with modifications to our vocal tract, lips, tongue and jaw to sing notes, articulate words or express feelings: the lovelorn sigh, the lover's moan, the joyous laugh.

Our pulmonary ventilation system isn't just a courier for vital gases. It's the conveyor of our deepest thoughts and feelings – the primary mechanism for human expression and identity. It sustains and conveys human personality and health through interaction with the environment. When this mechanism goes wrong, it can also be an indicator of both physical and emotional malady.

Perhaps the best-known medical problems relating to pulmonary ventilation are those concerned with constriction of lung capacity, or breathlessness. One of the most widespread of these respiratory conditions is asthma. Asthma is an inflammatory disease affecting the airways of the lungs. When these become inflamed the breathing can be greatly obstructed, sometimes dangerously so. The chest feels constricted and physical energy is compromised. In the most severe cases it can be fatal, with a quarter of a million deaths worldwide every year. The causes of asthma are complex; there is no cure, and the severity of symptoms can vary from patient to patient. Most often it involves a trigger reaction to common allergens like dust and pollen, or aggravators like pollution or exercise. It strikes many healthy children in their early years of development, leaving them wheezing and weakened.

The causes and consequences of asthma in childhood can also have a psychological and social dimension. Pre-existing anxiety or stress can exacerbate the physical symptoms of asthma, while the inevitable curtailing of group sporting activities or frequent absences from school may lead to isolation from peers and arrested social development. If a child has severe asthma early in life, forced to spend extended periods in hospital, then how will they be able to engage fully in the intentionally breathless and highly physical world of the childhood street, playground and school?

Having asthma can also make the young sufferer more prone to other serious pulmonary maladies. A chronic swelling and sensitivity of the airways can place one at increased risk of dangerous infections like pneumonia. Pneumonia is an acute bacterial or viral infection of the alveoli in the lungs, and in severe cases it requires immediate hospitalisation. It causes four million deaths worldwide every year.

Onset of pneumonia is often rapid; presenting within one or two days. It might start as a simple upper respiratory tract infection like a sore throat or sinus infection, but it soon moves into the lungs, where inflammation takes hold and fluid begins to collect. It produces a thick, congested cough and a suffocating feeling of breathlessness. The very young and very old are at particular risk of pneumonia, and help must be sought immediately if their life is to be preserved. Thankfully, medicine now has the means to help. Before the antibiotic age, pneumonia was such an efficient killer that in 1918 the eminent Canadian physician William Osler described it as the 'captain of the men of death'.

A traditional way to help patients suffering from a condition like pneumonia is to use an oxygen tent. This was invented by French physician Charles Michel at the turn of the twentieth century and consists of a tent-like covering placed over the hospital bed to seal the patient inside a specially controlled breathing environment. Oxygen is pumped into the tent, while high humidity is maintained in order to prevent the lungs drying out. The patient's depleted lungs are now able to receive more oxygen with each constricted breath.

If an asthmatic child can survive bouts of respiratory illness like pneumonia then the long-term prognosis is often good. Half the cases of asthma affecting young children will clear up within a decade. As these children become teenagers, their lungs will clear and become more responsive to exercise. The profound hormonal changes also affecting these young people will soon lead to new and more thrilling lung constrictions: the breath-held thrill of a first kiss, the projected voice in the school play, the lung-bursting joy of a victorious sports-day race. Unfortunately, those fresh lungs can also be compromised by youthful complacency. If a teenager is unwise and easily led, they might inflict serious damage on their breathing by cigarette smoking.

Smoking amongst teenagers usually begins as a wheezing passport to peer-group conformity, yet the effects are felt long after the peer group has disbanded. Most adult smokers started in their teens, and half of them will go on to be killed by it. Damage to the respiratory system from cigarette smoking begins immediately, as a result of the damage caused to our lungs' natural cleansing mechanism called the respiratory cilia. Cilia are tiny hair-like projections protruding from our bronchus tubes which help to sweep away foreign bodies and impurities from our lungs. The mucus we produce traps the dirt and dangerous organisms, while the cilia sweep them up to our mouths to be expelled. Cigarette smoking has an immediate suppressant effect on the functioning of these cilia. If we carry on smoking, the cilia will stop working altogether. This is the cause of the classic 'smoker's cough', as the cilia can no longer expel the accumulated mucus that's gathered in our chest. Yet this is only the start of our problems. A regular smoker's breathing becomes increasingly congested, which leads to conditions like bronchitis and emphysema, the symptoms of which are breathlessness, fatigue and wheezing. Eventually, the damage can change the very cell structure of the lungs, leading to cancer. The shy young smoker, eager to belong, ends up as a lung-blackened statistic. Flaws in our youthful psychology can have a direct and physical effect on the quality of our breathing.

The relationship between flawed human psychology and breathlessness is subtle and many-faceted. Anxiety conditions such as agoraphobia, for instance, can induce a profound breathlessness and panic in a sufferer without any physical or rational cause at all. Agoraphobia is an anxiety disorder in which a sufferer fears being exposed to public places where escape might be difficult, or help won't be available if an attack sets in. Agoraphobia usually appears between the ages of eighteen and thirty-five, and affects up to 3.5 per cent of the population. A common misconception about agoraphobia is that it's simply a fear of open spaces. The truth is more complex. The term derives from the Greek word *agora*, meaning a city's public gathering place – an indication that agoraphobia's causes are more social than spatial.

When a sufferer is exposed to a public place or situation in which they feel vulnerable, it triggers feelings of dizziness, nausea or faintness – and a sensation of suffocation that leads to an increase in the rapidity of breathing known as hyperventilation. Hyperventilation removes too much carbon dioxide from the blood via the lungs, which then upsets the acid–alkaline balance in the body. This in turn adds to the agoraphobic's feelings of dizziness – a vicious cycle that leaves them in a spiral of increasing panic. The sufferer flees back to a place of social safety such as their home and is subsequently fearful of revisiting the place or situation that induced the initial anxiety. Future events can induce a panic simply by their mental anticipation, sparked by the painful memory of that former incident. This interesting phenomenon, known as 'fear of the fear', means that once agoraphobia is initiated it can become a self-perpetuating condition – one that anticipates terror more than it experiences it. The malfunctioning mind becomes a prison for the body.

Agoraphobia can afflict a sufferer for months, years, or in some cases a lifetime. Sufferers are confined to their homes, with any journey outside involving panic attacks, breathlessness and feelings of suffocation. These attacks can occur in the most innocuous and enjoyable of public places – in bars, restaurants or parks – turning places of rest and leisure into places of danger. Worse, if the sufferer's life or work involves communicating directly with others, such as public speaking or performing arts, then this becomes a source of terrified anxiety. The idea of walking onto a public stage in the critical view of hundreds of strangers is a living nightmare for any agoraphobic.

Agoraphobia is slow to shift once established. How do we tell our protective but malfunctioning mind that it has nothing to fear but itself? Treatments for agoraphobia require us to unpick and reprogramme the internal cognition that has short-circuited normal behaviour and responses. One effective strategy is to expose oneself by increasing degrees to the conditions that induce panic. Over time, one becomes less and less susceptible – eventually retraining the brain not to associate those places and situations with fear.

For all of its fear and pain, the malady of my own teenage agoraphobia brought about one of the most positive experiences of my life. It taught me at a formative age about the power of the human mind and will – its ability to serve or constrain our best interests and intentions. It left me with a lifelong interest in neuroscience and the complex workings of the brain. It forced me to embrace my fragilities; not as shorthand characteristics, but as the valuable constituents of a larger and more complex personality. My malady became a teacher, a catalyst for empathy and the source of a wiser strength. The thing that stopped my teenage breath eventually became the means for me to breathe more clearly in adulthood.

Breathing is an exquisite mingling of body, mind and spirit

that sustains and conveys the human personality through an interaction with our environment.

Breathing is the sound our humanity makes.

History

Learning to Breathe: The McGann family, 1960–1983

The winter of late 1962 and early 1963 was known as 'the Big Freeze'. It was an extended period of arctic conditions that lasted well into the spring. Huge snowdrifts blocked streets. The sea froze. In a small terraced house in Birstall Road, Liverpool, a heavily pregnant Clare McGann sat out the cold with her three young children, Joseph, Paul and Mark. Her husband Joe trekked through the snow to his shiftwork at a copper factory on the outskirts of the city. Clare had given birth to three kids in under five years. Now there was another. Soon she'd add a fifth. She inhaled motherhood like fresh air. It energised her. It surprised her with its force. It motivated her in ways the changing world couldn't yet see.

As the Big Freeze went into February, Clare McGann went into labour. The midwife was called. By the time the woman had struggled on her bicycle through drifted snow her mood was less than charitable. My mum told me that she was grumpy throughout my delivery. It's funny to think that the baby she delivered would later play a doctor in a television drama extolling the bedside virtues of sixties bicycling midwives, yet his own birth would be afforded no such virtue. My first breath in the world was a wailed apology for any inconvenience caused. That's showbiz.

When my birth was announced there were apparently dissatisfied murmurings from the in-laws. They were impatient for a girl. Mum's response was iron love smelted in defiance. 'You were beautiful!' she said. 'Perfect just as you were – and you were *mine*.'

To be honest, what I looked like when I was born can politely be described as 'bonny'. Less politely, it looked as if I'd been inflated like a balloon in the hands of an overenthusiastic children's entertainer. I was nine and a half pounds in weight – the heaviest child my mother had given birth to. The modern average is seven and a half. The mothers around my pram cooed delightedly. 'Ooh, what a *bonny* baby!' The word was synonymous with 'healthy'. I wear that title with pride because a child that was bonny was a child that was taking its food – growing strong. At the turn of the twentieth century, 145 children in every thousand were dying in Britain before they reached their first birthday, according to the Office for National Statistics.* The post-war welfare state had reduced this number to fewer than thirty, yet the bitter memory of personal loss was still carried as inherited fear in those mothers' heads. To eat was to thrive.

The McGanns were thriving, if modestly. It was a hundred years since they'd stepped onto the Liverpool dockside from Ireland. For most of that century they'd merely subsisted – but now they were recipients of a system of nationalised health, welfare and education at the height of its post-war confidence: well funded, well regarded and fired by progressive zeal. For

---

* http://webarchive.nationalarchives.gov.uk/20160105160709/http://www.ons.gov.uk/ons/rel/hsq/health-statistics-quarterly/no--18--summer-2003/twentieth-century-mortality-trends-in-england-and-wales.pdf

thwarted scholarship kids like Joe and Clare McGann, the system offered their children protections and opportunities that they'd been denied. They were going to grab them with both hands.

The little terraced house we lived in was bought, not rented. Joe McGann was the first holder of a mortgage in our family's history. The house had been purchased for the princely sum of seven hundred pounds – a serious undertaking for a factory worker in 1960. It had three modest bedrooms up a steep flight of stairs, a cramped living room, a front parlour, and a tiny kitchen that ran out into a back yard with an outside toilet. Away from the fireplace, and in the days before central heating, the house was freezing – a cold that penetrated the sheets and misted the windows, congesting our chests and stealing our breath. But it was ours. Our little piece of the world.

My first few years of life were full of clear breath and sunshine. It would be more than two years until my sister Clare was born, and so for a time I had my mum's undivided attention: a rare luxury in a family of our size. I never went to nursery, and so was the full recipient of Mum's ecstatic zeal for parenting. I was introduced to the world through her shining eyes, and wouldn't be exposed to the feral squint of the urban playground until I was five years old. Those times were idyllic, though I've often wondered if their warm insularity was a hindrance to me later on; a dependency on the breathless love and security of home that left me ill-prepared for the wider world and the changes it necessitated. Perhaps it was significant that my later teenage problems saw me running back in panic to the safety of that house. The redbrick womb that breathed for me when my life was at its zenith of simplicity – an umbilical bond that required no gasping breaths of courage or defiance.

Sister Clare came along in 1965, and I adored her. Before child safety outweighed our society's belief in the health-giving power of fresh air, a Liverpool mother thought nothing of leaving her baby unattended in a pram by the front door for hours while she did the housework. The terraced street pavements were an assault course of perambulator awnings, knitted woollen blankets, chatting wives and flying footballs. I'd climb up onto the side of Clare's pram and sing snatches of Merseybeat songs to her while the miniskirted mothers strolled by on their way to the shops, their husbands' cash stuffed into scuffed leather purses. Working-class sixties Liverpool was a patriarchal cash economy. Dad got paid every Thursday in a small brown packet and provided mum with 'housekeeping' – the money necessary to fulfil her wifely duties. He never disclosed his earnings, and the idea of a married woman running her own bank account was unheard of. Mum couldn't sign a hire purchase agreement or take out a mortgage. She was as dependent on her husband as we were on her.

Despite my love for my sister, her birth nudged me out of my mother's sole affections. I now had to make my own way. It was at this time that my chest began to feel constricted. Nights were the worst – wheezing and coughing and making my brother Mark fret in the nearby bed. The mathematics of three small bedrooms with a family of seven meant that the children always shared rooms. It was a wonderful privation; stacked bunks, four kids together – chatting, whispering, giggling in the curtain-dimmed, streetlight yellow while our parents shushed and scolded. It was the closest we ever were.

Now it was a place where I struggled to breathe. Mum would prop my head up on pillows to aid my airways, while

Dad rubbed Vicks menthol vapour onto my chest to clear the sinuses. There were constant visits to the Royal Liverpool Children's Hospital clinic – hours of crying infants and surnames barked by fearsome matrons with clipboards. Those long appointments gave time for Mum and me to be alone again, chatting and thinking and waiting – her attentions undivided. I loved it. The doctor said that my problem was asthma, aggravated by an allergy to the house dust in my bedroom. It seemed to affect more than my breathing. My weight began a descent from 'bonny' to skinny. My little ribs spiked through my pale torso. The other siblings nicknamed me 'Bone'. Affectionate but blunt. A new identity to go with the new antagonist. Weakling. The names we give to things become the things we are.

Dust wasn't the only antagonist hanging in the air in Birstall Road. My father's neurosis and melancholy was a miasma that the McGann children inhaled from their earliest perception. Sometimes you could taste it in the air like acrid smoke – tiptoeing around his chair where he dozed following a long shift, hoping he wouldn't wake, or else confining our exchanges to careful pleasantries. It wasn't a fear of violence, or drunkenness, or the brisk lash of rage. My father was never the kind to trouble the police or bring the priest to the door. Instead it was a brooding cloud that seeped through the gaps in our optimism, bleaching the colour from our childish world. Our home life became attuned to his melancholic rhythm – meals without him were clean-lunged breaths of raucous laughter, inane argument, unfinished sentences, school news, clannish conversation. When he was there it was tight-chested bonhomie and watchful glances. Saddest of all were the times when he tried to break through the fog and join in the family laughter. The effort was heartbreaking. He loved us and we loved him, but we were an insufficient lighthouse for the rock-strewn sea of anxieties in his life. Eventually he'd doze in his armchair exhausted from the effort, and we'd escape to play outside with our optimism intact.

Outside. Hours and hours on cobblestone or stone-chipped tarmac – chalked goalposts, skipping ropes, hopscotched paving stones. We were the children born after Attlee and before the microchip age; long hours of outdoor physical activity with free treatment for our broken bones, and without the sedentary temptations of text messages or gaming consoles. There were bicycles and races and matches and chases and vast opposing teams of nail-grimed, pre-teen warriors bursting their lungs to demonstrate prowess in the only way that mattered. Physically.

My lungs were weighed in the balance and found wanting. My asthma meant I'd always be at the back in sprints, and be left coughing and wheezing by the sidelines in ball games. And it wasn't simply breathlessness that marked me. I seemed to be too self-absorbed. I'd be distracted and miss a pass, or overthink a catch and drop the ball. I lacked that easy courage that helped the other kids win reckless dares or swing bruising punches to settle disputes. I hesitated on the diving board of the urban childhood to which I'd been assigned. The other kids were perfectly amenable to my lowly prowess – a tribe as accommodating as it was competitive – yet my weakness was now an identifier, to me as well as others. A one-line biography, or the brand on an animal's skin. A brute synecdoche for my unformed self.

My asthma soon became a placeholder for my childhood personality within the large family to which I belonged. It marked a defining characteristic amongst five children struggling to make sense of their own identities within the knee-scraped arena of working-class Liverpool. It became a label of convenience for parents distracted by their separate needs and their shared unhappiness, and it also became a way for me to define myself. 'The sick one'. 'The weak one'. The one of whom too much must not be expected. There was a certain comfort in surrendering to the convenience of its modest expectations. Family identity, however assigned, becomes like inhaled oxygen – an unconscious function of our self-survival.

Sometimes I'd abandon the knee-scraped arena altogether, and return indoors to watch my father work. Dad had a peculiar hobby that absorbed him on free weekends. He'd repair old transistor radio sets – all broken Bakelite dials and cracked motherboards – rescued from some workplace friend or scrap bin. They rattled when you shook them. It seemed an impossible task, but Dad sat there stubbornly in his armchair, week after week, glasses balanced on his nose, fiddling and soldering. I'd sit at his feet and ask him about the different parts. He'd tell me about his time as a wartime telegraphist. Radio had been his technology – the time when his prowess had mattered. He loved it, and I loved to watch him loving something so simply, without shadows.

It was Dad who first told me how transistors worked. Transistors are the building blocks for radios and computers – the tiny alveoli that make our modern world breathe. It's an electronic switch or amplifier that's made from a three-layer sandwich of silicon. You put electricity through the silicon layers to make the electrons flow where you want them to. But the secret of transistors lies in their flaws. One must deliberately place impurities into the pure silicon layers in order to make them conduct electricity properly. Without those flaws, the element is pure but unexceptional. By integrating impurity, the power of the whole is amplified and the world listens.

Eventually, after weeks, and without fail, Dad's old radio set would burst into crackling life. He'd smile with quiet satisfaction, the impurities in his world briefly integrated.

We learned our first vocal harmonies as children from the songs we heard on those radio sets. My family have been credited with various talents, but back then there was little evidence of any innate gift. Except for the singing. As young kids we could harmonise together really well. No one taught us. We'd simply hear a song on the radio a few times, and then one of us would start singing the melody. A sibling elsewhere in the house would join in with a harmony above it. Another would add a third. Then someone else an octave. Finally my sister would find an impossible seventh, or a haunting sixth. By this point the child who'd started the melody would complain of harmonic mugging by a dystopian version of the von Trapp family. The McTrapps?

Our hierarchy of harmonies was an analogue for the subtle hierarchies of age and status that began to impress itself on us all at that time. My sister and I were never the melody line – never the foundation on which the song of our family was constructed. We had to find our own notes in the gaps and pauses left by more established voices. In the crude pecking order of working-class Liverpool family life, each sibling required a label with which to describe them – a sustained musical note allotted to each child in the chorus of family identity. Joe was 'the eldest', big for his age, his sensitivity hidden by his stature and frowned on by my father; Paul was 'sporty' and 'confident', encouraged to hide his fragility and doubt beneath an athletic skill and an assumed nonchalance; Mark was the 'middle child', regarded as insecure, but possessing enormous resilience, courage and compassion; me – the 'sick one' – my potential both excused and denied by my role as the family's weakling; and Clare was the 'baby girl', her prodigious intellect and academic skill constrained by her relative youth and gender. All of us in our allotted places. None of us adequately served by them. A tight skin we'd each be forced to shed later in order to grow.

Looking back, I smile at my own assumptions. I'd considered myself the only child who couldn't breathe. Yet all of us were gasping for air in our own way.

Why did our loving parents permit this blunt shorthand to take hold? Was it convenience? Oversight? Or was it us who needed it? The only way that the kids we were, crammed into an enforced proximity of bunk bed and shared bath, could carve out some space of our own?

Soon I carved out my own unorthodox space away from the pecking order. As a young child I was forever in and out of hospital. But I loved it. It conformed with my role as the sickly one in the family, yet also gave me time to be alone. To read and think and breathe. Hospitals weren't supposed to be pleasant places and, yes, sometimes it involved the inconvenience of needles, anaesthetic or operations. But there were advantages too. I was fussed over at strict visiting times, given toys, sweets and kind words, and then left to my own devices. The sixties National Health ward was a regimented barracks of care – spotless floors, starched sheets, fearsome ward sisters, the clank of silver bedpans and the enduring aroma of disinfectant. There was warmth and security in this orderly kindness. It was in hospital that I first found solitude and a sense of self. I could hide in plain sight – an anonymous child amongst the oxygen bottles and the beakers of Lucozade. I was free.

Not for long. Once back on my feet it was time to attend school. St Anne's was a gothic sandstone institution of polished wooden floors and stern, black-cloaked nuns, close to the tenements that my father's family lived in. It catered for inner-city Catholic children from infancy to factory age. All of the McGann children went there, although it involved a near-mile walk from our home. Mum and Dad valued its educational standards, and we quickly realised how important this was to both of them. Our parents shared so few things. They rarely socialised, and their conversations were often conducted with a caution and mutual incomprehension that ended with heavy silence. Any physical contact between them was brief, and agonising to watch. Yet there was our education; their mutual aspiration for us to do well and progress to a grammar school. It united them in a way no other part of their lives did. And it was an aspiration that we could do something about.

The Tripartite System of state-funded secondary education in the UK was now in full flow following the Education Act of 1944. This grand post-war experiment made it possible for children from our background to be fully funded at a selective grammar school if we passed a single key examination at eleven years old. Any young child failing this test was filtered either to a vocational technical school or, more likely, to a 'second-ary modern', an academically unchallenging environment that prepared its pupils for motherhood or the unskilled workforce. It was opportunity measured out in the blunt binary logic of sheep and goats.

It was clear which flock our parents wanted us to join. They greeted every glowing report the children received with a hope and pride that lit the room. My mother still cherishes a hand-written poem penned by my brother Paul back then – rhyming couplets in wide-looped primary-school cursive. Paul pays ostentatious tribute to his recent academic results, and those of his siblings. It's tender and funny on first reading, but becomes more moving on reflection. The poem isn't written in conceit, but with a wide-eyed eagerness to please. Paul is offering our academic success as a collective gift to our parents; a peace offering to fill their silences with a noisy new pride and purpose.

I progressed fast at St Anne's, as did my whole family. I excelled in my school reports, yet found the rough social world hard to adjust to. The catchment area for the school was diverse but socially deprived. Bright and gentle children shared desk space with kids whose homes were battlegrounds and whose lives were scarred by neglect. There is a particular smell to poverty in children that I still remember from that time. A warm-biscuit odour of unwashed cotton and low-level depression. The halitosis of young untended teeth. The dried sweat of endless subsistence with permanently narrow horizons. My home, though simple, was always safe. There was love and order in it. My baby teeth were brushed and my clothes were ironed. Yet that biscuit odour in my nostrils could easily have been my own if circumstances had been slightly different. The McGanns were only inches from their past. This was the odour of my recent ancestors. It was the smell of the kind-hearted but luckless school friends next to me. Those who think poverty is just a want of money have likely never been required to breathe its air as an equal.

By the time I got to junior school, my asthmatic frame and teacher-pleasing character singled me out for punishment in the predatory hierarchy of the playground. My dinner money was often stolen, and I was a constant target for the calculated cruelty of small boys in large numbers. I remember once trying to fight them back. It still brings a wry smile. There was a genuine amusement from my tormentors – an admiration for the wheezing runt of a bear they baited – until, patience thinning, they kicked me harder for my impertinence. I was left choking for breath on the cracked tarmac.

I'd soon have more than wheezing to contend with. In the early months of 1971 my chest started feeling more congested than usual. A terrible pain in my left lung kept me awake. It felt different to the normal breathlessness. Sharper. A devil I didn't know. The doctor was called. It was severe pneumonia. He called an ambulance, and I was escorted to the back of it on a stretcher, wearing a look of saintly stoicism while the neighbours watched from nearby doorways. This was the sport I excelled in. Peak weakling.

By the time I arrived at the hospital, my mother's ashen face told me this was no ordinary rest break. I was very ill. I couldn't stay awake. They put me in an oxygen tent – a large polythene enclosure placed over my bed to encourage me to sweat out my fever, into which they pumped oxygen-enriched air to help me breathe. It was unbearably humid and my sheets were soaked with my own perspiration. The movements of the nurses were reduced to ghostly, condensation-smeared silhouettes through the plastic barrier. Every few hours, a nurse pulled back the plastic sheet, turned me over, and injected my buttocks with intravenous medicine. I'd cry with each injection, my resolve evaporating by the hour. One night the nurse pulled back the sheet again to reveal my father sitting there. He'd been keeping silent vigil. His look of worry was washed by an expression of such gentleness. The nurse prepared the needle again and I began to cry. Dad placed a tender hand on my head. 'Shh. There, there, son,' he said. 'It's penicillin. It's wonderful. It'll make you better.' I looked into his face, so often clouded by melancholy and doubts I never understood. There was no doubt. Just love and certainty.

Penicillin was the one thing in my father's life that had never disappointed him. It had been the gentle hand on his own head when he'd most needed it. Now it was back to save his son. Penicillin was the messenger of a larger mercy. The McGanns were no longer a pestilence to the country they were born in, diseased and incurable. Joe McGann's son was worthy of the finest attentions of medicine. It was a right he fought for and one that his children could now assume without violence or cost. Penicillin was dignity and gratitude. It was ingenuity and compassion. It was the sound of a civilised society breathing. It was a child's life.

I lived. My lungs cleared. I returned to my junior school and continued to do well academically, although my asthma became worse and my absences more frequent. Looking back, there was more to my wheezing than simply allergy or genetics. I was progressively more anxious and unhappy at school, which gave my asthma a psychosomatic dimension. As the crucial eleven-plus examination approached, I punctuated bouts of fruitful work with extended sick days. I was acquiring a habit of escaping the stresses of my life by seeking the security of home.

When the eleven-plus finally arrived, I was calm despite the pressure. It tested our intelligence in the narrow puzzle-based style of an IQ test – a format I found easy. We were little lab rats running within the maze walls of uncomplicated metrics. If we sniffed out the correct path with sufficient accuracy we would be deemed worthy of reward and transferred to a more gilded cage. If not, the bars that confined our lives would be reinforced. I was deemed sufficiently accurate. I passed my exam well and was offered a place at a Catholic grammar school in Liverpool's leafy suburbs. It was a bus ride from my home, but a million miles away from the life I'd known.

All of the McGann children passed their eleven-plus examinations, and all were educated in suburban faith-based state grammar schools. It's no exaggeration to say that in a century and a half of McGann family history, the education that we received as a result of those exams was the single decisive factor that transformed our family's fortunes. More than any talent or occupation; more than any wage or medicine or mortgage or experience. It was the education that mattered. Education as ideas. Education as other worlds. Philosophy and physics and the sound of a bow on a violin string. Debate and doubt and challenge and poetry and the endless possibility of books. It was the thing my mother had tasted, and the thing my father had been denied. Without it we'd never have been able to dissect a script or build a character. The brutal method of selection by which children like us achieved our education and others didn't has rightly been criticised. But the fact of it can't be denied. It changed everything for my family, and everything that followed came as a result.

* * *

I arrived at Cardinal Allen Grammar School for boys in a uniform my father had struggled to afford. My brother Paul was already a pupil and had shown a keen talent in sport – his school athletics records were listed proudly on the notice board in the corridor as we filed in. The games master singled me out and told me he was expecting great things. I took a nervous breath and felt the rattle of the wheeze in my chest. Ah.

Thankfully there were other subjects I could shine in. Most of my new classmates were from lower-middle-class suburban families. They had semi-detached gardens and company cars and inhaled the prejudices of their parents with barely a pause for breath. Yet I wasn't intimidated. We sounded equally terrible in orchestra rehearsals. My early school results were encouraging and my parents were delighted.

There wasn't a lot that delighted them at this time. My parents' marriage – never the smoothest surface on which the children could stand – was now showing wide cracks. Mum had enjoyed the child development aspect of motherhood so much that once her kids were at school she'd resolved to take it further. She trained as a nursery nurse while I wheezed my way through St Anne's, and was now employed at an inner-city nursery school. Dad hated it. He regarded his wife working as a mark of personal shame. He'd mock her low wages, and accuse her of neglecting her children. It was vindictive and cruel, a neurotic insecurity turned into a sulking meanness, designed to wear her down in the same way as his relentlessness had done in their early marriage. But this time my mother stood her ground. It was now the seventies. Women of her generation had begun to inject their own desires into the closed world of men's expectations. Clare McGann had done her marital and maternal duty beyond reproach, and now she was going to pursue her modest dreams in spite of her husband's obstructions. It was a battle she'd ultimately win, but at a cost to her marriage and her children's peace of mind.

By my second year in Cardinal Allen the shouts and arguments were terrible. My parents had embarked on a war of attrition that tore away any veneer of peace in our home. Meals were spent in sullen silence. Dad would embark on long periods of hunger strike, while Mum would take us away in summer without him. My oldest brother Joe abandoned our home and moved away. Paul cultivated a self-protective confidence that revealed little of his feelings. Mark, wrestling with adolescence, struggled to be heard in all the shouting. My sister Clare became a high-achieving scholar – each glowing school report a desperate peace offering to parents too distracted by their own unhappiness to see her quiet despair.

And me? Perversely, my asthma began to ease. For all the tension at home, my developing lungs could take a deeper breath. Yet there were more things I needed from that environment than a lungful of oxygen. My body was changing. I was now growing hairs in interesting places and feeling the first confusion of pubescent sexual awakening. There was a new knot of tension in my stomach. A mounting panic that distracted me. The little house in Birstall Road had provided me with a protective womb from which to comprehend the world. Now it had ruptured. My schoolwork nosedived, and my teachers were baffled by my uncharacteristic passivity towards it. I looked lazy and uncommitted. I wasn't. I was crying for help.

I drifted on through the early years of adolescence as my parents' marriage crumbled. Nights were an escape. I dreamed about those pretty girls I'd spied at the bus stop or watched gliding piously down the aisle at Mass, storing up enough pneumatic sins to keep the priest occupied in the confessional for a month.

By day those same young women would stare back at me like something unpleasant discovered on the sole of their elegant shoes. I was hardly love's young dream. Just as my asthma had lifted, acne had arrived to take its place. My limbs and other appendages grew rapidly, and in all the wrong directions. I was shy and clumsy and hopeless at the kind of flirtatious confidence required to turn breathless dreams into reality.

Then one day at school I did something uncharacteristic. I walked into an audition for the new school play and offered my services. I was painfully gauche, yet I'd seen the previous school play starring my brother Paul, and had been inspired by his wonderful performance. Paul had shown things in public that he'd never shown at home. Strength and sensitivity – courage under the glare of strong lights. I wanted to find that. What's more, girls loved him for it. The fact that he possessed preternatural good looks and flawless skin doubtless helped. But hell, it was worth a try ...

The part I auditioned for was small and manageable. The teacher who directed the plays was an English master called Joseph Hartley – as crucial to the brothers' later careers as anybody who came after. He liked what I did and offered me the part. The rehearsals were wonderful. I was part of something I'd never felt before. A collective endeavour. A gang that didn't beat me up. When the performance finally came I grew terrified. I only had a few lines, but ran them ceaselessly in my head for fear I'd clam up in the spotlight. When my entrance arrived I could hear my footsteps on the floorboards and the thump of my heart banging in my chest. I stood, frozen, as my first line approached. The moment of truth. Run or fight.

I opened my mouth. My diaphragm descended and air flooded deep into my lungs. My chest muscles tightened to funnel the exhaled air towards the larynx. My vocal chords resonated. My throat and lips, tongue and jaw worked in harmony to articulate projected words to the back of the school hall. I heard my first line. My voice was painfully thin and untrained. But I heard it. I hadn't run. I'd stood my ground.

The English master was encouraging. He gave me confidence

in myself at a time when my life was full of doubts. He suggested that I had a talent for drama, just like my brother Paul. Mr Hartley had encouraged Paul to become an actor, but Paul didn't know how. He'd left school soon afterwards and started to drift. Mum decided to take him in hand. She dialled directory enquiries and asked for the number of the only drama school whose name she knew. It was called the 'Royal Academy of Dramatic Art'. The rest of us had never heard of it. She rang the number and requested an application form. Paul needed a bit of persuading to fill it in. The school agreed to help him with a Shakespeare piece and a speech from *My Fair Lady*. The audition day duly arrived, and Paul went off to London on the train. That night he returned. The outcome seemed inconclusive, so Paul shuffled back into his provincial life.

After that, the main drama switched back to home. Mum had reached the end of the line in her marriage. Dad had rejected every suggestion of counselling. When she asked for a separation, he refused to leave. Mum sought the parish priest's help, but my father wouldn't budge. Mum and Dad, despite their troubles, were devout Catholics. Marriage to them was an indissoluble thing. It was therefore with the utmost pain that Mum finally went to a solicitor and filed for divorce. Still my dad refused to go, and so Mum was forced to take out an injunction on him. The pain and guilt of it still stings her. In the end, the priest came round to help Dad pack. Dad, shattered by the results of his own inflexibility, moved back in with his brother and sister.

My sister and I were caught in the crossfire. We were now required to perform that sad dance of fractured families everywhere. The children of separated parents – hasty experts in fixed-smile diplomacy and the negotiation of divided loyalties. Clare, with extraordinary courage and discipline, buried herself in her schoolwork – her academic performance excelling even as her home life dissolved around her. I drifted on, the knot in my stomach being the only consistent application of my energies. To escape the suffocating effects of home, my brother Mark had discovered a wonderful new creative outlet at the Everyman Youth Theatre. This was a young people's drama group run in warehouse space at the back of Liverpool's Everyman Theatre. The kids who attended were tough, smart, brilliant, blunt and utterly compelling. I'd never seen anything like them. Pugnacious young poets, beautiful, brittle punkettes, ascerbic young gays and smirking sink-estate scallywags. I quickly followed my brother into regular weekly attendance. It would have a lasting influence on our lives.

Soon after I joined the Everyman, a letter dropped onto our doormat from the Royal Academy of Dramatic Art. Paul had passed his audition – one of about twenty people in over a thousand applicants. Paul was dumbstruck. We were astonished. A working-class Liverpool factory worker's son with just a couple of school plays' experience had been accepted into one of the world's leading drama schools. Up until that moment drama had been something my family had encountered by accident and indulged in without ambition. It had been an alternative means of escape – a source of creative oxygen and structure. We'd never been to the theatre as a family. There were no actors we knew, and we had no knowledgeable acquaintances we could confer with. Yet, thanks to an English teacher's encouragement and my mum's tenacity, one of our family was now to be trained for a career in drama. Paul was the first McGann male in history to follow a profession – a job free of coaldust, bullets, factory grease or soil-grimed fingernails.

But what was I to do with my life? My O-levels were fast approaching and I was spending every spare moment either in school plays or at the Everyman Youth Theatre. I started under-age drinking in the few pubs that would serve me, my pockets laden with guilt money procured from my divorcing parents. I remember my first cigarette. The tightness in young lungs barely clear of asthma. The stab of nicotine in my undeveloped brain. The naive vandalism of elective self-harm. A gesture of defiance to a future I couldn't yet believe in.

My drifting was just one symptom of the wider forces shaping my family at that time. The McGanns had reached an interesting crossroads in their history. Education had delivered us from the brutal simplicity of our labouring past, but it hadn't provided us with the means to negotiate the more complex world we'd reached. It was as if we'd been dropped off at the gates of our parents' post-war promised land without a key. We had to pick the lock ourselves. Who were we exactly? We weren't like our mum and dad any more – or like theirs. But we also weren't those people who taught us, or auditioned us, or shared our classrooms. We were something else. Something Owen and Susan might have recognised. Immigrants, scrambling for a foothold in a strange new place. Our education was the boat that brought us. Now we had to get ourselves off the dockside.

* * *

My O-level results arrived and I was astonished to have scraped seven of them. Lacking any clear plan, I decided to stay on for sixth form. I signed up to study music, while devoting all of my spare hours to the brilliant, brash world of the Everyman Youth Theatre. It was the beginning of the eighties. Liverpool arts culture was thriving, even as the city's economy plummeted: Liverpool bands filled the music charts and Liverpool theatre brimmed with a vibrant joy and anger. Our youth shows were the backdrop to our coming-of-age in a city that was determined to go down fighting. It was breathless and exhilarating.

I fell in love for the first time. She was an art student. She was beautiful and funny and worldly and kind, and I was still shy and scared and a virgin. When I finally found the guts to kiss her, I didn't want to stop. We'd spend our nights at wild parties in the derelict merchants' mansions that bordered Toxteth's Sefton Park. The ostentatious palaces of Liverpool's Victorian mercantile classes were now the crumbling playgrounds of its penniless punk students. Owen might have enjoyed the irony. We made love for the first time in a room full of people too stoned to notice or care. We held our breaths when the climax came, suspending the joy for as long as possible. Holding off the future.

My future crept towards me regardless. In order to study A-level music I was required to be proficient in a musical instrument. My music teacher suggested I should undergo crash-course training as a tenor singer. To help my sight-singing, he also suggested I should apply to join the Liverpool Philharmonic Choir – an excellent amateur chorus attached to Liverpool's world-renowned city orchestra. So I found myself a local singing tutor and I auditioned for the Liverpool Phil. To my great surprise I was successful.

The singing lessons were tough. Really tough. I'd collected a legion of bad breathing habits in my short life. Shallow, strangled gasps and tight-throated top notes. Now I had to undo it all and learn to breathe properly. For most of our lives, breathing is just an automatic process. But *directed* breathing – breathing with artistic purpose – isn't. Without adequate breath, it's impossible to sustain a note or project a full voice. Without control over the things that connect us to others, we can never be in possession of our intent. We can never project the best of ourselves into the wider world.

For weeks and weeks I barely sang a verse of anything. It was all breathing. Hour after hour of deep-lunged breathing until my head span with the excess of oxygen. Gradually I was able to harness the power of my diaphragm and the huge column of air it controlled. I finally produced notes that could resonate and sustain, rather than thin out and die towards the end of a phrase. I could now make myself heard in a way that didn't shame me.

I needed to. My early time with the Philharmonic Choir was a white-knuckle ride. The expert choir needed little rehearsal, effortlessly wading through vast screeds of complicated sheet music with barely a glance. I was reduced to aping their fast-turning pages and miming their confident vibrato. But the music they made was magnificent – Beethoven, Bach, Vaughan Williams, Elgar – and we had great conductors like Sir Simon Rattle to direct us, and venues such as the Royal Albert Hall and Royal Festival Hall to sing in. The tenors performed in bow tie and dinner suit, which wasn't exactly my standard wardrobe. Mum dug deep on limited income to purchase the best she could. I really looked the part, although I didn't feel it. The other choristers were older – elegant, affluent, and totally unlike me – yet also warm, kind and funny. A different world, but not a hostile one.

My life was now increasingly full of jarring notes – irresolvable themes that didn't fit together in any kind of harmony. I'd go straight from genteel choir performances to the bawdy anarchy of a youth theatre party, or from the breath-sustained discipline of music lessons to drunken cigarette-tainted kisses in parks. I was still drifting, still standing outside of myself, miming life's confident vibrato while the pages turned without me. I could feel a creeping acceleration in the speed at which the separate pieces of me pulled apart. The edge of the waterfall was drawing closer.

The two oldest McGann brothers were now settled in London. Joe had gone into the music business as a singer and songwriter, while Paul was confidently ensconced as an actor in RADA. Mark and I were spending all our waking hours at the Everyman. Entirely without forethought or planning, the performance arts had injected themselves into the centre of my family's collective story. It remains a mystery to us why it should have been the arts – rather than, say, business, or science, or a million other things. It seemed to be a common means by which we tested and defined ourselves. A lonely melody that we each attempted, and to which each sibling added a specific harmony. A way to understand our lives in the absence of a key. A way to pick the lock and leave the dockside. But it would still require good fortune: a moment of serendipity for each of us that would break the chain and propel us forward.

Mark's fortunes suddenly found their moment. He'd been singing John Lennon songs for a band that was accompanying the Everyman's main house production of Ken Campbell's *The Warp*. Mark's incredible characterisation of Lennon in those songs brought him to the attention of the theatre's artistic staff.

The next show they mounted was to be a musical biography of John Lennon. They selected my brother Mark to star in it. The show was a huge success, later going on to enjoy a successful West End run. Mark was simply phenomenal as Lennon – full of fire and passion and heart. Overnight, my brother went from an amateur youth theatre actor to a career professional. His chain was broken, and forward he leapt.

My A-levels arrived, and I failed them spectacularly. I was finally ejected into the adult world. Still unprepared. Still running, not fighting. At least for now there was still the choir. There was still my girlfriend's warmth and wit. Still the social magnet of the youth theatre. But the city I lived in was in the midst of a deep depression. There was no work – not even the most casual job. I was unemployed, collecting my benefits with the rest. The streets of Toxteth were rioting. I drank my dole away. I screwed and smoked and drifted and ran and waited for some magical leap of fortune to make sense of the discordant music in my head.

I'd reached the edge of the waterfall.

I travelled to London with the choir to sing a piece of Elgar in the Royal Albert Hall. The choir stalls in that auditorium are curved, high, and very steeply raked. As I made my way back to the tenor section after the interval, I looked down at the concertgoers in the audience. Suddenly my breathing became rapid and shallow in my chest. I was overwhelmed by a terrifying dread. The sound of the chattering in the auditorium became distorted in my ears – the voices of the choristers next to me were loud and jarring. I felt dizzy. I started to panic. My exit to left and right was blocked. I couldn't escape. The ceiling of the Albert Hall was pressing down on me. I was totally exposed. What if I collapsed and fell? What if I fainted during the performance?

After what felt like minutes of agonising petrifaction, my breathing slowly calmed. The music started. The choir sang. Yet I could only mime and turn the pages, unable to sing a note, still shocked and confused by what had happened.

The drifting was over. The falling had begun.

TESTIMONY

'Are you okay?'

My girlfriend is standing with her coat on in the living room of Birstall Road. She's waiting for me to walk her to the bus stop. I'm not moving from my seat. I'm trying to control the agitation wriggling in my gut.

'Fine. I'm just – tired. Hungover. D'you mind if I don't walk you tonight?'

She looks at me. I feel the pulse beating in my ears as she watches me.

'Sure. See you tomorrow.'

When she's gone I feel my breath easing. The terrible dread that stalks me like a murderer from the window has withdrawn for now. The relief mingles with guilt at letting her go alone. My mind dispels the agitation it causes. It's nothing. I'm not well, that's all. A hangover. A cold. Fatigue. Something physical. Nameable. Easily explained. Nothing to be worried about. Nothing . . . else.

My mind can't say it. It doesn't possess the vocabulary. The names we give to things become the things we are. I can't be that. My mind has been my mental strength in a life marked by physical weakness. It has consoled me through a bullied child's tears and loneliness. It's been my companion in solitude – the truth against which the fictions of my world were judged. It doesn't lie, and it doesn't judge itself.

I'm aware that the fear I have of stepping outside has no rational justification. The likelihood of sudden death is minimal. Yet the fear remains. It grins at the futility of my logic. Only in my house do I feel safe. Yet even here it haunts me. The terrible dreams at night. The permanent anxiety in my gut that I can't shake. The dizzy unreality to my daily perception, like I was gazing at the world from behind dimpled glass. The slow asphyxiation of my future.

It's 1982. I'm nineteen. I've been out of school and unemployed for a year, and housebound for a few months. Leaving the safety of my home, even for a quick visit to the shop, is an ordeal I must prepare for and one I rush to conclude. Yet I'm not diagnosed with anything. I haven't seen a doctor and I haven't acknowledged the facts of my condition. It doesn't have a name.

Distant trips are the worst. To London, especially. I get nervous days in advance, and spend the whole time trying to control the panic that descends on me in crowded bars or theatre stalls. Paul is newly out of RADA and blazing a trail as a young actor. He's appearing in a Trevor Griffiths play called *Oi For England* at the Royal Court. The family trek down to see him and we go for a meal afterwards. There's a photograph of us smiling at the dinner table – grins and booze and family pride. Mark is there, now an actor himself. The clan are going places. The boys share a theatrical agent – a flamboyant and ambitious businesswoman who wants to unleash my family on an unsuspecting world. London has become a magnet for our dreams; a new destination for our cultural emigration.

When I look at my grin in that picture, all I remember is the pain it's disguising. The crowded restaurant is suffocating me. I've developed a mask for my anxiety that gets me through the worst of it, but it's exhausting to maintain. I'm longing to go home. At the same time I'm full of hate. I hate the merciless cruelty of it. I'm a hostile slave to its constraints. Running, not fighting.

It's my girlfriend who first names it. She looks at me one night and says its name out loud.

'I think you've got agoraphobia.'

I jump to my feet in agitation. The word ricochets around the tiny room in Birstall Road. I refute and scoff and deflect. After she's gone I lie in bed, the room spinning. The word has come to life and reaches out to grab me in the darkness. I try to regulate my breathing. I try to remember those music lessons – breathing from my diaphragm, taking the air deep into the base of the lungs to loosen the tight muscles and shoulders. It's no good. I'm still falling. Falling and falling and not waking up.

Then something stops me falling further. Anger. A white-hot furious anger, free of impurities. God, I'm angry! Angry at myself. Angry at the world. Angry at my weakness. It burns like potassium in the darkness. I'm *furious* at my agoraphobia. I can see the demon's face in the potassium light. It's the bully in the childhood playground who stole my lunch money. It's the gang's boot in my solar plexus. It's the games teacher's contemptuous grin in the school gymnasium. It's the merciless asthma gripping my infant lungs, holding me back from my life's potential. The one-line family biography, its blunt shorthand still suffocating.

The weakling. The one of whom too much must not be expected.

No. I've had enough. My mind has lied. Life has lied. I'm not this. I'm something better. I want to breathe. I want to be those full lungs of fearless air; the ecstatic suspension of breath when I make love; the diaphragm-powered courage of words delivered to the back of a packed auditorium. I want to sing a melody to which others can harmonise, to let the world hear all of the good and kind and strong things I can be. I don't want to be agoraphobia. I want to be something else.

From that moment on there's a new voice in my head. It startles me to my feet and drills me into positive action.

Get up, Stephen. Get up and fight.

* * *

Next to our house in Birstall Road is a small park over a cov-ered reservoir. In the morning I walk down to the newsagent's next to it and I purchase a newspaper. With every step I feel the bang of my heart in my ribs and the shallow, rapid fire of hyperventilated breathing. I wait in the queue with my coins in trembling hands. I take my newspaper and walk with deliberate care to the park. The sky lurches above me. The passers-by stare. I find a park bench and I sit. I breathe deeply to calm my heart rate. I take the newspaper and read the front page. All of it. Slowly. I steady my hands as the paper shakes. I read on. When the first page is done, I do the same with the second. Then the third. Garish headlines, advertisements, small-print gossip. Dog walkers pass my bench. Skipping children, their lungs clear, oblivious to my combat. Only when the whole paper is read do I allow myself to return home. I don't run. I walk. Every step deliberate. Fighting for control. I get back to my house and I collapse on the bed, exhausted but resolute.

The next day I do the same. Then the next. Then the next. On and on until the knot in my stomach becomes a devil I know. An enemy territory I can reconnoitre without the blindness of shellshock. It's a lonely melody sung without the expectation of harmony.

One day, my father arrives at the house. Mum must have said something – or else he identified something in my eyes that he recognised in himself. He tells me that he's booked a private appointment with a specialist doctor in town. We travel there on the bus. Dad doesn't discuss the appointment. He doesn't say anything. The brittle worldview that he clings to doesn't possess the vocabulary for shared fragility. He simply rubs my hair. The way he did when I had pneumonia. The doctor chats with me. I tell him about my drama interests. He tells me that it's not unusual for people with artistic sensibilities to exhibit cognitive vulnerability. 'It's part of who you are,' he says. An excess of reflection. Low self-image. He tells me I need to get out of my own head; take up a hobby, work with my hands. Have I considered sport?

He gives me a prescription for tranquillisers. My father and I leave the chemist's without comment. On the bus home, the silence is painful. I long for Dad to tell me that he feels it too. I long to hear a single piece of wisdom that can help me complete the broken circuit of my thoughts. Make my life flow again, like the current in one of his old radios. Transmit my voice to the world. But he can't. He can't help solder the broken pieces of me together without admitting that he too rattles when shaken.

That night I take one of the little blue pills. The smog that descends on my brain is as suffocating as the anxiety I feel. A blunt instrument. I throw the pills away. I take a deep breath and return to my lonely melody unaided.

The summer passes in the park. Then, without warning, a moment of serendipity alights on my battlefield. Mark and Paul's theatrical agent is throwing a party at a posh restaurant in London. It will be attended by the great and the good of London's theatre scene. She hatches a plan to use it as a way to introduce London to her new protégés, the McGann brothers. She requires a band to provide the music for the night, and suggests that all four brothers do it. 'Just to see what happens,' she says.

The idea is terrifying. London. A strange room crammed with hostile eyes, watching me as I attempt to control the enemy in my head. Trying not to run. I hear the voice in my head again. *Get up, Stephen. Get up and fight.* I agree to do it.

That night in the restaurant, our band is truly terrible. Truly. We're ill-rehearsed, out of tune and liberally sprinkled with strong drink. I try not to meet the eyes of the people I recognise from television as the amplifier feeds back over the party chattering. Eventually it's over. I'm still alive. As I head to the bar to quieten the knot in my guts, a drunken theatre director blocks my path to tell me how great we were. I smile politely. He tells me that he wants all the brothers to be in a musical he's doing at a theatre in east London. He's slurring his words. I suggest he rings tomorrow. I watch him stumble away, and I shake my head. Tomorrow. He won't remember his own name tomorrow.

Tomorrow. I wake on the sofa in my brother Joe's London flat. I feel the tight, familiar intake of breath as I realise I'm not in my home bedroom. I breathe deeply to control the panic that builds. My head is banging from the booze. Joe's telephone rings. It's the director. He remembered. He was serious. He offers me a part in a musical with my brothers. I'm speechless.

'I don't have an Equity card,' I tell him.

In those days, one couldn't walk onto a professional stage in the United Kingdom unless one was a member of the actor's union, Equity. A union card was almost impossible for an amateur to acquire. One or two were handed out each year by selected theatres to the lucky few.

'I've got one to spare at my theatre,' he replies. 'D'you want it?'

For a moment I can't reply. And then I do.

'Yes – yes please.'

And that's it. I'm a professional. A moment of serendipity has broken the long purgatory of my newspaper vigils and my stolen breath. A way to pick the lock and leave the dockside.

Maybe.

Will my anger be enough to propel me forward? Or will the mounting terror of what I've just agreed to do make me flee back to my home once and for all?

* * *

October 1982. The Half Moon Theatre, Mile End Road. A part of London's thriving fringe theatre scene. The musical is called *Yakety Yak* – a glorious, foul-mouthed homage to the music of fifties songwriters Leiber & Stoller. I sleep on the couch at Joe's flat and we take the tube to rehearsals. I breathe hard through the unscheduled stops in tunnels, squeezed tight against oblivious commuters.

Rehearsals are brilliant and scary and exhausting. We're drilled by a choreographer – hour after hour until the weight drops off me like sweat. I can see my pale cheekbones and my hollow eyes in the bathroom mirror after nights spent drinking away the knot building in my belly as opening night draws near.

The theatre is very small. A few hundred seats at the most. There's a reassuring cosiness to it. It feels like the youth theatre shows I did. If I squint my eyes I can convince myself that it's not a very public place, and that my mounting terror can be deferred for a different battle. I can blend in – not be too exposed. Get it all over with. The boys are all crammed into a tiny dressing room together. It's lovely. Like we were back in our old bunk-bedded room. The Four Musketeers. All for one and one for all. All of us bemused by where our lives have dropped us.

The first night passes and I survive. I don't faint or die or run from the stage, despite the screaming in my head and the clawed breaths struggling to throw my constricted voice to the back of the tiny room. Surviving it feels thrilling. Fighting, not running. And something else. Barely detectable. A strength hiding inside the frailty, not yet brave enough to speak.

The audience goes crazy. Within days we've sold out the short run. The reviews are wild with praise. Hip magazines arrive to photograph us for glossy features. I see faces in the audience from television: newsreaders, alternative comedians, musicians. Columnists seek exclusives. For the first time since James McGann stood on the dockside in New York in 1912, the media has taken an interest in what my family has to say. I stand outside of it all – hiding in plain sight, not daring to believe that it can endure.

The demon is still my nightly visitor. It's only the potassium anger that gets me through. A fury with life stronger than the weakness. Every day is exhausting. Like an extended trip to that park bench – newspaper in hand, reading every line and feeling every constricted breath. But I tell myself it's not for ever. The run will soon end. I can return to the safety of home, my duty done.

Then, in the last week, the director calls a surprise meeting. He's very excited.

'Great news! We're transferring to the West End!'

After just a few weeks' break, we're going to take the show to a huge new theatre. Hundreds more seats. The glare of new critics. A cavernous stage, looking out into impenetrable, lurching darkness.

Everybody cheers. My breath seizes in my chest.

I can't. Not again. Not there. Not every single night for months and months. My anger won't be enough. I need something else. Something more complete. A kinder voice. A deeper reason why. A better name for what I am. The strength that I can feel hiding inside my frailty. The thing my father can't find the words for.

I need a better way to breathe.

* * *

January 1983. The Astoria Theatre, Charing Cross Road. The opening night of *Yakety Yak*.

The Tannoy in the dressing room picks up the expectant chatter of the audience. I'm in my costume and I'm staring into the mirror. Five minutes to go.

Four.

Three.

My stomach lurches. The breath catches in my throat.

My father is out there somewhere with my sister. He's come to see his children unveiled to the wider world. He's come to see a vindication for all of those years of duty and suffering. He's come for an answer. I think about him at my age, running for his life in France. The courage of it. The fear of it.

Two minutes.

I think of him on that bus back from the doctor. Unable to share his own frailty with me. Unable to marry the courage in his life with the fear. His world brittle and mute. Me at his feet, listening out for some word of wisdom as he soldered in silence. Him like one of his broken radios, unable to transmit. A broken transistor, unable to integrate the impurities of his character into his own personality – the thing that every adult needs to do in order to turn the bricolage of childhood fears and needs into a flowing, flawed, complete, amplified human being, crackling with new life and singing their brave truth to the world.

One minute.

Then the penny drops. The simple wisdom delivered, unwittingly, all those years ago.

How transistors work.

How could I not have seen it? That gentle voice hiding beneath the cold purity of my anger and the breathless fear. The strength inside the frailty. The integration of my impurities into an amplified courage. A clean, strong melody funnelled through imperfect weakling lungs. The sound of my humanity breathing.

My brothers move around me in the crowded dressing room. Hands in mine. All for one and one for all. I watch their controlled nerves. I watch their private preparations. Now I see how each of them was drawn to the same career in the spotlight's hard gaze. They did it to test their own lonely courage under strong lights. To gauge the nature of their strength and frailty by an exposure to strangers. To ask a question of life. To sing their own song in the hope of an answering harmony. To understand themselves in the absence of a key. To transmit. To breathe. To be a transistor.

Drama is human transmission. The communication of universal human vulnerabilities and strengths to others so that we might understand ourselves better. To transmit those things you have to see yourself as *all* of yourself – the impure as well as the pure – the warrior as well as the weakling – the fear as well as the confidence. You have to integrate your own impurities as a human being into all of the strong things you are. You have to amplify yourself. You have to be a transistor.

'Act One beginners please. Stephen McGann to the stage.'

I walk to the dim-lit stage. I hear the band preparing. I peep out through a hole in the set at the chattering audience. I see the faces of iconic pop stars and fearsome theatre critics. I think of Birstall Road, all those miles away. I feel the knot in my stomach tighten.

Yet I smile in spite of it.

'Stand by.'

I am my agoraphobia, but it isn't all of me. I am that asthmatic, but he isn't all of me. I am so much more. I am humility, and courage, and shyness, and love, and the ecstatic breathlessness of climax. All of them necessary. All of them the things that make me into myself.

The names we give to things become the things we are. Yet I'm not my father. Instead, I'm one of his transistors. I can embrace the impurities that permit me to transmit the best of myself to the world.

The audience goes silent. I walk onto the stage and into the spotlight's glare. I look out into the impenetrable, lurching darkness. I'm scared. But I'm not going to run any more.

I open my mouth. My diaphragm descends and air floods deep into my lungs. My chest muscles tighten to funnel the exhaled air towards the larynx. My vocal chords resonate. My throat and lips, tongue and jaw work in harmony to project words to the back of the theatre. I hear my first line. It's clear and frail. Vulnerable and strong. A new skin. A new way to breathe.

6

HEART PROBLEMS

Heart n.

1. A muscular chambered organ that pumps
   blood through the human circulatory
   system.
2. The symbolic seat of human love; the
   essential essence of something.

MEDICINE

The human heart has a unique place in our medicine, history, language and culture. That fist-sized, metronomic lump of muscle, blood and valves has preoccupied surgeons, lovers, artists, executioners, priests and poets for centuries. So ubiquitous is the word 'heart' in our vocabulary that it's almost surprising to remember it describes a discrete physical organ – one with a specific role to play in the maintenance of human life, and one whose maladies can profoundly affect the lives and families of those afflicted by them.

The heart is the central driver of our cardiovascular system – a coordinated set of processes that circulate blood through the body and transport the nutrients, blood cells, hormones, oxygen and carbon dioxide necessary to maintain life. At its most basic, the heart is a system of two pumps – left side and right side – working in close harmony. Each side has two blood chambers – a small atrium at the top to receive the blood, and a larger ventricle below it to pump it back out again. When our blood has finished delivering oxygen and nutrients to our tissues and organs, it returns to the heart carrying the waste carbon dioxide. It enters the right atrium, and is then pumped towards the lungs by the right ventricle to be replenished. As we breathe, our lungs take the carbon dioxide and deliver fresh oxygen to the depleted blood. The newly oxygenated blood now re-enters the heart via the left atrium, and is pumped back out to the rest of the body by the left ventricle.

This continuous cycle is regulated by specialist cells in the right atrium called the sinoatrial node. It's the heart's natural pacemaker, firing an electrical impulse that causes sensitive muscle cells in the atria to compress, pushing blood into the adjacent ventricle. An associated impulse in the ventricle then squeezes the blood back out to the system, and the sinoatrial node fires again. A human heartbeat. This cycle repeats between fifty and a hundred times every minute for a resting heart. Every hour of every day, every day of every week, every week of every year: from the first bright pulse in a five-week-old foetus to the terminal monotone of the geriatric's electrocardiograph.

To keep blood moving smoothly through the four chambers of the heart, each has a valve to prevent blood from flowing backwards once pumped out. The valve linking the left atrium and the left ventricle is called the mitral valve. This seals the path to the left ventricle when new oxygen-rich blood arrives in the atrium from the lungs, and then opens again to allow this blood to flow to the ventricle for pumping onwards to the body. In healthy circumstances we'll never be aware of the church-organ symmetry of opening and closing valves taking place in our chest. Yet if our valves become defective, we soon notice it.

One serious defect is called mitral valve stenosis, or MVS. This is a condition where the mitral valve fails to open fully due to damage such as stiffening or scarring. The constricted passage-way prevents the blood in the left atrium from being pumped efficiently through to the ventricle and so the body gets a reduced supply of oxygen-rich blood. This leads to fatigue and breathless-ness in the patient. The backed-up blood also increases pressure in the atrium, which can result in a build-up of fluid in the lungs. In severe cases, the restricted flow can cause heart failure.

A common cause of MVS has its roots far away from the ailing heart itself. It's often a consequence of rheumatic fever as a child – a disease that starts as a simple streptococcal infection like a sore throat, but develops into nasty fever, rash and joint inflammation. An insidious side-effect of rheumatic fever can be the undetected scarring of the mitral valve, leading eventu-ally to MVS. The early treatment of streptococcal infection by antibiotics is now routine in developed nations, but this wasn't always the case. A pre-war child of deprived means in the years before public medicine might easily have fallen victim to rheu-matic fever. Then, many years later, long after the childhood malady was forgotten, their adult heart would begin to fail.

The cause of some heart problems can even predate child-hood. Congenital heart disease is a medical term that embraces a range of structural heart problems present at a child's birth; like a hole between the heart's chambers or a constriction to the arteries that supply it. The genes we inherit play a part in our heart's fortunes. One genetic condition that can have a devastating effect on the structure of a baby's heart is Down's syndrome. This is a genetic anomaly that results in an extra copy of a chromosome being produced in the baby's cells – something that affects more than 750 infants in Britain every year. The anomaly has well-known effects on appearance and learning ability – but less well known is the damage it can inflict inside the body. Down's children are prone to congenital heart defects, and a particularly unfortunate manifestation of this is Fallot's Tetralogy.

Fallot's Tetralogy is a cluster of four interrelated heart problems that lead to leaks in the chamber walls, constricted valves and a depleted level of oxygen in the blood. The deoxygenated blood supply can give the lips, tongue and flesh a telltale blue tinge, and the sufferer is prone to frightening bouts of breathlessness, choking and infection. Major corrective heart surgery is needed to repair Fallot's Tetralogy if an affected child is to have any length or quality of life. Short-term surgical procedures may ease the worst effects of it for a while, but unless the underlying abnormalities are tackled, the child is likely to die of heart failure. The damaged organ then ceases to be the beleaguered supporter of a child's life, and reverts to an inanimate lump of muscle, blood and valves, its value now gone.

Or is it?

The human heart has always had an emotional and metaphorical value greater to us than the sum of its medical properties. The ancient Egyptians believed it to be the seat of human morality. Aristotle thought it was the location of our intelligence. Catholic symbolism presents the suffering of a divine heart as the ultimate expression of virtue and devotion. Even in our secular age, the heart remains a potent symbol of romantic love and human emotion. The language we use endows the heart with a powerful transactional value – one that motivates the most profound feelings, actions and choices. For instance, we choose to 'give' our heart to someone, or it can be 'broken' by the actions of others. In some cases, it can even be 'stolen'. We don't have to delve too far into the metaphorical life of the human heart before we're confronted by ideas of ownership and the choices it gives us. Yet do all these flights of metaphorical fancy have any relation to the value and custody of a *real* heart?

More than we might think, perhaps.

A deceased child's heart with complex abnormalities such as Fallot's Tetralogy could provide a valuable specimen in medical research. If medics were quickly able to remove the organ and preserve it for study, then some good might come from the problems that affected it. After all, the poor child doesn't need it any more. Medically speaking, it seems logical and practical to allow medics the freedom to remove such an organ whenever they feel it's appropriate.

Yet legally speaking, things are not so simple. In England and Wales, the Human Tissue Act of 2004 sets out the rights and permissions governing the use of organs after a person's death. Enshrined in this act is the principle that organs can only be used for medical research if specific consent is sought from the family of the deceased. If medics want it, they have to ask permission. And that means permission can be refused. Regardless of any value to science, the ultimate custody of that dead child's heart lies with the family whose love helped to nurture it.

Why? Why does a rational society, as reflected in its laws, choose to empower the emotional symbolism of a grieving family over the imperatives of medical science when it comes to possession of a dead organ? Does that serve the greater good?

I think it does. The key word in law is not 'possession', but 'consent'. The state doesn't wish to preclude organ donation – in fact, it strongly encourages it. Yet it recognises that there is choice involved in the value placed on a human heart by society – a choice that goes far beyond matters of medical utility or genetics. By giving a grieving family the choice to gift their cherished heart to someone else, society acknowledges a wider healing function in the love that was poured into it. Love becomes most powerful in healing when it's freely given, and not just when it's assumed. The unseen families helped by that donated organ become bonded by love to the family that freely chose to donate it. They are joined to a wider family of collective care. A greater good.

In matters of the heart, choice is the way that love best reveals itself.

HISTORY

Sacred Hearts: The McGann family, 1983–1990

When we talk about family history we often define it in terms of shared 'blood' – a metaphor for the genetic inheritance passed on by our forebears over time. We might speak of similarities in appearance, character traits, or common susceptibility to certain ailments. It's a seductive idea. The twisting chromosomes in our cells imply an infallible certificate of authenticity for clan membership. They're the product of our parents' contribution to our construction, and a breadcrumb trail to the contributions of their parents, and theirs, and theirs – backwards through time in a single straight line to the beginnings of life itself. In this metaphor, inheritance is something given to us by others. It's assigned, established before our birth, and transferred to our children without their consent. If a family is defined by common blood, and blood means genetics, then DNA must be the heart of it all – the single beating source of identity flowing through our passive veins.

But is that really all a family is? A shared code passed on to us by others? A passive inheritance?

When we look at our family trees, a different truth jumps out. The branches aren't just populated by people to whom we're related genetically. There are also many people who have no direct DNA link to us – people like our in-laws, or the spouses of our siblings. Yet most of us would still refer to those people as our family, and include those people in our bonds of shared 'blood'. Take my uncle Billy, for instance, starving in that Japanese prisoner-of-war camp. Just seeing his name written there on my family tree gives me a sting of sympathetic pain – a keen jolt of shared kinship. He's *my* uncle Billy. My childhood clown, speaker of profanities, eater of flowers. Yet Billy was only related to me by marriage to my mother's sister. If a scientist made a DNA comparison of that man's blood and my own he'd find no link. In biological terms we're strangers. Similarly, I have bonds of love and affection with my in-laws stretching back decades. My brother-in-law Johnny is one of my closest relatives; our fraternal bond is more than a quarter-century old. His brother David's life and heart form a central part of this chapter, and my own family's story. Yet he doesn't share my genetics. The blood in our veins is medically incompatible.

A family isn't simply a passive inheritance. It's defined by the bonds its members *choose*, and not just the bonds assigned by genetics. Each time a family member joins their life to a biological stranger in marriage, adoption or through having children, a new clan joins itself to our family tree at the junction point of the union. New ancestors are fused with ours. New descendants are sired by the mingling of separate genetic codes. Without this chosen love our gene pool would stagnate. Without this new family, an assigned inheritance couldn't continue. Genes might specify the way we're put together, but without our human will to love beyond those specifications, a family can't be all the things it might be.

Family blood is a versatile thing, capable of inhabiting many different vessels. It's capable of choosing the arteries in which it flows. Capable of self-replenishment. Capable of transfusion into the hearts of strangers who share its vitality. Capable of new love. New family. New identity.

* * *

January 1983.

My dad was wonderful on that opening night of *Yakety Yak* at the Astoria. Full of glowing pride and dry humour. He'd watched his four sons on a West End stage. He'd spent the after-show party swapping stories with members of Spandau Ballet and chatting gamely with punk pop star Hazel O'Connor. We watched him soak it in, and it helped us to stop for a moment in our own frenetic lives to soak it in too.

Dad's years of melancholy and inflexible duty had delivered

an unexpected consolation prize. A clinching retort in his bitter dispute with life. He found himself the father of a family of celebrity acting brothers. We were appearing on chat shows and in tabloid articles. Dad took the torn-out press clippings to his local church club to show his fellow snooker players. We were 'Joe McGann's lads'. Local boys made good. His surname was now pasted across headlines and glowed in theatrical neon. It meant something to him. A new lease of life – or perhaps simply a balance paid on the old one.

As he progressed through his fifties, Dad's heart had begun to give him trouble. He'd not been a smoker since his navy years, and was fit for his age. Yet he became short of breath and found it difficult to walk any distance. The doctors diagnosed a heart valve problem, and asked him about his childhood rheumatic fever. Dad denied he'd ever had it, but it was likely to have been forgotten in the wider maladies of his tough pre-NHS child-hood. The evidence was written on his scarred mitral valve. He was given valve replacement surgery, but after a few years it failed. The cloud of grey that had always attended him began to darken. He looked weary. Isolated by his infirmity from the new energies that surrounded him.

It was a bitter shame, because at the same time his wider iso-lation had finally begun to thaw. In a touching postscript to my parents' divorce, my mum had invited Dad to move back in with her. He and Mum had re-established polite relations after the kids had moved to London, and although he never swallowed quite enough pride to concede he'd been wrong, the regret he experienced in the years of separation had softened his stubborn-ness. The war was over. Mum had never wanted to divorce Dad in the first place, so when she saw his fading condition she was glad to assuage the quiet guilt that had clawed at her ever since the last solicitor's bill had been paid. Divorce was still taboo in their shared faith, whatever the justification. Mum's break for freedom had placed her outside of the church's higher laws. So now she simply declared it void. No legal papers or ceremonies necessary. She invited my father back home one day, and he came. When the kids arrived back from London on a visit, Dad was sitting in his old chair like nothing had happened.

We loved this arrangement. We loved its quiet compassion and compromise, its wise eccentricity. A state-divorced Catholic couple living 'in sin' together as unmarried singles was an amusing moral conundrum. If you asked Mum how she explained her unorthodox marital status to the world, she'd simply shrug. 'The Catholic Church doesn't recognise divorce,' she'd say, 'so we're still married in the eyes of God.' This showed a logical dexterity worthy of Sir Thomas More. What God has joined together let no lawyer put asunder. It was also a reminder of the other heartbeat that had propelled my family through the veins of time to the present day; something that had specified my family's nature well before the potato fields of Roscommon had turned bad. There were bonds of loyalty beyond the family that we could see – a wounded heart more worthy of worship than our own. Religious faith.

One of the first encounters that any Catholic child has with matters of the heart is the livid image that greets them in every relative's household, and in every church they attend. The image of the Sacred Heart of Jesus. The Sacred Heart is one of the most popular and enduring of Catholic symbols – an ancient vision representing Christ's humanity, and his suffering for the forgiveness of our sins. It's quite an eyeful for an impressionable infant. Jesus is displayed facing us, arms open, revealing His exposed heart sitting in the middle of His chest or, better still, held out in one of His hands. The heart is a deep raw red and drips with blood from a gaping wound. Around the heart is a ring of thorns piercing the exposed muscle, while tongues of fire can be seen bursting from its top. It's a gruesome and elaborate collection of heart problems symbolising Christ's crucifixion. Despite the evident cardiac distress, Christ's expression remains calm – wistful. His free hand indicates the bleeding heart held in the other. He stares at us as if to say, 'Look what I did for you. For your sins. Don't you care?'

To a young mind it's a powerful message. The sweetest, gentlest man who ever lived suffered for me. Suffered horribly – his heart lacerated and burned. All because of my faults. Because I was born in sin. Because I don't love my mother and father, my brothers and sister, as much as I should. Because I haven't learned the cost of what it means to be a full member of that wider family he's specified for me. It's love as debt. Compulsory love. Owed, not freely given. It's a duty, like my father's relentless work ethic. Faith as a deeper rhythm. It overrides any pleasures of the flesh, or the legal arguments of divorce courts.

Yet the image of the Sacred Heart is regarded by many good, decent people as a comfort and strength, and I can understand that. A debt is also a bond. Those who owe a debt of kindness also feel the warmth of the kindness given. There's fellowship in it. A tribal unity. A family connection. The assigned genetics of established faith.

The McGann children had been steeped in the family rites of the Catholic Church since our earliest childhoods. We were educated in its schools, and had spent every Sunday fidgeting in the pews of its churches. Before we were old enough to construct arguments about the deeper nature of the world we inhabited, we were handed a prefabricated moral framework for it all. A system for living. We were hardly exceptional. Much of the planet's population is born into a religious culture of some kind, and many into mine. Many stay in it for life. Some, like me, don't. But I can still feel its cultural heartbeat in my chest.

The moral framework of family faith suffused our home. It was there in my father's patriarchal assumptions; in the pill-free multiple births; in the unshakeable guilt of divorce. Liverpool's Catholicism was rooted in the gothic sufferings of the emigrant Irish. There was a ravishing, martyr-burned beauty to it all. A rough tribal faith born in the pestilent brotherhood of the slums, and fought for by our ancestors. It wasn't simply a belief system, it was the compulsory bond of clan membership. The sacred heart of a shared family order.

Now this sacred heart risked being scarred by contact with our separating futures and our sensual new experiences. The young McGann children were beginning to seek different answers. The boys were fresh-faced actors in a vibrant and permissive artistic industry. My younger sister Clare had been accepted at London's prestigious Imperial College to study science. After 120 years the McGanns were emigrants again – but this time sailing towards something of our own, and not away from something suffered in common. This would ultimately bring the sacred custody of our hearts into conflict with older hierarchies. And, for a time, with each other.

The geographical and economic dislocation of British families like ours became a common feature of the country's sociology from the eighties onwards. Many northern parents like Mum and Dad watched with a mix of pride and sadness as their kids moved away for new lives and careers elsewhere. They'd had their own relatives close at hand when they were young. They may have been financially poorer, but they'd been rich in other ways. The support of family, church and community was a binding force that gave extended families a moral purpose and a social cohesion. Now it was gone. Post-war parents hardly saw their busy professional children, and would have little contact with their gadget-rich grandchildren. Meanwhile, those heavily mortgaged sons and daughters could no longer depend on the child support of a nearby aunt, or the familiar consolation of the family priest. Church attendances declined with an increase in the more purchasable deities of the new consumer age. The post-war promise of free education had delivered for working-class parents like mine, but it was achieved at another kind of cost – one their hearts had never budgeted for.

For now, though, there was still Dad sat in his old chair when we returned for our occasional visits – the melancholic constant around which our family formatted. As long as he sat there at its centre you could believe that the old order we'd grown up with still endured. An unshifting rock against which we could hurl rebellious teenage kicks in order to propel our new identities forward.

It wasn't to last.

The call came late one evening. I was sitting in Mark's flat in London. It was Mum. Dad had been rushed to hospital. It was his heart. The doctor said it was serious. He said he was unlikely to make it through the night.

The world shifted. I was just twenty-one; Mark only nineteen months older. Like most people of that age we thought life existed purely as a theatre for our own unique joys or sufferings. We didn't yet comprehend that subordinate part we all play in life's more significant commonalities. Like the death of a parent.

We dashed back to Liverpool. We were in luck. Dad hadn't only survived the night, but he'd rallied. The vision of his children turning up beside his bed seemed to galvanise him. Dad's heart was finished, the doctor told us. His mitral valve had failed, and his other organs had started to wilt under the burden. It would only be a matter of days.

As it happened, Dad lived for another week. And I can honestly say that I got to know him better in those last seven days than in the twenty-one years that went before. A change slowly came over him while he lay there in that hospital. At first he approached his declining condition like a challenge. 'If I could just eat something I'll feel better,' he'd say. But gradually he absorbed the truth of it. I watched his shoulders drop – a life's worth of tension and anxiety released. He was just sixty, and still without the resolutions he felt his past courage and pain had warranted. It gave him a quiet, dry smile – a vindication of his belief in life's capacity for disappointment. And yet he was strangely liberated by it. Once his life had truly amounted to the sum of all of his anxieties, he found himself free of its tyranny. He didn't just walk open-eyed into the shadow of that valley, he strolled.

Dad became unusually talkative and reflective. One or two of us would be there at any given time, so we'd each get some time alone with him. It was wonderful. In one such moment,

I asked him to recount his war experiences to me again. He'd told me it a dozen times when I'd been younger, but now I wanted to hear it in the spirit of a definitive account – an oral record that I could take with me after he'd gone. Dad knew what I was doing. He smiled and ruffled my hair. Then he began to talk. Quiet and unhurried – from the very beginning of his service to his demob. There was none of the old tension that came with it. Just the memory. A final testimony free of emotional chains. Compassion for his comrades. Fear expressed with honesty. Courage described simply. Now, when I think of him, it's this man I remember. The kind, wise, reflective, brave man – standing at that fearsome threshold in all of our lives, but responding to it like he did on that beach. Rising to meet the worst of things with knowledge of his mortality, and a courage that comes from somewhere else.

Eventually the daily visits reached their sad conclusion. Dad slipped into fitful semi-consciousness, and the family gathered for a final vigil. It lasted through the night and into the next day. We watched his failing body still fighting the inevitable, still stubborn, his beleaguered heart refusing to surrender. Towards the very end he wanted to go. He was ready for it. It just wasn't quite ready for him.

The end came around noon. His breathing grew intermittent: snatched gasps, seconds apart, decreasing gradually until we listened for them like echoes of a distressed voice on a distant hillside. Then they were gone. My father's body underwent a profound change. The physical transformation between the two biological states of life and death – from person to corpse – is startling to witness for the first time. Within a minute the cheeks grew hollow, the jaw dropped, the blood drained from the flesh. Wherever my father had been, he certainly wasn't there now. By the time the nurses answered our bedside alarm they found my family staring at kilograms of inanimate skin, sinew, muscle and bone.

Dad's funeral Mass took place in Sacred Heart parish church. We were surprised by how packed it was. Strangers told us how Dad had personally helped them or shown them kindness. We thought of the man in that chair and his stubborn melancholy. This new person was a revelation. Someone he'd never shown to us. For years afterwards, my work in drama was informed by the father I discovered at that funeral. Every human being possesses facets to their nature that can't be accounted for in the hasty character assessments of others – dimensions of character that are a mystery even to themselves. Dad was more things than the role the family had assigned to him, and far more than the role he'd assigned to himself.

When the funeral was done, there was only the sombre bureaucracy left; an unassuming paper trail left by the dead. These documents seem so trivial when our grief is fresh – discarded refuse that demeans the enormity of our loss. Yet history knows the value of these unregarded things; the broken pottery thrown into a Roman well, or an unassuming death record in an archive. We imprint ourselves onto this world in so many tiny ways, and this incidental refuse can later be invaluable to a wider understanding. I'd been an amateur genealogist for about four years by the time my dad died and I'd learned the hidden value of what the past can throw away. My mum knew this too and so she bestowed a small honour on me. She asked me to go and sign my dad's death certificate at the local register office.

Application Number 5623084-1

QBDZ 373805

CERTIFIED COPY OF AN ENTRY

| DEATH | Entry No. 115 |

Registration district *Liverpool*   Administrative area *Metropolitan District*

Sub-district *Liverpool*   *of Liverpool*

1. Date and place of death *First August 1984.*
Broadgreen Hospital, Broadgreen

2. Name and surname *Joseph McGANN*   3. Sex *Male*

4. Maiden surname — of woman who has married

5. Date and place of birth *25th May 1924*
Liverpool

6. Occupation and usual address *Quality Control Inspector (Retired)*
4 Birstall Road, Kensington, Liverpool 6

7. (a) Name and surname of informant *Stephen Vincent McGANN*   (b) Qualification *Son*

(c) Usual address *79 Chatsworth Road, Kilburn, London*

8. Cause of death
I(a) Left Ventricular Failure
(b) Mitral Valve Disease

Certified by GN Russell MB

9. I certify that the particulars given by me above are true to the best of my knowledge and belief   *Stephen McGann*   Signature of Informant

10. Date of registration *Second August 1984*   11. Signature of registrar *R G Hollis Deputy Registrar*

I have the document in front of me now. Dated 2 August 1984. Dad's heart, and his life, reduced to terse diagnosis: 'Left Ventricular Failure'. There's my twenty-one-year-old signature, careful and unworldly. Qualification: Son. On the surface it all looks so bloodless – so lacking in human warmth. But look closer and it pulses with life. This was my genealogical love letter to Dad – a document bonding our two names together forever, stuffed into a bottle and thrown overboard into the ocean of time for our descendants to find. It was the first time my signature had ever appeared in public records. I was telling posterity that someone called Stephen McGann had lived in this time and place, and had wanted the world to acknowledge the life and beleaguered heart of the father he'd loved.

A single record in the public archives is like the single beat of a family's heart over time. In isolation it tells us very little about the health of the wider organism. Yet when the beats are combined across the years, an underlying rhythm is revealed. The flow of declared love pumped through the arteries of history.

Following Dad's death, there was a shift in the balance of my family. Subtle at first, like the erosion of a familiar coastline, but visible over time. Dad had provided a fixed reference point for the extent to which the rest of us had progressed. Because he'd been so unable to adapt himself to the changes in our lives, he came to stand for the past we'd all escaped – a staid home port that each of us had abandoned for a new promised land, our chronometers synchronised to his distant longitude. To Mum he'd been the anachronistic patriarch she'd divorced to become free; to the children he'd been the caring but melancholic parent, baffled by the worlds we now moved in. Yet once this fixed reference point was removed, the remaining family members were forced to navigate their separate ways by reference to the positions and values of each other. This would prove a more hazardous ocean to sail.

The brothers shared the same theatrical agent, who watched over our public lives with a matriarchal flourish. It sometimes felt as if Dad's role at the head of our childhood table had simply been replaced by our agent at her office desk. She chose the career paths she believed each of us should take, and she selected auditions for us according to her own estimation of our talents. It was all rather odd. Novel at first, but increasingly discomforting. The private hierarchies we'd lived under since childhood had been reconstituted in the public realm – like a scratchy home movie projected onto a CinemaScope screen. One minute we'd been a family like any other – flawed children trying to discover who they were and what they weren't, with all the petty arguments, competing affections and contested statuses. The next minute we were 'the McGann brothers' – a motley conglomeration of lookalike siblings caught in the vague stare of the public eye. I'm not complaining. We'd all been very lucky, and as a living it beat the hell out of getting shot at or throwing coal into a ship's furnace. But we'd never planned it that way and it became increasingly difficult to resolve the two worlds we now inhabited. I remember once walking into a TV studio with my brothers to do a chat-show interview. As the assistant tried to focus our minds on the impending live transmission, two of my brothers were busy having a heated argument. One was accusing the other of stealing a pair of socks from his chest of drawers the week before. The argument only paused when the studio applause began, and it continued as soon as the interview finished. Back then, our public life was something that took place in the gaps between private disputes over underclothing.

And what about my sister Clare? The public perception of the McGann family as consisting only of acting brothers left little space for this brilliant, non-acting, high-achieving undergraduate sister. Her gender became a barrier to the public perception of what my family was, and her academic achievements were out of kilter with what now seemed most desirable as a career path for the children. All of that educational attainment Mum and Dad had worked so hard to give us now seemed rather passé.

I've often wondered what would have happened if we'd all pursued different career paths after school. I suspect many things would have been easier. But then I'd never have seen the wonderful things my brothers achieved as actors. I'd never have watched each of them wrestle with their courage and talent in the way they did. In the end, our response to life was the same as for our ancestors. The same as for immigrants everywhere. We did what we could with the things we'd been dealt.

The McGanns, for all their artistic fancies, were as itinerant as their seafaring forebears. We'd simply exchanged distant ports for provincial theatres and film studios.

The trouble with an itinerant life like drama is that it can lack a firm anchor – a way to understand oneself by reference to a fixed place or person. It's easy to drift from job to job, and to forsake personal character development for the thrill of playing other people. The boys all loved each other, but we needed to understand ourselves a bit more. Who were we, finally? What did our own kind of love look like? How did it reveal itself? Our careers might have specified the public things we were, but without the will to love beyond its specifications we'd never really be the people we could be, and never find that junction point for a new kind of family relationship on the stagnating branches of our tree. Our lives cried out for a bond we could willingly share, and not just one we were given. It was no longer enough to accept the compulsory loves assigned to us as children. It was time for us to choose a love of our own.

I watched as the older boys embarked on new relationships outside of the family. I was fascinated by the way that these new partners exposed facets of my brothers' characters I'd never known before, and how the romantic choices they made shifted the nature of their relationships with the rest of us. They were now anchored to someone they'd chosen to love, and it was allowing them to see themselves more clearly. To see what their love looked like.

My own love life was rather less revealing. I had relationships, some of them committed ones, but all of my romantic involvements seemed to lack an essential element of conviction. An anchor.

Then, suddenly, I found her. And from that moment everything was different.

* * *

Firstly, I don't believe in love at first sight. I find it a rather trite idea – a self-confirming post-hoc justification for a love we build by hard endeavour.

Secondly, love at first sight is exactly what happened to me when I first met my wife. So what do I know?

It's 1986. I'm twenty-three. A young actor. My dad's been dead for two years. I'm living in a council flat in east London, and I'm auditioning every day. One day I get a call from the agent about a play in Liverpool Playhouse called *Shamrocks and Crocodiles*. It's by a new writer. They've asked to see me in Liverpool for the lead part later that day. I look at my watch. I have a hundred things to do, and getting a train to Liverpool isn't one of them. I'm grumpy, but agree to go.

I'm due to meet the writer and director at six in the evening. I pick up a copy of the script from an address in London and catch the train at Euston. I'm tired. I grab a cup of instant coffee from the buffet carriage and settle down to read the script before the meeting.

Then I wake up. The play is brilliant. Searing, intelligent and thoughtful. So elegantly written. Poetic and brutal. A story of a Liverpool family torn by the sudden death of their father – something that feels resonant to me. I turn to the front of the script to read the name of the author.

Heidi Thomas.

She's new, the agent had said. I've never heard of her. I try to imagine what she might be like. The themes in the play are far too mature and deftly crafted for her to be a young writer, so my guess is that she's a mature woman who's begun writing late – perhaps a mother returning to work after raising children, or a wizened academic on a second career.

I'm met at the stage door of the theatre by the director and taken through into a small room. As I enter, Heidi Thomas rises to greet me.

I'm speechless. She's young – early twenties like me, but with a complexion and elfin figure that makes her look like a teenager. She identifies as a Liverpool native, but sounds like the head girl of an Edwardian convent school. This woman – this *girl* – wrote that beautiful, brutal, black-humoured script?

We begin to discuss the play. Heidi starts to speak, her high-toned staccato sprinkling the room like birdsong. It's easy to assume that the rapidity of her words denote a lack of reflection or acuity. But I quickly see it. Elusive at first, then more clear. There's a razor-sharp edge beneath the rapid-fire song, planted there like tripwire in the warm grass. A devilish wit beneath her verbal camouflage.

Heidi is one of the most subversive people I've ever met. She sports a surface gentility, while hiding a penetrating emotional voice in the spaces between her words. There are many clever people who still don't hear it, who assume that surface tone is a reliable indicator of content, or that assumption is the same thing as insight. Heaven knows I've been wrong about so many things in life. But I was always right about Heidi Thomas. I saw her qualities right away – and my heart was soon banging so loudly in my ribs as I sat in that interview that I feared she'd hear it.

It soon becomes clear where the raw emotion in the play comes from. I can see it behind her eyes. There's a restlessness. Something that wants to be seen, as well as wanting to see. Our eyes keep flashing a look to each other as we talk. In those moments she holds her exposed and wounded heart out to me in one hand while indicating to it with the other – wanting me to see the sacred parts of it, wanting me to know she'd heard my own heart's beating.

When the interview is done I leave the theatre in a daze. That night I lie in bed with my heart still pumping. I had to get that job. I had to see Heidi again. Had she felt it too, or had I imagined it?

She had felt it. When I'd left the theatre that evening, Heidi had raced out into the nearby city square to find me. In her head a single word repeated itself over and over.

Found. Found. Found.

* * *

I got the job and in those weeks of rehearsal for the play, Heidi and I fell irredeemably in love. We'd stay in the rehearsal room during lunch breaks, and we'd talk and talk. Heidi had lost her father suddenly a few years before, as well as her brother David. Her bloodline was Irish and Suffolk labourer. Her humour ambushed you with its wicked edge. We knew we loved each other, but we both had partners. Although we could have concocted some justification to go with the desire we felt, it mattered that we didn't. What we had was something else, something requiring a different kind of bonding.

The play was a great success. It concluded, and we went back to our separate lives. Heidi went to Stratford-upon-Avon as the youngest writer ever commissioned by the Royal Shakespeare Company. I went back to my east London flat, my girlfriend and my biological family. We wrote to each other for a while – extravagant twenty-something prose that we still have in an attic trunk to make us laugh. Then the letters stopped. Being young and stupid, I convinced myself that the momentous things I felt for her must be a recurring feature of life, rather than its greatest vindication. We lost touch. Two years went by.

Then, unexpectedly, we met again.

I was filming a comedy series in Liverpool and staying at a riverside hotel. One of the guest stars knew Heidi through a mutual friend. When I walked into the hotel bar one evening, Heidi was sitting with my colleague. My heart thumped in my chest. We exchanged pleasantries. She told me she was soon to fly to the Soviet Union on a journalistic assignment for a national newspaper. She looked lovely – newly confident. She was also newly single.

My heart was telling me the facts. Banging against my ribs like a Victorian schoolmaster thwacking a ruler on a slow boy's head to impart salient information.

Tell her you fool! Tell her how you feel! Say something! This is *important*.

What did I do? I started an argument with her. A silly, petty, stupid argument about nothing. The only excuse I have for my behaviour is that the romantic tension between us was so intense it required an outlet. I just happened to pick the worst possible one. Quite an achievement, really. I watched her eyes brim with tears as we bickered, and I could feel the headmaster's ruler thwacking me ever harder. I was screaming at myself to stop, but couldn't.

We parted frostily, and I returned to my hotel room, shell-shocked. I closed the door. It was at that precise moment that the truth became clear. Heidi was the love of my life. My anchor. I'd never find anyone else like her. I wanted to join my family to hers on our respective family trees. I wanted to hold her sacred heart in rhythm with mine.

Except I'd just blown it. She was now lost to me.

I slept fitfully, and rose early to work. When I came back to my hotel the next evening there was a book of love poetry by Brian Patten pushed under my door, and a card inserted at a particular page. I read the poem printed there:

> *Doubt shall not make an end of you*
> *nor closing eyes lose your shape*
> *when the retina's light fades;*
> *what dawns inside me will light you.*

My heart stopped. The schoolmaster in my chest gave one last almighty thwack. Enough was enough. I needed to find this woman and ask her to be my wife. And this time I needed to be something other than a complete idiot. She'd left her number on the card, so I rang her mother's house in Liverpool straight away.

'Can I speak to Heidi please?'

'She's gone to the USSR.'

'Already? Have you got a number for her?'

'She's in Siberia. Behind the Iron Curtain. It's not like ringing the council.'

'I see. Well ... if you hear from her, could you tell her that I rang?'

I was stunned. Heidi had left for the provincial Soviet Union straight away – one of the few places on earth where it was impossible to contact her. I'd have to wait weeks before I could say what I needed to, and before she could respond. The moment was hers to choose, not mine. My doubts had not made an end of her, but what dawned inside of me was now in her ultimate gift to complete. It's almost as if she'd timed it that way ...

Heidi smiles wickedly when I recall this detail. 'Serves you right for being an idiot.'

She came home eventually. Within two years we were married. We've been married ever since.

Soon after I started my relationship with Heidi, I began to get to know her brother David. David was born with Down's syndrome, and had died due to the damaged heart it had given him. He'd been dead for a few years by this point, so I never actually got to meet him in person. Yet in all the important ways we became acquainted as brothers.

How can you know your brother without ever actually knowing them?

Easy. A family relationship is about more than physiology, blood, or the sum of chromosomes; it's more than living tissue, or physical interaction. A family member lives on in the refracted tones of memory and words that the prism of their life throws onto those who follow. When someone we love dies, the ability of that person to self-generate new points of human interaction ceases. But their part in future interactions doesn't. They're carried in the minds of those who love them, and transferred in the artefacts and language chosen to define their lives beyond death. They're shared with strangers as stories, and preserved in oral testimony like a seed in amber. They live on in the words that love chooses.

Words are important. Words can carry the important parts of us inside of them.

Compy.
Slimp.
Niney.

These are David words. These are words my young brother used as a child, and which were passed on to me by Heidi in our daily conversations over the years. We use at least one David word every day. My brother had a unique vocabulary. 'Compy' meant comfortable. 'Slimp' was his way of saying slim. The mispronunciations weren't simply an effect of his Down's, but related to his hearing difficulties. My favourite is 'Niney' – his way of saying Heidi. I use that one a lot.

The thing about David words is that there's a story attached to each one. Each word refracts a tone of my lost brother, like a record in the archives might index the character of an ancestor, or the words in this book reference the collective story of my family. His words convey a part of him and by using them he lives in our house with us. Over the years, his family have added their own elements to David's story, so that now I have a collage of David's remembered self that I can converse with. My wife is always surprised when she remembers I never actually met him.

I spent those first days with Heidi in her newly purchased house in south Liverpool – back when a playwright's paltry income could still stretch to the deposit on a mortgage. David's old school photograph had pride of place on her sideboard, and his grinning face would watch over us as we began the gentle process of fusing our lives together. Heidi would tell me about David's life – his beleaguered heart, the laughter through the breathlessness. This was our sacred space – a new love growing like mistletoe from the junction point of our respective family trees. Something chosen, not assigned. Something beneath which new kisses can be made. David was a part of that space. A sacred heart beyond inheritance.

* * *

Back in my own family, things felt a lot less sacred. On the surface all was fine. My sister Clare had graduated with first class honours and had taken a big job in the City of London. Paul was starring in the peerless film *Withnail & I*. Mark was flown to New York on Concorde to give a press conference about his amazing performance in a US biopic about the life of John Lennon. Joe was drawing attention on British TV as a detective in the peak-time drama *Rockcliffe's Babies*; I was in a lavish TV drama in Austria and starring in the West End. Yet the common career the boys had chosen now felt as cramped as that old house in Birstall Road. There were unique qualities each of us had that couldn't be reduced to a single theatrical biography. Drama encourages a culture of competition – daily auditions, where one's self-worth is constantly tested before strangers. It's hard enough when you're pitted against friends and colleagues, but when you're also being judged alongside your own family it gets a bit tedious. It was too easy for this new arena to superimpose itself onto the old family hierarchies – impelling the brothers to measure their personal value or status according to the blunt imperatives of the industry we'd joined. Worse, it tempted us to believe that in order to succeed, our status or achievements must somehow dominate the lives and achievements of those closest to us. A culture of competition insinuated itself into the family's heart just at the time when the siblings should have been forging healthy, divergent paths as young adults. Those petty arguments, competing affections and contested statuses of childhood had congealed into something more corrosive. Our inherited heart had developed problems.

Things could get quite petty at times – and being at the bottom end of the family pecking order didn't exactly help. One particular status game the brothers used to play makes me smile now. I call it 'tomcat spraying'. Have you ever seen how cats mark their territory? They strut onto a perceived rival's ground and spray their own scent onto its prominent landmarks – vandalising their rival's sacred space, and forcing the other animal to live under a more dominant scent than their own. It's a private message meant only for the initiated – other species can't read it. But for those genetically bonded creatures the message is clear: 'Your territory belongs to me. I can demean it if I wish.'

The brothers had their own version of tomcat spraying. It might involve a condescending remark about another brother's home or partner – perhaps a veiled critique of their work or ambitions, or a cavalier disregard for their personal space or feelings. Nothing too overt; this was a game strictly for the genetically bonded. Friends and strangers might miss it completely. But it was there, and its message was as strong as musk. Of course, many families will be familiar with some or all of this kind of petty behaviour. Yet my family had perfected its own particular brand of feline vandalism, and it was one that now attempted to appropriate the sacred space inhabited by my new partner. That would be a territory too far.

* * *

As a keen genealogist, I've often wondered if there's a particular moment in the story of a family when the fusion of in-laws or genetic strangers into one's clan is felt to be complete; when the hearts we've chosen become indistinguishable from the hearts assigned to us by inheritance. A marriage might mark the legal joining of two families, but it can't enforce the mutual love and loyalty necessary for their meaningful coexistence. This has to be given freely by all concerned. A family's heart is more than the things assigned to us by society or the law. It's what we *choose* to give that makes us who we are. Was there a specific moment when Uncle Billy became *my* uncle Billy? I can't recall. Was there a single moment when my feelings towards Heidi and her family transformed from a shared vocabulary into the raw single heartbeat of biological union?

Yes. Yes there was.

1990. Heidi and I have announced our wedding. It was to be

a traditional Liverpool church wedding, rather than a swanky London affair. In this way we could offer hospitality to those who'd always known and cared for us in a way that they'd respect. A marriage to us wasn't simply a party or a personal statement. It was one of those great moments in family history; a joint declaration of love by two people in front of their own flesh and blood. It belonged to the whole family, not just to its instigators. Who are we to dictate the means by which those many additional family bonds are formed?

As our wedding approached, my family gathered in Liverpool. The ceremony presented a challenge to the normal sibling dynamics. I was, unusually, installed as the undisputed lead male in this particular drama. It wasn't a pecking order my family were very familiar with – and, as preparations continued, I realised how rare it was for me to be at the centre of significant family events. Some seemed to find it harder than others to adjust.

I was in Heidi's house in south Liverpool, making final arrangements for the wedding, when the bell rang. It was one of my brothers. He'd not rung ahead. He strode straight past me and into Heidi's home like he owned it. Heidi, polite as ever, offered coffee and kisses. I watched my brother suspiciously, anger rising as he paced about. I could read the body language. He strode through the room, manhandling Heidi's records, smirking at the artwork on her walls, casting little half-smiles at the modest furniture. Tomcat spraying. Laying his scent onto my new territory. But this wasn't just mine now. This was Heidi's. And Heidi deserved no part of this.

He picked up the little cast-iron statuette of a Soviet sailor from the mantelpiece. Heidi had brought it back as a souvenir from her journalistic assignment in Russia; one of those grandiose Bolshevik symbols peddled by street-sellers. He'd never been to Russia himself, let alone travelled to darkest Siberia for work, as Heidi had done. Heidi, making polite conversation, described the experiences she'd had there and then playfully pondered what our own lives might have been like if we'd all been thrust as artists and intellectuals into the October Revolution of 1917.

'I'd love to have taken part in the Russian Revolution,' Heidi mused.

He smirked at her. 'Doing what? The catering?'

There was silence. His remark was so blunt and dismissive, it left nowhere in the conversation to go. Heidi looked towards me for support; offended, but also confused.

The catering. In a movement of artists and intellectuals, it was the only work he regarded as worthy of her. Heidi was substantially more educated than we were. She was already a successful playwright, a published author and a writer of broadsheet feature articles. What's more, he was a guest in her home.

Heidi didn't yet understand what was happening, but I did. For all her talents and success, she was considered merely my partner, and therefore a part of that territory of mine that could be demeaned at will by any passing family tomcat. I knew that in a thousand other situations he'd never have said such a rude thing to a host. But this wasn't other situations. This was tomcat spraying. This is what my family did. A compulsory love and hierarchy I was expected to accept, and that my partner was supposed to adopt.

We drank our coffee in discomfort until he left. When he'd gone, I explained to Heidi what had happened. She was genuinely curious as to how the partner she valued so much could allow himself to be treated in this way. Needless to say, she was never going to accept it. 'How have you let this happen to you?' she said.

I couldn't answer. But I knew it was the right question to ask.

That was the moment. The single moment in time when my feelings towards my wife and her family transformed from a shared vocabulary into the raw single heartbeat of a biological bond. I looked over at David's photograph on the sideboard. He looked back at me with a request in his gentle eyes.

'Protect her. Keep her heart safe.'

The love I suddenly felt for that little boy's sister chased all of the tomcats from my sacred space. Heidi was *mine*. My flesh and blood. A decent, loving, caring woman. Mine to protect. No tomcat on this earth was ever going to disparage her like that. No one had a right to the things we'd both chosen. It's the hearts we choose that make us who we are.

From that moment, I knew the real value of the choice I'd made. Blood is a versatile thing, capable of choosing the new arteries in which it flows. Capable of self-replenishment. Capable of new love. A new identity. A new family.

TESTIMONY

I remember waking up for school and Dad telling me that Mum had gone to the hospital in the night to have the new baby. I was very excited. I was seven and my brother Johnny was just four. As we ran out of school later that day, Dad was waiting in the car – he said, 'You've got a little brother called David, and he's got ginger hair!'

It's the present day. A winter evening in our home, the low sun fading over distant fields of frost. Heidi has returned from a busy day of television production meetings in London. She's tired. She lies on the sofa with her head close to my lap, and reclaims the earliest memories of her brother David from the tangle of her daily concerns:

He used to be put down for naps in the front room where nobody went – it was kept for best. I'd creep in when he was asleep and try and kiss him because I thought he was so gorgeous! Then I'd have to sneak out again and pretend I hadn't been in there because we weren't meant to disturb him.

It was only later that the first inklings of David's disabilities began to peep through:

I remember being aware that something wasn't right. Perhaps some strain in my parents. But nobody ever put a name to it, and I didn't connect that strain with this gorgeous baby that Johnny and I adored.

In the end, the first name she heard given to her brother's condition was delivered in the savage vocabulary of the school playground:

Someone at school said to me, 'Your brother's a mongol!' I denied it vehemently. To be a mongol seemed like something so terrible – yet nobody had ever told me that anything was the matter with my beautiful brother.

David was officially diagnosed with Down's syndrome at three months. But the more concerning diagnosis for his family was the news of his heart defect: Fallot's Tetralogy.

The fact that he had Down's syndrome was neither here nor there. I don't think we ever thought of that as a 'problem'. That was our normal. Love grows to fit the space available. He fitted brilliantly into our family, and we were insanely proud of everything he achieved. But his heart was the real problem.

The effect of David's heart condition was immediately apparent. His skin constantly betrayed the blue tinge of cyanosis due to his deoxygenated blood, and he'd suffer frequent attacks of cardiac asthma – gasping for breath and choking while the children listened anxiously. Nights were the worst:

He had a tin lantern burner device beside his bed that burned Wright's coal tar to help him breathe. It cast a flickering light, and the smell of it would pervade the whole house. To this day I love the smell of Wright's coal tar – if the lantern was burning there was always a sense of relief. We knew that David was asleep – at peace – not suffering. But there were times when the coal tar just wasn't enough.

Yet short-term help was soon on its way. When David was six years old he was offered a surgical procedure called a Potts shunt, to help relieve the pressure on his cardiac system. It wasn't a moment too soon:

Potts was a stopgap. It wasn't a cure, but I don't know how long he would have lived without it. David went down to the operating theatre wearing his favourite knitted hand puppet, which he called 'rag puppet', to keep him company. The operation took all day. I remember us sitting watching TV that evening – Mum and Dad chain-smoking, waiting for the call from the hospital. Then the phone rang. They said he was out of theatre and doing well. I can remember both of my parents crying with relief. When they came back from the hospital they told us that David still had the little knitted puppet on his hand, so we knew he was okay.

The effect of the surgery was immediate, and felt miraculous:

I'll never forget it. He was just a completely different colour – his hands, particularly the tips and nails, had always been purple, like the colour of a varicose vein. But I can remember turning his hands over in mine and saying, 'Mummy! He's got pink fingers!' It was like he'd been mended. He looked like a sort of angel version of himself.

The respite would prove to be all too brief:

For a little while he was more mobile. He could walk as far as the top of the road with the dog. He could get up the stairs at bedtime. But by the time he was ten his abilities had faded. My brother Johnny used to have to carry him up to bed on his back.

David went onto the waiting list for further surgery – this time to tackle the underlying problem of Fallot's Tetralogy. The waiting took forever, and as each year passed David's heart grew more damaged. The family were desperate – and when they witnessed younger children being treated ahead of David their desperation turned to frustration:

He'd be admitted to the hospital ward for monitoring, and I remember my mum saying, 'That child over there in that bed wasn't even born when David went on the waiting list, and he's just been treated!'

245

When the date for David's operation finally came through, there was a genuine feeling of optimism – a bright new start. On the night before the operation the family gathered around David's bed in the hospital, laughing and joking. Heidi was happy to leave him there and return home.

But later that night, tears began to roll down Heidi's face.

I suddenly thought, 'I'm never going to see David alive again.' I just knew. Maybe deep down I'd been suppressing the knowledge that this was a very risky surgery. Maybe deep down I knew that.

The next day, the family went to the hospital to wait for David to return from surgery, but Heidi didn't go with them. Instead, she spent the day painting a small boxroom that she used for her writing. She needed something to occupy her. She glanced at the clock repeatedly as the hours ticked by:

He went down to surgery early in the morning. We were told it would be about eight hours. They'd all gone to the hospital after lunch, as he was due out around two. Then I saw their car pull up outside. They seemed early. I came down and I said, 'How is he?' Johnny said, 'He didn't make it.'

The open-heart surgery had required David's heart to be temporarily stopped in order to perform the necessary repairs. Yet once the surgery was complete, the surgeons weren't able to restart it. It had deteriorated so much over the years of waiting that it couldn't be persuaded to beat again. My brother-in-law died on the operating table.

His shellshocked family returned home. They continued to receive 'good luck' calls, and 'how-is-he' visits, and 'get-well-soon' messages from David's friends, teachers and neighbours. Each time they had to relay the simple, terrible news to fresh tears. David was gone.

The next days were overtaken by a new urgency. David had died on the Tuesday before Easter. They wanted him back home for burial before the long Easter break, or else he'd be alone in the morgue all that time. He belonged with his family. Yet there was a frustrating two-day delay in getting the documents from the hospital necessary to release his body, leaving them with a desperate dash on Thursday afternoon to get the death certificate so that the undertakers could collect him.

It was only years later that they learned what had happened to David and his heart in that unexplained two-day delay.

The burial took place the next week. Heidi's mum wanted David buried in his own clothes, so she and Heidi picked out some of his favourite things to wear. It turned out to be a positive experience for them both:

> There was a pair of cords he looked nice in, and he had new slippers for the hospital that he'd been particularly delighted with, so we buried him with those. There was also a He-Man action figure that he loved, so that went in too. After that we felt better about things. We'd got him back. We were looking after him again, even though he was dead.

The funeral service was moving and very well attended. David had touched a lot of lives in the parish. Yet the burial was harrowing. It poured with rain at the graveside. The family were all soaked to the skin.

They didn't have a large gathering afterwards. In the evening, the family went for a sombre meal in one of David's favourite restaurants. They reminisced quietly about the son and brother they'd lost. They tried to make sense of what David had meant to them all:

We weren't really physically demonstrative with each other as a family. We weren't very 'huggy-kissy'. But the thing is, everybody hugged and kissed David. We all told him we loved him. David was a touchstone for our family, a nodal point for our collective love. When we lost David we lost so much more than a person – we lost our means of communicating with each other. People talk about a child like David having 'special needs'. But David was himself special; he fulfilled our special needs.

David had been her family's sacred heart. The rhythmic beat of a demonstrative love pumped through the arteries of their world. He'd replenished and sustained the best parts of them. And now his sacred heart had been taken from them.

In more ways than they knew.

* * *

January 2000. It's my tenth year of marriage to Heidi, and we have a four-year-old son. Reports about the Alder Hey organs scandal have been peppering the television news for months. It's shocking stuff. The organs of dead children had been removed from their bodies without the knowledge or consent of their families for the purposes of private medical research. The practice had been particularly widespread in Liverpool, where it was discovered that Alder Hey Children's Hospital had illegally retained and stored 2,080 children's hearts, 800 other organs and 400 human foetuses over many years. A pathologist called Dick van Velzen had authorised the harvesting of children's body parts on an industrial scale. Organs were kept in a crowded basement. The body parts were inadequately documented and badly preserved. The practice had become routine procedure – long established, and increasingly estranged from any ethics, family dignity or legal rights.

Being from Liverpool, we felt a particular empathy with the families. Yet David had never been treated at Alder Hey hospital, so we didn't feel directly involved.

Heidi recalls the night that changed:

One night it was announced on the news that children who'd been treated for heart problems at David's hospital were also affected. It gave a number you could ring to make enquiries. I rang the number straight away. The lady on the phone was kind, but businesslike – clearly well trained. I gave her David's dates and details and she said she'd be in touch. But we heard nothing at all, and after months went by the matter drifted from our minds. We assumed that everything must be all right.

We assumed wrong. After almost a year, the telephone rang:

I was in our kitchen standing by the cooker, chopping something. I picked it up. 'Is that Heidi Thomas?' It was Alder

Hey. 'We've been trying to get hold of you. It does appear that your brother was involved in the organ scandal. We've found his heart.'

I remember the rush of blood to my head. The lady said, 'We can assure you it's been kept in very respectful circumstances. It had its own jar.'

The hospital had stolen David's heart after his surgery to use as a research specimen. They'd conducted an unauthorised postmortem on him in that two-day gap when the family had been waiting to bring his body home. They'd taken David's heart without asking, or providing any information. We found out later that, relatively speaking, David's heart had, indeed, been well kept. Van Velzen had harvested organs so haphazardly that many were stored in appalling conditions – piled in buckets and badly documented. Yet David's heart was logged and exhibited as a prime example of Fallot's Tetralogy, and so had been successfully traced.

The next ordeal for Heidi was how to tell her mother. She'd come to babysit for us one evening when Heidi broke the news. It was an agonising scene:

My mum just ran out of the room. As though the news was an animal from which she had to escape. When she could finally speak, her anguish spoke for all of us. 'It was the first time I'd ever let him out of my sight,' she said.

In spite of these events, the hospital then asked if David's heart might be retained by them for medical research. The family, perhaps not surprisingly, weren't inclined to turn a medical theft into a donation. They requested the immediate return of David's heart for burial. Later that month, two women arrived at my mother-in-law's home in Liverpool to complete the necessary formalities – a legal administrator and a counsellor. Heidi sat with her mother in support:

They brought out a sheaf of legal papers an inch thick – so many documents. They told us we'd have to sign two forms so David's heart could be released. My mother's face was like thunder. She told them: 'You didn't ask me to sign when you took his heart away. So why should I sign to get it back? His heart is mine. It was always mine!' She wouldn't sign. The women were respectful. Kind. I knew that the only way we'd get his heart back was to sign those forms, so I offered to do it. In the end I think Mum and me signed one each.

Alder Hey paid for the funeral and the casket: a small polished pine box about a foot square. David's grave was reopened. The box arrived in its own hearse – it was so small that the undertaker carried it on his knees. Heidi's brother John carried it from the car in his arms. The graveside ceremony was short and intimate:

It was a winter's day. And the thing I remember most is that as the box went into the ground the sun came out, bursting through the clouds. When we'd buried him it had poured with rain. And now the sun had come out.

Tears well up in my wife's eyes as she remembers:

It felt as though it was finally completed. That first time – that terrible rain – he wasn't complete. Because we didn't know his whole story. We didn't know what had happened to him. You can't bury the whole person if you don't know their story.

Afterwards, the Alder Hey Trust offered every family a settlement of five thousand pounds. My family took the payment, and the matter was finally closed. Heidi's mum gave Heidi a portion of the money and told her to buy something to remember David by. Heidi bought an exquisite pair of candlesticks – delicate silver stems that now have pride of place in our home.

Every Christmas Day Heidi places a ribbon on the stems and a fresh candle in each. She places them at the heart of our table as the family gathers to celebrate. Heidi calls them 'David's candlesticks':

When I put them on the table now, I never think, 'Those are the Alder Hey candlesticks.' They're David's candlesticks. The crime of Alder Hey was to not perceive a child as part of a family. Most of the children whose organs were harvested had been ill or disabled all their lives. Because of that they were exceptionally well loved and protected by the siblings and parents that cared for them. Those families were going to feel that child's loss incredibly keenly – and if you ransack the child's body without consent you don't just cause pain, you deny that family a considerable gift in their hour of bereavement: the choice to give something of the love they felt. That would have helped so much in healing, and I expect it would have been more helpful to medical science than organs spilling out of buckets onto a laboratory floor. Now when I look at those candlesticks, Alder Hey doesn't enter my mind. We've taken repossession of him. Now his life speaks as loudly as it ever did – but of the things that mattered when he was alive. Love. Light. Family. That's our victory.

The scandal of Alder Hey was one of consent, not idle sentiment. My family, like many others, are lovers of medicine and keen organ donors. If asked, we would likely have allowed David's heart to be used to help others. But our consent was not considered relevant. David's failing organ wasn't seen as belonging to him or his family any more, despite years of heroic nurture. Someone felt sufficiently entitled to take David's heart without asking. This attitude was a self-inflicted wound dealt to medicine by its own narrow assumptions, and not by the emotions of its victims.

A 'greater good' without the free consent of all parties is neither great nor good.

The lessons of Alder Hey are central to the credibility and survival of public medicine in our society. Public health is nothing if it can't speak directly to the hearts of the humans it serves. To do this it must understand the true nature and rhythm of human care beyond a heart's narrow function. A family's heart is about more than physiology, blood, or the sum of chromosomes. It's more than the things assigned by genetics or accidents of biology.

It's what we choose that makes us who we are, and the people we choose to love that governs the health of the hearts assigned to us.

7

NECROSIS

Necrosis n.

1. The death of cell tissue due to disease, injury, or failure of blood supply.
2. From the Greek νέκρωσις, meaning the state of death, or the act of dying.

MEDICINE

You will die.

That's the beautiful, terrible, simple truth of it. A biological fact, a medical reality and a genealogical axiom. You can walk around it, rationalise it in faith or medicate against it, but it won't change the ultimate outcome. Implicit in the fact of your existence is the inevitability of your extinction.

You will die. Maybe soon. Maybe not for many years. But you will.

It's little wonder that this fact holds our species in such a metaphysical grip. If malady is the antagonist that drives the heroes of a family through the chapters of their story, then death is the implacable judge that subjects all of our life's actions and

255

choices to the summary verdict of others. In the end, our free will is as worthless to us as our possessions. The capacity to tell our own story ceases. We become the narrative property of those who follow.

In medicine and science there are many different kinds of death, and many dimensions to it – from the microscopic expiry of an organism's cells to the mass extinction of a species. Death in nature is a process as well as a tragedy. It's intimately bound to the life it extinguishes, and the change it induces can be productive as well as painful.

At the cellular level, death has a natural role to play in the functioning of the wider system. Apoptosis is the name given to a naturally occurring process of programmed cell death in our bodies. Sometimes our cells need to die for the greater good. It might be that they've become damaged, infected by a virus, or their destruction is required to make way for new growth or development. In these cases an orderly death of the cell takes place. Proteins and enzymes break down the cell components, and then specialist roving phagocyte cells move in to mop up and remove the debris. This leaves adjacent cells healthy and unaffected. Menstruation in women involves cell apoptosis, as does the development of separate fingers and toes in foetal growth. Constructive death plays a part in the very stuff of human life.

That said, some kinds of natural death feel anything but constructive. Early-stage foetal death, commonly known as miscarriage, is one such example. The chance of losing a baby after less than twenty weeks' gestation is reasonably high – about one in ten for women under forty. The body can spontaneously abort a foetus if there are problems with its development and

genetic abnormalities are evident in more than half of the foetuses miscarried in the first thirteen weeks. As with apoptosis
at the cellular level, a foetal death may serve a greater biological
good, yet it can bring a lasting emotional cost to those who
suffer it.

One kind of biological death can be very costly indeed.
Necrosis – the unnatural death of living cells – occurs in the
human body when an external agent causes a cell to decompose
and die prematurely. This might be due to bodily infection, a
venomous poison or an injury like frostbite. The affected cell
swells and bursts, and its contents are dispersed. This disorderly
destruction of the cell, and the subsequent response produced by
our immune system, prevents the phagocyte cells from mopping
up the cell debris in a controlled way, as happens with apoptosis.
Material released by the destroyed cell can then damage nearby
healthy cells, spreading necrosis and placing the whole of the
human organism at risk. A well-known example of necrosis in
human tissue is gangrene.

Gangrenous necrosis develops when the blood supply to
tissues is blocked – often in the body's visible extremities –
depriving those cells of the oxygen and nutrients they need to
survive. This can happen through poor circulation, or due to
medical conditions like diabetes or high blood pressure. It can
also be induced by severe cold or damage to our blood supply
through injury or surgery. The most common kinds are dry
gangrene and wet gangrene. Dry gangrene, though serious,
rarely results in human death because the damage is localised,
non-infectious, and slower to spread. Removal of the dead tissue
at the affected extremity will normally lead to full recovery.
Wet gangrene is more dangerous. In this case, the gangrene

becomes bacterially infected or 'wet' – so-called because of the stinking pus that quickly builds in the affected area. This can lead to sepsis, and if the gangrene and infection isn't treated and removed immediately the patient may die.

But perhaps the most fearsome necrosis of all is one that hides itself from sight. Gangrene of the skin on fingers and toes has a ghoulish but helpful appearance. Blackened flesh is easy to notice and diagnose. But what if the gangrene is hidden deep inside our bodies? What if an essential part of our functioning system suddenly suffers a loss of blood and begins to die inside of us? Would we know what was happening? Would medics be able to diagnose the problem in time, and excise the essential tissue before the infected gangrene ate our life away?

A necrotic crisis like this can occur as a side-effect of acute intestinal obstruction. An intestinal obstruction is a condition where the passage of digestive waste along our intestines suddenly becomes blocked. The intestines connect the stomach with the anus, and serve the key function of absorbing nutrients and water from the food and drink we consume, while discarding the waste products. Food is pushed along the eight metres or so of our bowel by a synchronised and unconscious process of muscle contractions called peristalsis. It passes through three sections along the way. The first is the small intestine, which absorbs most of the nutrients in our food; then the large intestine, where water is removed from the waste, thereby creating a stool that's eventually passed on to the rectum to be ejected.

The intestine can become blocked in a number of ways. It might be obstructed by a cancerous tumour that forms in the abdomen. It may be caused by a condition called diverticulitis – a severe inflammation of bulges in the lining of the bowel. It may even be the result of a foreign object ingested by the patient. Yet one of the more common causes of intestinal obstruction is the presence of abdominal adhesions.

Abdominal adhesions are fibrous bands of scar tissue that form as a result of previous surgery, and can attach themselves to organs and tissue in the abdomen. When a patient's abdomen is cut open and operated on, injury to the internal tissue will inevitably occur. A gluey substance called fibrin forms over the internal wound to help seal it, but this can sometimes collect into a permanent sticky adhesion that then attaches itself to nearby body parts. If these bands of scar tissue attach themselves to the intestine and pull it out of shape, then it can become knotted like a twisted water hose, cutting off the flow of waste. This will lead to the complete breakdown of the digestive system, and require urgent medical intervention. But that's not the only problem. The adhesion can also cut off the blood supply to the twisted part of the bowel. This means that the intestinal cells get starved of oxygen, and become necrotic. Gangrene then spreads along the blocked intestine and perforates the intestine walls, becoming infected or 'wet' due to the highly microbial content of the bowel. Peritonitis – a serious inflammation of the lining of the abdomen – will likely follow. If untreated, the patient will soon slip into septic shock; their body overwhelmed by the infection now assaulting their immune system. From perfect health, a sufferer can be dead of an intestinal obstruction within a matter of days.

This kind of malady is no respecter of wealth, age, celebrity or talent. Singer Maurice Gibb of the Bee Gees died suddenly

following a constriction to his bowel in 2003. Elizabeth Branwell, the Brontë sisters' much-loved aunt, fell ill with a bowel
obstruction in 1842 and succumbed in the most agonising
manner. Without the mercy of modern surgical intervention or
painkilling drugs, she took a whole four days to die. Her nephew
Branwell Brontë, who was at Elizabeth's bedside, described the
horror of it: 'I am incoherent . . . I have been waking two nights
witnessing such agonising suffering as I would not wish my worst
enemy to endure.'

In 1956, US President Dwight Eisenhower was taken critically
ill with an intestinal obstruction. Adhesions were discovered
from an earlier operation on his appendix, and his life was saved
by timely emergency surgery. Surgical intervention to repair a
constricted and necrotic intestine usually involves cutting away
the gangrenous parts of the bowel and stitching the shortened
healthy parts back together in a procedure known as an anasto-
mosis. Yet even if this is successful, a patient won't be clear of
danger. The associated infections caused by a bowel obstruction
are, in themselves, enough to kill. Septic shock claimed the lives
of actor Christopher Reeve, boxer Muhammad Ali and composer Gustav Mahler.

It's sobering to think that scar tissue left by an earlier surgeon's good intentions can go on to wreak such damage in our
abdomen. Perhaps it was the earlier removal of a troublesome
appendix, or the timely excision of a cancerous tumour. Or, if
one is a woman, it might have been to increase the chance of
new life, by removing obstructions to conception.

Endometriosis is a condition in which the tissue normally
seen in the womb lining or endometrium develops abnormally
outside of it, in places such as the fallopian tubes or ovaries. This

alien tissue can block the normal functioning of the reproductive system and prevent conception. Endometriosis is an incurable condition that affects an estimated two million women in Britain. In some cases endometriosis can lead to the growth of an endometrioid cyst – a large, non-cancerous lump of endometrial tissue that accumulates around a woman's ovaries and renders her infertile. These cysts can grow to many centimetres in diameter; however, if they're surgically removed, a woman might gain a priceless window of fertility before the endometriosis reasserts itself once more.

Yet the scar tissue that results from a procedure to bring life into the world can ultimately be the agent of a life's destruction.

Death and life are intimate dance partners in the music of time – the double stave on which we write the libretto of our collective history. Every narrative requires an antagonist to move its hero to action, and an inevitable coda by which their actions are given meaning and structure. We all die. Maybe soon. Maybe not for many years. Yet implicit in the fact of our expiry is an acknowledgement of the unique and transient melody that precedes it. Everything that dies also lives, and life is the single orchid-frail composer that pens the deathless music of our family through the ages.

History

The Boat that Didn't Sail: Heidi and Stephen McGann, 1990–present

I married Heidi in the summer of 1990. It was a beautiful day. The setting was an Anglican church in south Liverpool where

Heidi's ancestors had married and been christened. To a keen family historian like myself, it seemed especially fitting. It was also the union of an Anglican with a Roman Catholic – an ecumenical service involving so many different clergy on the altar that it was surprising the bride and groom could even squeeze on. We were amused to watch the church's divided congregation during the service – groom's Catholic relatives to one side, bride's Anglican family to the other – ostentatiously crossing themselves or not depending on the petty distinctions of their faiths. But everybody was united in all the important things. Two families were joined, and a new branch of McGanns was created at its junction point.

I remember signing the register in the church. I placed my erratic signature on a public document for posterity once again. I recalled my barely adult scribble on my father's death certificate six years before, and felt the gentle turning of cogs marking the passage through the documentary milestones of my genealogical lifespan. In centuries to come, a descendant might retrace this small breadcrumb trail of legal documents as the only clear evidence of my life. The only information left of me, like the bleached bones of some ancient villager found by archaeologists – a fragmented skeleton from which a living human must be invoked. As I've done the same thing with my own ancestors, I find the idea strangely comforting. There's humility and practicality to it. All that lavish passion and struggle we experience in life dissolves away like soft tissue in soil over time, until only the bare documentary bones are left – a modest skeleton whose story future generations are free to imagine for themselves. Our immortality is a distracting fiction. Narrative is the privilege of the living, not the dead.

My brother Mark was my best man, my sister was a brides-
maid, and my other brothers entered into the spirit of the
occasion wonderfully. Despite the tensions that could simmer
in those days, there was always a love between us. There were
also new McGanns. Joe had a young daughter now, and Paul
a son. There were separate partners, separate homes – separate families to forge with our common surname. Despite the
cramped public persona our chosen career had chained us to,
the boys were beginning to feel the same cogs turning. We were
all growing up, and this meant growing away from each other.
Old hierarchies were dying, and deep down we all knew it was
a death that served a greater good.

Champagne flowed, tears fell, and music played. Afterwards
Heidi and I honeymooned in Tuscany before returning to our
newly purchased cottage in rural Essex. We were both twenty-
seven years old, and life was full of bright new narratives.

One professional narrative that came to dominate those
first years of married life had been brewing for some time,
and it had a moving resonance for my family and its history.
The genealogical work I'd done up to that date brought me
back time and again to the subject of the great Irish famine
of the 1840s. All the Victorian Liverpool records I'd traced
were haunted by the ghost of that one cataclysm. Although I
didn't yet know where in Ireland my family came from, I was
curious to find out more about the events that led to such a
mass exodus. The Irish famine had never been included in my
school's history curriculum, and despite its huge influence on
western history, no major screen drama had ever been made on
the subject. So, being young and filled with reckless optimism,
I set about making my own.

I took a research trip to Kerry with my brother Joe, and we developed the idea of a television famine drama based around a rural Irish family – to be played, conveniently, by the McGann brothers. I went home and typed up a treatment for a TV series, and the brothers formed a production company to develop it. We gave the company the name of the little park near Birstall Road where we'd played as children, and where I'd struggled to confront my agoraphobia. We partnered with expert Irish co-producers Little Bird, and in the early nineties BBC Northern Ireland agreed to fund and broadcast it. The brilliant Allan Cubitt was recruited to write the scripts, and by 1994 we found ourselves filming a major four-part fictionalised historical drama about a rural family enduring the horrors of the Irish potato famine in 1847. It was called *The Hanging Gale*.

We filmed *The Hanging Gale* for four months in the beautiful county of Donegal in Ireland's wild northwest, and we were supported by an astounding range of Irish screen talent – not to mention wonderful supporting artistes, local businesses and communities. Their involvement really mattered. We quickly realised why nobody had attempted to dramatise these events in Ireland before. The famine was still an open wound – a source of historical, personal and cultural pain deeper than any story some long-emigrated Liverpool brothers could tell. Yet our sincerity was real. We wanted to tell a famine story as authentically as we could, and tell it to audiences that had likely never heard it before. Owen, Susan and their children deserved no less.

So, in the strangest of ways, my family's history came full circle. Our famine was repeated; not as tragedy, but as public theatre. The McGanns who'd fled that island in penniless starvation a century and a half before now returned to it as chauffeur-driven, make-up wearing, cosseted TV actors. The blighted potatoes we farmed were props. The pitiless deluge that fell on us was delivered by a rain machine, and not by grim fortune. Narrative is the privilege of the living, not the dead. The real pains our ancestors suffered were now the narrative property of those who followed. Many of the characters in the drama died, and those who didn't emigrated like our forebears had done. My own character met a gruesome death, hanged on the gallows as an Irish rebel. It was grimly fascinating to watch a stuntman dressed as myself descend through the trapdoor to hang, wriggling on the noose. A narrative apoptosis – the programmed death of a character to serve the greater dramatic good.

The drama was a great success, with high ratings and awards to follow. Yet, looking back, it marked another kind of family death – unseen at the time but nonetheless appropriate. *The Hanging Gale* had been perhaps the best chance my family ever had to collaborate in a true 'family business'. We had an opportunity as co-producers to use the experience gained to collaborate on new drama projects – to work together as a single team on the cerebral and collective challenges of film production, and not simply compete as separate actors. When I attended the BAFTA awards in 1996 I was asked by a very senior television executive, 'What are you boys going to do next?'

It was already pretty clear to us that there was never going to be a 'next'. We'd had a great experience making *The Hanging Gale* – it had been moving, funny, challenging and reward-ing. We'd all worked hard, and we'd come away with shared memories that we'll keep forever. And yet bringing the brothers together to work on one large-scale project had made it obvious how separately we now saw ourselves – how far that public family persona really was from the private needs of its members, and how different our interests and our talents really were. Ultimately, any true family business requires a degree of collective endeavour and distribution of skills; something we simply weren't able to muster. Seeing this demonstrated so clearly in production meetings or publicity engagements was, I think, a good thing. Our shared past contained necrotic elements that it was wise to cut away. It was an orderly apoptosis that enabled new growth to form in the separate families we made, and with the separate partners we'd chosen. Although the brothers would work together again in future years, it would always be with the modest ambition of colleagues, and not with any illusion about a collective professional destiny.

Heidi was my family now. Like Owen and Susan all those years before, we'd embarked on our own journey to a different future. We'd abandoned city living for the timeless peace of rural Essex, far away from relatives. Heidi had expanded her career from theatrical playwright to television scriptwriter – regular, well-paid work that helped to smooth out the all-or-nothing nature of my actor's employment. The money that *The Hanging Gale* brought in enabled us to move into a larger house in the nearby market town of Saffron Walden. The property we purchased needed the sort of building work that only the young feel equal to – tearing up floorboards, demolishing walls, freezing in unheated winter bedrooms while we waited for central heating, and cooking meals on rickety gas stoves while earning the money for a kitchen. Yet that freezing old house was full of new promise. It had four bedrooms: our room, a study, a guest room . . . and one more. A nursery?

We'd been married for five years, but up till then we'd never felt financially ready for a child. Our previous old cottage had been too small to contemplate a baby in it, and my frequent absences for work had meant that no serious plans had been made. That said, we'd abandoned contraception eighteen months before, and we took a fatalistic view of pregnancy. If it was going to happen, it would happen. However, now we had a new home and a designated nursery, and it seemed like the perfect time to try in earnest.

But as 1995 rolled towards its end, the hoped-for pregnancy didn't materialise. It wasn't a cause for immediate concern. We knew that conception doesn't arrive to strict order – there are many couples who find this natural process elusive, and there are many biological reasons for it. But when Heidi did the sums in her head, she felt the lack of results warranted further investigation. She went to see the doctor.

Her GP examined her and said, 'I think you've got an ovarian cyst.' A visit to a specialist followed, and ultrasound confirmed the presence of a huge endometrioid cyst on her right ovary. We were stunned. We cupped our hands into spherical shapes and tried to imagine how something ten centimetres in diameter could grow undetected in an abdomen for so long. Heidi had minor pain, but nothing much. She was lucky. There are different kinds of cyst – some fast-growing and fluid-filled, twisting and bursting inside and causing unseen trouble. Her cyst was solid, slow and benign – the result of long-term endometriosis. Yet this cyst had laid siege to Heidi's reproductive system and it had rendered her infertile. The specialist was hopeful, though. If it was surgically removed it might present us with a short window of opportunity for conception. We wasted no time. Heidi was admitted to hospital in late October.

The severity of the surgery took us by surprise. It was a major procedure – akin to a hysterectomy or a Caesarean section. The surgeon had to cut through multiple layers of abdominal tissue in order to access the problem. It resulted in a long, movement-restricted recovery for Heidi. But it was successful. There was a short window of opportunity for us to conceive – maybe six months, the specialist said.

Heidi came home to recuperate in a house that still looked like a bomb had hit it. She was sad to place her fingers on the deep-lying, still-livid scar that now interrupted the smooth line of her lower abdomen. But I loved it, and I still cherish its now-almost-indiscernible shadow. When we're young we think of a scar only in terms of a blemish: a permanent defacing of some assumed perfection. But youthful perfection is really just the bland white canvas on which we later smear a more vibrant description of ourselves. Scars are like strokes of a palette knife, tracing out small features that give sense to the whole. Or like one of those archive records I love: a permanent certificate of a moment of experienced life. It might be just a minor incident – a gash from a nail or a trivial accident. It may be major – like a surgeon's wound or the signature wheal of survived trauma. But like those modest registers of death or the names on crew lists, each one has a story to tell, and collectively they build into a portrait of narrated life. Life isn't the featureless canvas a scar defaces; it's the sum of scars that give the blank canvas purpose.

By Christmas Heidi was feeling better, and we knew the time for idle procreative fatalism had passed. We'd been given a lucky break as potential parents, and we intended to seize its yielding flesh with every convenient free hand. The clock was ticking. It was time to make a baby!

We were successful almost immediately. In January Heidi brandished a positive pregnancy test. A hole in one! We were overjoyed. We tried not to get too excited. Early days. But we allowed ourselves to imagine the house echoing with new cries. Sadly it wasn't to be. After only six weeks, the pregnancy terminated naturally. We cried real tears for that unformed little vessel of our hopes. It was easy to feel despondent, after the travails Heidi had endured on our account. Yet there was consolation too. We now knew that conception was possible. We just had to be organised and resolute. Try again.

At that point our plans went west, in more ways than one. I landed a job in a theatrical touring version of the cowboy musical *Calamity Jane*, playing Wild Bill Hickok. We were in no financial position for me to turn it down, and so we carefully planned our baby attempts for those weeks when I'd be playing theatres in the southeast of England – close enough to commute from home. When the curtain came down, I'd whizz back in my car to continue my night's work. Members of the cast, aware of my efforts, would encourage my hurried exit from the theatre with cries of 'Break a leg!' and 'Yee hah!'

Once again, we were successful almost immediately. It was now late spring. I had a free week on the tour and the builders had started dismantling our bathroom at home, so we'd decided to escape to a rented house in Norfolk for a few days to avoid the mess and mayhem. Heidi performed another pregnancy test while we were there – and it was positive! As the weeks rolled by, things felt better. Different to last time. More secure. Our confidence slowly grew. This pregnancy felt like it was going to last. We were going to be parents.

We walked along those wide, pool-strewn coastal estuaries as the Norfolk breeze blew and our child grew as a tiny foetus in my wife's womb. It would one day grow to become my son Dominic – a talented philosophy undergraduate who now grapples with the deepest questions of existence in his studies. It's a source of childish amusement for me to answer Dom's deepest metaphysical ponderings with a simple theatrical fact. Regardless of the high-minded reasoning he employs to interrogate the nature of his reality, he wouldn't be here at all if *Calamity Jane* hadn't played a convenient week in Woking. So take that, Descartes.

The early pregnancy felt unreal. Heidi didn't get sick, and didn't start to show for six months. We'd watch the calendar nervously as the weeks ticked by – each week a new milestone, each week closer to the time that we knew the baby would be safe. I remember that first ultrasound scan in June; the faded ghost of movement glistening like interference on an old black-and-white television screen. The assistant pointed out the baby's tiny fingers moving and flexing on cue. 'It's a right little performer, this one!' the assistant said. I thought about my own performance career – the petty struggles and disappointments. Not if I can help it, I thought. My child was now a real thing I could see. I wanted its life to be as free from anxiety and as fully flexed as those little fingers. He remained an 'it' for now. We didn't want to know the baby's sex until we were properly introduced at the end of the year. If we got that far.

We took a holiday in Menorca in the summer, and by the time we returned Heidi had really started to show. I'd listen to her tummy and hear the sound of bubbling movement through water. It was easy to imbue our anonymous submariner with all sorts of human characteristics. 'Ooh, look!' we'd say. 'It's kicking because it likes this music!' We must have known that our child's movements were most likely random and instinctive. Yet we'd begun that process of narrating our as-yet-unborn child into full humanhood by ascribing motivation to the baby's embryonic mind. Narrative is the privilege of the living.

At twenty-nine weeks, Heidi started getting some mild but unsettling labour-like pains when she walked short distances. The doctor advised complete rest, as some women can go into premature labour following these warning shots. There were still three weeks to go before the magic thirty-two-week mark when a baby is considered pretty safe, even if premature. We watched the calendar nervously until the milestone was passed. We were told the baby was likely to be early, which would place the birth comfortably in mid-December – yet as Christmas approached, nothing. Heidi grew bigger and bigger. We banished all seasonal relatives, hunkered down and prepared for a Christmas on our own with the hospital suitcase packed. Then, on Christmas Eve night, some contractions. A Christmas baby? Heidi got herself ready, and I looked for a suitable bright star in the sky. But it was a false alarm. My child possessed a seasonal sense of humour.

Finally, in the early hours of the twenty-ninth, the real thing. Heidi took a relaxing bath, and I did a little aimless manful pacing. We drove to the hospital in Cambridge through a white-frosted early morning. The midwife examined Heidi and declared her well dilated and in 'established labour'. She spent the time between her infrequent contractions pacing the small, hot room and moving slowly into the primeval self-absorption of a woman in labour; reducing her world by degrees into the confines of the room, and then deeper into her own body. It was inspiring to watch. My life's companion had retreated somewhere I could never go – somewhere that those female ancestors had visited before her – a place of ancient pain and, before medicine could blunt nature's brute mathematics, a place of frequent death. I began to comprehend the fitting redundancy of a man in all of this. The pomp and assumptions of my gender are valueless in life's most crucial moment. We're as useful as we can be useful to the women we love. No other contribution is necessary. It's an education in humility I'm still grateful for.

The first stage of labour dragged. Three hours went by and Heidi was still no further on. The midwife suggested that she should artificially break Heidi's waters to 'speed things along a bit'.

It did rather more than that. The moment Heidi's waters were broken, things moved very fast. Within minutes she was fully dilated and the midwife was urging her not to push straight away. From a slightly-too-leisurely labour, things developed into a medical situation – not a crisis, but something from which an orderly control had been lost. Medics began to appear beside the bed, and I was pushed further to the side, my redundancy more obvious by the minute as Heidi lost awareness of her surroundings in the new waves of pain assaulting her.

Soon there was another problem to occupy me. The rapidity of the labour into the second 'push' stage had not allowed the baby's head to fully engage in the correct position. Its head was tilted towards one shoulder – known as asynclitic – placing it out of correct alignment. Also, the body was in what's known as right occiput transverse – meaning that it was facing Heidi's left side rather than aligned with the birth canal. The foetal heart monitor began to show that the baby's heart rate was dropping abnormally. I saw the concerned professional looks exchanged between the assembled medics even as their words continued calm and reassuring. The baby was becoming stressed. They needed to get it out. A young obstetrician brandished forceps and my wife was cut open. Things moved in a blur of gowns and scrubs – barked instructions punctuated by Heidi's animal cries. The forceps were clamped to my child's skull, and Heidi can still remember the obstetrician's focused brute force as she tugged and tugged to pull the infant's twisted body free and out into the world.

Time stood still in the cacophony. And then a single adult voice was heard – professional relief devoid of emotion.

'It's out.'

There was no cry. Wasn't there supposed to be a cry?

I caught a blurred glimpse of blue-coloured flesh – like a little dolphin – as the staff huddled around the newborn and carried it to the resuscitaire to clear its throat of mucus. A bustling silence.

Seconds went by. And then at last I heard it. Not a full cry. More of a slow, bruised groan.

Heidi's look of relief and joy cut through the agony and delirium. The midwife carried the little groaning thing over to me so I could announce its gender. I saw its face for the first time. Red and bruised from the grappling tugs of forceps – grimacing with pain and the glare of lights.

A boy. I had a son.

We'd chosen two possible boy's names. Patrick and Dominic. Heidi couldn't see his face, so asked me which one he most looked like. 'Dominic,' I said, resolutely. 'Definitely Dominic.' It's possibly the only major family decision Heidi has ever entrusted to me, and I think she still regrets it. But my son seems very happy with his name.

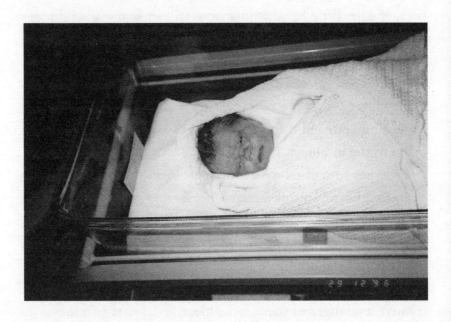

Heidi had to be whisked away to be stitched up, so I was surprised to find myself alone in a recovery room with my new child. Dominic. The 'it' now had a name. The name now had a real face and eyes and tiny fingers. Full humanity. Dominic lay wrapped in blankets on the bed while I sat beside him in a chair. It seems astonishing to me now, but I didn't pick him up in that room. Not once. In truth I was too nervous. It was like I'd been given a delicate instrument to handle with no instructions for operation. I sat really close to him and lightly stroked his battered face. The forceps had left him looking like a prize fighter after a bout. Every ten seconds or so he'd make a sad groan.

'There, there, son,' I said.

A son. I'm a father. A parent. I was going to know this little prize fighter for the rest of my life. He'd be someone I'd love beyond all things. I knew this already. Yet sitting there felt ... strange. That little bundle of bruises and fingers looking up at me seemed so unfamiliar. Who is he? Who, now, was I?

My brother Paul gave me what I still think is the most useful advice any parent ever bestowed on me. He said:

Meeting your child for the first time is like meeting any other human being. They're not just a projection of yourself – they're a brand-new individual, with all of their own unique likes and characteristics. Some parents say the instant you meet your new baby it's like you've known them all your life. Well good for them! But for the rest of us I suspect it's a bit more like real life. Don't be surprised if your kid feels like a stranger to you at the start – they are! But you're a stranger to them too. Imagine if I told you that a stranger was about to walk into the room that you'd know and love for the rest of your life. What would you do on that first meeting? You wouldn't sit there worrying about how little you knew about them – you'd start to get to know each other!

Love isn't pre-written, just like a family isn't pure genetics. It's the thrill of discovering a common new joy in lives beyond our own experience. Something found, not something always known. Eventually Heidi was wheeled into the room to join us. Our new family was united at last. She looked askance at me through her exhaustion.

'Haven't you picked him up, yet?'

'We've just been getting to know each other,' I said.

Over the next days and weeks, Heidi and I got to know our beautiful new son a whole lot more. We took him home to our new house, and placed him in the Moses basket at the bottom of our bed, listening for his hungry snuffles in the night. We'd lie with him between us in the evenings – exhausted and ecstatic – not quite able to believe that the doctors had allowed such a complex creature to leave the hospital in our amateur custody. His bruises quickly faded, and his little body began to put on healthy weight. We learned how to bathe him together – an operation that resembled a tricky bomb disposal in the hands of new recruits, but gradually became second nature. There was, however, one task I felt eminently qualified to do alone. I went to register my new son's birth.

In those days, the picturesque local register office was housed on the first floor of a small timber-framed building on Saffron Walden's medieval high street. I was greeted by a charming but formidable registrar of middle years and eminent heritage, who looked at my casual attire over half-rimmed spectacles as she filled in the details on the register. I recalled that last visit I'd made to the register office, to certify my dad's death. That vast municipal edifice in Liverpool, ringing with the sound of heels on stone and the flattened vowels of overworked northern public servants. Now here I was in a tiny building older than the United States, opposite a woman whose family my ancestors would have been pleased to clean for. I shared a quiet smile with my father.

'Place of birth?' the lady asked.

'Cambridge,' I said.

Cambridge. Centuries-old seat of learning on the edge of the English Fens. What a lovely place to begin one's journey as a McGann. This would be my child's first piece of primary data. He was being written into existence as a citizen of the state. He now had a beginning to his story. A future narrative.

The registrar stopped writing and looked up. She gave me a particularly stern glance over her glasses as she asked, 'And what is the name that you would like your child to *go through life with?*' Her emphasis amused me. She'd clearly had to endure frequent birth registrations by parents who chose outlandish names for their offspring, and she wished me to know she didn't approve. I told her Dominic's full name, and she seemed relieved. I must say I can sympathise. A name doesn't belong to those who do the naming. Like any fine ambassador, it should bring honour to the post without attracting unnecessary attention to itself.

When everything was in order I signed the register. Just like I'd signed for my father's death. Just like I'd signed for my marriage to Heidi. My genealogical journey through documentary time had now achieved a full cycle. A birth – a marriage – a death. Each one a key moment in my own family narrative. Each one bearing my spidery, scrawled signature. Another breadcrumb for the trail. Another turn of the cog.

In the following months we watched our son thrive and grow. We heard his garbled sounds begin to coalesce into vowels and consonants. We saw his first smile, and heard his first full-throated chuckle – surely the greatest sound nature has ever created. By his first Christmas and birthday he'd begun to attempt his first baby steps – wobbling across our living room in pyjamas as his relatives cooed and cheered, the lavish toys of an only child scattered all around.

It looked like Dominic would be our only child. The window of fertility had closed as quickly as it had opened, like the specialist had predicted. But we felt blessed. Medicine had gifted us a single new narrative, and we knew how fortunate we'd been. We've never wished for more. In any previous age the medical problems we'd had would have been undetected and untreatable. It's impossible to tell the history of a family without a tribute to the great matriarch of medicine – a mother whose mercy spares so many of us to thrive when we would have failed, or live when we would have stayed ungrown. It's the dragonfly of hope that flutters free from Pandora's box of grim maladies.

By the end of February, Dominic was beginning to scamper around with such resolution that we felt it was time to buy him his first proper pair of shoes. So one bright Saturday afternoon we put him in the car and took him to Cambridge.

It was a lovely day. You could feel spring around the corner. We went to the city's shopping mall where we knew there was a reputable childen's shoe shop. Dominic was mercifully well-behaved. He had his little feet measured, and we purchased a lovely pair of blue lace-ups for him. Afterwards Heidi and I strolled around the shops with Dom in his buggy, enjoying the perfection of the moment. A family in frozen time. Health like mercy. Happiness like the delicate filigree on the dragonfly's wing.

In less than seventy-two hours from this perfect moment, my wife would be close to death.

TESTIMONY

When we got back from shopping that Saturday evening, Heidi had a dinner engagement in a friend's house across the road. I agreed to stay in with Dom. She got back at about half past ten, and we had an early night, knowing that our young charge would have us up early the next morning.

As Heidi lay there, she began to feel the first stirrings of stomach pain:

> I remember thinking, 'I must have eaten something that disa-greed with me.' I went to the toilet and I was sick. I suddenly began to feel quite ill, so I went into the spare room in order not to disturb you if I was sick again in the night.

Heidi started to retch constantly. Then the stomach pains grew worse – the worst pains Heidi could remember – coming on like contraction waves throughout the night between each bout of retching. By Sunday morning, Heidi was moaning with the pain. I got up with Dominic, and told her to stay in bed to sleep it off:

> I still thought it was food poisoning at that point. But then I started to vomit huge quantities of bile. I didn't have nausea any more. The greenish bile started to turn darker and

darker and the waves of pain were becoming unbearable. I went up and down the landing on all fours because the pain of it was so terrible. It was like I was trying to crawl away from it.

Looking back, it seems inconceivable that we still thought it was food poisoning on that Sunday morning, and didn't immediately realise it was something much worse. I still shudder at my own carelessness – my willingness to believe that her pains were awful, but not untoward. Yet there was no precedent for what was happening. We were young and our new life simply couldn't imagine any horror so sudden or so severe. We were wrapped in the dragonfly's wings. Or so we thought.

By lunchtime things hadn't improved. I called the locum doctor out to the house. He arrived in the afternoon. When he asked what the problem was, we gave him the only explanation we could think of. Food poisoning:

He examined me, and confirmed that it was food poisoning. He went along with our diagnosis for what we believed was happening. He gave me a single Valium tablet and two paracetamol. He said, 'Have one paracetamol every four hours, and by tomorrow you'll feel better.'

It was a serious misdiagnosis. If he'd listened carefully to Heidi's intestines he'd have detected no sound of activity – a sign of serious malfunction. It was an oversight we'd later overlook in light of the medical efforts that followed. An overworked locum, forced to draw hasty conclusions from the information provided by a patient who didn't wish to make a fuss.

By the evening of Sunday it was obvious the paracetamol wasn't going to do the trick. The pains had actually become less extreme – but the vomiting of bile continued. And the pains had now been replaced by fever:

I had a feverish night with episodes of vomiting bile. I was back in our bed, but I was drifting in and out of consciousness. By the Monday morning, I . . . I'd just never felt so ill in my life.

Deep inside Heidi's body, there was a gruesome unseen reason for the easing of her stomach pain:

The reason that the pain had stopped is that my intestine was dying off – and as it rots, it kills off the nerves that cause the pain. There I was thinking, 'Oh good, it's gone off a bit.' I remember the roof of my mouth was covered in this sort of slime, and I couldn't get warm. That was the beginning of sepsis.

Wet gangrene was spreading along her small intestine, killing nerves and infecting her blood. Heidi was slowly starting to die. On Monday morning, our childminder Janet turned up to look after our son. She left Heidi in bed and brought her some mint tea. Heidi couldn't touch it.

It was now twenty-four hours since we'd seen the doctor, and clearly Heidi was worse. I was getting agitated. It wasn't right, and I knew it. Yet I still didn't call the doctor out.

Why not? Was I a complete idiot? Maybe. All I can say is that when you're in such a situation, the wildly unlikely nightmare is hard to imagine and harder to embrace. I had no experience to draw on, and I was still young enough to believe that such tragedies are things that happen to other people. Yet there was another element too – something that would prove almost catastrophic. Heidi is incredibly stoical in the face of illness, something she combines with a very strong dislike of excessive fuss. She hates to put people out, and has a strong will – something I love her dearly for. It means that when she decides on a course of action, it's very hard to dissuade her.

Yet on that Monday those characteristics had combined into a dangerous form of delay. Heidi – though profoundly ill and feverish – still insisted that her condition was something that could be endured, and that it would all pass. She didn't want to bother the locum again, and waved away the idea. I hadn't yet reached that stage of grim resolution that would override her self-diagnosis. If Heidi said she was okay, then she must be. I trusted her with my life. Trouble was, it wasn't my life that was in danger . . .

By Monday night, things finally snapped. Heidi had been in bed all day. I locked up the house and came upstairs. It was around midnight. When I arrived in the bedroom, I was shocked by her condition. Heidi recalls the moment:

I remember you looking at me. My hands were really cold and apparently my lips were blue. You said, 'Look, are you better or are you worse? Because if you're not better then I'm calling the doctor again.' You were frustrated with me – agitated. Pacing around. I kept saying, 'I'll be fine. I just want to sleep . . .'

Heidi went off to the toilet to be sick again. I sat in bed in an agony of confusion and rising concern. When Heidi arrived back at our bedroom door she was crawling on her hands and knees, tears rolling down her face. She didn't even have the energy to climb back into bed.

That was the moment the veil finally lifted. The moment I finally stopped listening and started doing something. It was the moment that probably saved Heidi's life.

I telephoned the locum immediately. A different locum answered. I explained Heidi's condition and the previous doctor's insufficient advice. By now the floodgates of my agitation had opened into frustrated anger. The locum – doubtless busy with a dozen other urgent calls – felt the need to interrogate me further, lest I be wasting valuable time. 'Look, exactly how ill *is* she?' he said. I said nothing, but simply held out the telephone receiver towards our nearby bedroom. At that moment, my wife was giving out a chilling scream of pain that rang around the house. I put the receiver back to my ear. There was a stunned silence on the other end. 'I'll be over right away,' he said. The doctor arrived and examined her, this time listening for sounds of abdominal movement. When he'd finished, he said to her: 'You're very, very poorly. There are no bowel sounds – you have peritonitis, but we don't know what's causing it. You have to go to hospital, and I'm going to stay until the ambulance comes.'

I asked the doctor what it could be. 'If you're lucky it's a burst appendix.' I remembered that such a malady had delayed Edward VII's coronation, and very nearly killed him. It didn't seem such a lucky thing to wish for.

Janet arrived to look after Dominic just as the ambulance

pulled up, the mute blue lights bringing the neighbours to their windows. We got to A&E at around one or two in the morning. They were waiting for us. Heidi was wheeled to a cubicle and the nurse took a sample from her:

> I remember doing the urine sample, and it was a deep, dark red – I've never seen anything like it. I remember thinking, 'That's not right . . .'

Nevertheless, Heidi clung to a strange and touching hope, based on the date:

> It's 2 March, I thought. It's the anniversary of David's birth-day. It's a lucky day.

The nurse fetched some pethidine to give Heidi her first relief from pain since her malady had set in. Heidi drifted in and out of consciousness as we waited for her condition to be diagnosed and prioritised. A junior houseman arrived – newly qualified and courteous. He examined Heidi, and quickly fetched the senior houseman – an irrepressibly bright and enthusiastic practitioner called Mathew – who could barely disguise his relish for the challenges of his onerous job, despite hours without sleep.

'We've got your tests back, and there really is something on,' said Mathew. 'You've got peritonitis, and your white blood cell count is off the charts. We're going to have to send for the registrar.'

The registrar was woken from his sleep – just one hour of sleep after a hundred-hour shift, we later heard – and he gently pressed his hand onto Heidi's abdomen. When the pressure was released, Heidi screamed with the pain.

'We'll have to operate,' he said. 'We need to open you up to find out what's going on.'

At about four in the morning Heidi was wheeled through to the operating theatre on an upstairs floor. I followed on – as redundant as I was in the delivery room a year before, but still wanting to be all the things I could for her. It was the junior houseman, Mathew and the registrar himself who pushed Heidi's trolley – no porters being around at that unearthly hour. She'd never have more qualified attendants in her life.

When we finally reached the doors to the theatre, the registrar quickly produced the necessary consent forms for Heidi to sign. But something on the form made her hesitate.

'I don't want a colostomy,' she said.

'Heidi ...'

'I won't sign.' She was quite resolute.

'Sometimes it's the price of life, I'm afraid,' said the registrar.

'No. I won't do it,' said Heidi.

I shared a helpless look with him.

'How about if I put this ...' said the registrar. He drew a little symbol on the form.

'This means that we can open you up and ... proceed as necessary.'

The compromise seemed to satisfy Heidi. She signed. I breathed a sigh. See what I mean about a strong will?

Then it was time. As far as I could go. I gripped her hand before she was wheeled away from me through the swinging doors of the operating theatre. My girl. My life. I'd first met her through the doors of a theatre. Would I leave her the same way? I watched her disappear amongst the scrubs and the harsh lights. The doors swung closed.

Mathew stayed behind a moment with me. 'Go home,' he said. 'Try to get some rest. We'll ring you when she's out.'

'How long will it be?'

Mathew thought before he answered.

'We don't know for sure. It's exploratory. If it's something relatively fixable like an appendix, we should be done in two hours or so. If it's longer than a couple of hours, it means ... something else.'

'Something else'. My mind tried to comprehend the horror crouching behind the merciful euphemism. Perhaps a rampant tumour. A vital organ obliterated, her body doomed and inoperable. My eyes fixed on the clock. It was four in the morning.

Two hours or so. Relatively fixable was two hours or so. Six-thirty.

I drove home in a daze through the black dawn. When I arrived back, the house had already started filling with relatives who'd heard the news. Dominic was up. My mother-in-law had arrived in the night and needed a bed. I gave her mine. I set up a camp bed for myself in Heidi's study and lay down, sleepless, to wait for the telephone to ring. I can remember staring at her bookcase as I lay there. It contained all of her favourite literature – her poetry, her plays, her university readers. Her life in coloured spines and copperplate titles.

Relatively fixable was up to two hours. Six-thirty. I looked at my watch. It wasn't quite five. I breathed deeply. I stared at the copperplated spines and waited.

When the telephone finally rang, it was eleven in the morning. Seven hours later.

Something else.

Something very else.

The nurse was polite, but gave no information except to say that Heidi was out of surgery and I would be told more when I arrived at the hospital. As I drove there I tried to comprehend what had happened. What they might have found. What it might mean for her future. If she had a future.

A nurse greeted me at the ward entrance, kind but reserved. 'I'll go and get the houseman,' she said. The ward was now full of daylight and activity. People brushing past me, busy staff, smiling visitors. Complainers. People having ordinary days. How I wished I was having an ordinary day.

Mathew appeared with the nurse. I smiled hopefully, but he assumed a professional distance from the enthusiasm and fellow-ship of hours before. 'Let's find somewhere where we can talk,' he said. He and the nurse led me down the corridor to find an available side room where we could be alone.

This was it. I was in that scene I'd watched in a thousand medical dramas. They take the next of kin into a side room to tell them the bad news. This was now my part. A part I'd never auditioned for. How will I play it?

I followed them, unable to breathe. Dragonfly hope flapping its wings desperately against my ribcage. The nurse tried the first room, but it was occupied. Then another – that too was full. We continued along the corridor, the ghastly farce of it stretched out. Eventually we came to a small stockroom. The nurse showed me in.

The room was piled with cardboard boxes full of medi-cal supplies. There was barely room for the three of us to fit. Mathew and I sat on the boxes while the nurse stayed on her

STEPHEN McGANN

feet. There was a moment's pause. I sat there – ears ringing – waiting for the inevitable, terrible, life-changing words.

'Well . . .' said Mathew. 'First I just want to say that your wife is a very, very brave and strong woman. Quite extraordinary.'

'Is'. He said 'is'. Present tense. Hope like frail filigree.

'Is she . . . okay?' I whispered.

He looked exhausted. 'The surgery was very long and complex. When we opened her up, we discovered that her small bowel had become constricted and blocked by earlier scar tissue. A large section had become necrotic – gangrenous. The smell was . . .'

After a moment he continued, professional detachment slicing through the olfactory memory. Their first approach had been to remove about seventy-five centimetres of Heidi's necrotic small intestine and attempt to reattach the healthy portions of it, but it didn't work. So then they performed a more substantial right hemicolectomy – removing the existing junction point between her small and large intestines, and then reconnecting the remaining small intestine directly to a newly reduced section of her large intestine.

He took out a Biro and a piece of paper from his pocket and sketched out a drawing of what they'd done. I saw tubes, and cuts, and curling sections of organs and removed appendages. I didn't understand and couldn't absorb it.

'But . . . is she okay?'

Mathew nodded kindly. 'She's recovering in a special-care ward. But she's still extremely ill. She has peritonitis, and severe septic shock. She was very close to death. The operation was a success, but there's a real risk of further infection. She's not out of trouble yet.'

My poor girl. So much to battle. So alone. Mathew must have seen my eyes brimming. He leaned in and smiled encouragement.

'She's strong, your wife. Stronger than any of us expected.'

'Has she got a colostomy?' I asked. I couldn't give a damn if she did or didn't. I just wanted to tell her first, if necessary. Console her in some way. Ease her lonely courage.

Mathew smiled wider, remembering our conversation in the night. 'No. We managed to avoid it. I expect she'll be pleased with us for that.'

* * *

The next thing I remember is the feeling of them putting the cannula in my bladder. I remember shouting, 'I'm awake!' and there was a sudden flurry around my bed. My eyes were still closed. I was wheeled into the recovery room, and I heard a voice say, 'This woman has had very considerable bowel surgery – we're waiting for a better bed for her.' I opened my eyes. I saw the clock on the wall saying ten forty-five. I was lucid enough to do the sum in my head. Seven hours. I'd been in there for seven hours . . .

Heidi lay waiting in the recovery room until a bed became available:

There was a poor little child on the bed next to me covered in bandages. He was crying and crying. I remember trying to reach out my hand to console him. The nurse said, 'Heidi, don't worry about that now, just press this.' It was a morphine dispenser. I didn't have the strength to press it, so she did it for me. I don't remember anything after that. Not until much later.

* * *

The progressive care ward was a dim, low-ceilinged room with no more than half a dozen beds. Heidi's bed was near the window, but there was no view to speak of. Not that it mattered now. When I entered the room and saw her, it took me a second to adjust to the shock of it. Heidi looked desperately frail – pale as death. It was difficult to see her beneath the mass of tubes and machines crowded in and around her body.

> I had a catheter for urine, an oxygen mask, morphine, saline, antibiotics, and they put a nasogastric tube up my nose and down my throat to drain the bile and prevent me from vomiting. The nurses would drain it off at regular intervals. There were so many wires and bags, I thought I must have had a colostomy, but by that point I didn't care.

She was heavily sedated, which was a mercy. It was the first peace she'd known for days, and her body was still under siege. Heidi would be there with me one moment, and then drift off the next. Then she'd wake again, and it was like she was seeing me for the very first time. The memory of her look of joy and surprise when she saw me sitting by her bed still breaks my heart.

Her close family came to see her over the twenty-four hours, and the shock at her appearance was barely concealed. My son was brought in and held up to the bed. He was too young to know the momentous fight taking place inside his mother, and was happily distracted by the sterile playground of the ward. Heidi tried to smile, her body so weak she could hardly move it. There were brave grins and bonhomie by her bedside, but we all knew the battle wasn't over. And the nights to come were the worst part of it:

The nights were just so long. The effects of the morphine mixed with fever were awful. Time would stretch out. I'd have frightening dreams, full of battles, fighting wars. I suppose I was metaphorically under attack – my subconscious telling me how ill I really was. The dreams would seem to last an age – but when I woke from them and looked at the clock, only fifteen minutes would have passed. It was torture.

You look at clocks in all the significant medical moments of your life. When you're in labour, you look at the clock. When you're really ill, you look at the clock. It's like sailors navigating by stars – we chart our way through the crises of our lives by time. It wasn't the blurring of night and day so much as the extension of day and night – the despair of seeing your world shrinking to the hands of a clock. I would live for the moment when your face came around the door.

I knew it – and I was determined to make my face as constant as possible. That was my sole purpose now. In those first days my life became entirely focused on that ward to the exclusion of the world outside. My son was being cared for by relatives, so I could devote myself completely to Heidi. I'd come to the hospital as early as I could, and simply sit there. All day. Staring at my wife while she slept. Watching her dreaming fitfully – so that when she woke each quarter-hour she'd see my face. She'd smile with relief, and know she wasn't alone. The nurses were wonderful – turning a blind eye to my constant presence out of visiting hours.

Despite the terrible circumstances, these days were a time I treasure. It's a great privilege to experience the full banishment of one's own concerns, to mute the endless droning voice of shallow self-interest in one's mind. I watched her face for hours and hours. Frail and brave and beautiful. I felt a love for her that still astonishes me with its force. There was no outside. No condition on the moment. She was everything to me – and I could feel it as a physical thing. I couldn't live without her. It was no longer a romantic notion, but a material fact. I didn't want to. And each hour that this wasn't the case was an hour stolen from a future I didn't want to imagine.

One day rolled by. Then another. The medical staff would visit her frequently, checking her temperature, hoping that the surgery would hold, and that the fever wouldn't overwhelm their best efforts.

She held on.

On the third day, Heidi remembers the nurses coming to take her for a shower. It was the first wash she'd had for days, but it would involve her first serious movement since the operation:

> They put me in a wheelchair to take me there, and then they placed me on a plastic chair under the shower head. I could barely move without assistance. It was two young women in their early twenties – I was mid-thirties by this time – and that was the moment I realised what real nursing was about, as opposed to medicine.

Heidi's eyes fill with tears:

They said, 'We're going to do this together, Heidi, because it'll
make it quicker for you, as you can't be out of bed for long. If
you can just hold your catheter bag and your nasogastric bag,
we'll do the rest.' So I held those two bags in my hands containing my bodily fluids, while they gently washed me. Just
to feel that water on my head and shoulders – the gentleness
with which they did it. It was just incredible.

Years later, that frail woman they nursed would go on to
write a hugely successful television series that had exactly this
kind of nursing care at its heart. If the burning love and compassion for medical practitioners in the writing of *Call the Midwife*
has any true birthplace, it was in that shower room. Their gentle
act of care in her darkest time was a medical humanity Heidi
never forgot.

Friday arrived, and Heidi continued to improve. The doctors
started to be more encouraging. With luck the worst would
soon be past. She might be able to move to another ward, away
from the intensity of progressive care. The dragonfly's wings
could be heard again.

Then it changed.

Heidi suddenly started to feel unwell. Her temperature
spiked in the afternoon. Her attention span started to fade. The
nurses began to hurry about, and the doctor was called. I could
see their frowns. I could tell their meanings. Vital signs were
wrong.

No.

Not now.

Not after all this.

The doctor told me she needed an urgent CT scan to check what was going on inside. The danger had always been there. Relapse. Reinfection. Failed repair. Now it was real.

Heidi was distressed. I held her hand tightly as the nurse wheeled her down for the scan. I watched her helplessly as she was taken into the scanning room. Our eyes met again. I was told to wait outside. I watched the doors close behind her again. Only this time my hope was spent. The box lid had closed on the dragonfly. There was nothing left.

No.

Not now.

Not after all this.

I rushed into the nearby toilet and I found a vacant cubicle. I sat on the seat. I started to sob – great gasping sobs twisting my face and smearing my sleeve. I cried like a baby – on and on and on. I wailed. I'm crying now, just at the memory of it. I will never, never feel so helpless as I did at that moment. Never so alone as in that place. I'd lost her. I could feel it in my bones. The brave one. My beautiful, brilliant, better self. My son would grow up never knowing his mother. He'd never see what I'd seen. What I'd shared. The cruelty of it was something I couldn't bear. My mind couldn't comprehend it. I started to pray – dredging up old Catholic prayers from childhood – all those years of comfortable agnosticism thrown aside in my utter desperation and despair. I begged whoever was listening for mercy. I offered any bargain for her returning health; any price I could pay, I would. Just please *please* don't make this happen. Not to her. Not now. Not after all this.

It took a while for me to calm myself. Eventually I bathed

my red eyes in the sink and went outside to wait. The nurse was there. Judy. She sat with me. She was so gentle. Calmly running through the hopes. I'll never be able to repay the simplicity of her kindness that day.

The scan was completed, and Heidi was returned to the ward. When the test results came back, they proved inconclusive. It was a mystery. No answer – but no bad news either. Heidi remembers the medics being relieved, but cautious:

They said to me, 'When you've been as ill as you have, your body can experience these sudden crises.' They were worried about lung problems due to the sepsis – pneumonia, as well as further infection. But they found nothing. The relapse was a bit of a mystery really – so frightening at the time, but ultimately it marked the turning point. The storm before the calm.

That night she had a peculiar dream:

It was the first dream I'd had all week that wasn't frightening. I was walking through a beautiful estuary – but instead of being a single channel of water, there were little springs coming up through the sand. Beautiful little fountains of life bubbling up all about. In the middle of the estuary was an upturned boat, its hull in the air. As I walked past this boat I remember thinking, 'I haven't got to sail on that.' It was like a Ship of Death. But it was turned upside down. I didn't have to sail on it. I carried on, walking away from the boat, through the beautiful estuary. Then I woke up.

The next day, Heidi was so much improved that she was able to leave the progressive care ward and move into a general ward. It had light and life and gossiping female patients and a lovely view over Cambridgeshire fields: 'I remember looking at it and thinking, "Ooh, I can live here."'

And she would. It would be another two weeks before she left the hospital, but she'd never go back to the darkness of those previous days. Her body started to expel the mass of fluids that had bloated her when the infection had been at its height. She lost twenty pounds in a few days. The nurses laughed at her shrinking frame. She now had to adjust to a new bowel, a new diet, and a new drug regime to clear her lungs of the detritus left by sepsis: 'I was going to have to learn some new digestive habits. Living with a modified bowel is quite an enterprise.'

I'll never forget the day I brought Dominic in to see her again. He'd become a proper walker now, and toddled along the polished corridor in those same little blue boots we'd bought him that day. When he saw his mum in bed I lifted him up and he hugged her. Knowing she'd been unwell, he patted his little hand on her back comfortingly – the same way we always did with him when he was unwell.

'Aaah,' he said. 'Poor Mum-mum . . .'

'Mummy's better now, darling,' said Heidi.

She really was.

There were regular appointments – weekly at first, then monthly as she gradually improved. By summer Heidi was told that it was safe for her to go on holiday. We booked a little trip to Crete, and I was able to watch the miracle of my wife playing in the water with my little son, unimaginable just months before. Not an estuary, but just as good. His laughter was like fountains of life bubbling up. It was a precious moment:

> I remember playing on that beach. That's when I truly felt better. As the mother of a toddler I'd felt anxious and disenfranchised because of my illness. So much of mothering a toddler is about catching them or lifting them – putting them in cars, prams, chairs. Having a fourteen-month-old is as physical as mothering gets. They still won't walk everywhere, but they can run if they want to! After my surgery I didn't have the physical strength to be the mother I wanted to be for him.

There was one more sweet moment of mothering she did that summer. Dominic was growing fast, and those little blue boots were beginning to feel tight on his feet. One day Heidi put him in the pram and strolled down to the shops:

> It was a warm, sunny day. Just me and him. I took him down to the children's shoe shop and I bought him a new pair of T-bar sandals for the summer.

The little blue boots that began it all were now outgrown – like the experience they'd led to. It was time for a new pair of shoes. New shoes for a new chapter.

* * *

Present day. Nineteen years on. The memory of it still has the power to stop our breaths. Heidi sits beside me on the sofa.

So much life since then. So much estuary walked. I ask her how she thinks the experience changed her. She's silent for a moment:

There are times when I've looked back on it and thought, 'My goodness! I could have died. You could have been a widower with a fourteen-month-old baby, and that baby would never have remembered me, except for a few photographs.' It was a very striking thought for a while, but now I can hardly believe it happened – I can hardly believe in that alternative reality. The great miracle of the experience was that life continued afterwards.

The simplest thing I can say is that it stops you being so afraid. When you've dealt with something completely terrifying and come out the other side, you can reflect on it and think, 'Well . . . I came back.'

Sometimes all you need to know about life is that there can be another chapter.

And me?

I still feel shock and a rush of raw gratitude when I remember it. And I'm grateful that a part of me will always be sobbing in that cubicle – stripped of all distraction, understanding clearly at that moment what was most important. To reduce the world to the simplicity of an outward love.

Every day we live is the cleansing storm before the calm. Every day is a day that the boat doesn't sail. Every day is beautiful and fragile. Every day has the possibility for love. Every day has the delicate filigree of the dragonfly's hopeful wings sewn into its fabric.

The boat will sail. For all of us. Eventually it will. But for each day that it doesn't, life's estuary is such a beautiful place to walk.

EPILOGUE

2017. I'm lying in my bed before a new day starts. One more to add to the breadcrumb trail of days stretching back to the early 1960s. Running total increasing. Final total unknown.

My name is Stephen McGann. In two weeks I'll be fifty-four years old. I'm the registered owner of the vehicle parked on the gravel outside my bedroom window. I'm listed as the joint owner of the house in which I'm lying. I have a pension number and a legal will. I have a credit rating and an undergraduate son. I have a wife sleeping beside me to whom I'm next of kin. Published books and television scripts have my name on them. Broadcast television programmes have my name in the credits. My voice can be found on commercially recorded music, and on archived recordings of old theatrical shows. My medical record lists a perforated ear, a dodgy knee, and minor aches and pains in my lower back. My doctor calls this 'wear and tear' – a polite phrase meaning 'normal for my sort of age'. I am now 'my sort of age'; someone for whom a malady can be considered a natural outcome. I'm registered for council tax and listed as the patron of charities. My master's degree certificate hangs on my office wall. My passport contains stamps from different continents.

Me as data. A mountain of accumulated facts and natural outcomes. Running total increasing. Final total unknown.

I rise and go into the bathroom. I'm confronted by my reflection in the mirror as I enter. I see my dad's face looking back at me. I smile. He smiles back. One of his dry smiles. 'You don't know you're born, lad.'

He's right. I don't. I love him for that. I love him for many things.

I've started to look like he did at my age. That same dark hair with flecks of grey. The same crow's feet around the eyes. I love the feeling of seeing him there in my face, his ghost inhabiting me, rather than having him disembodied in my memory. I love my fifties, too. Better than any age before. I'm so much more comfortable in my skin. Nearer to my end, but more secure in the value of the life that preceded it. I'm a happy man, because I now know why I'm a lucky one.

My siblings are showing similar signs of age. The creaking joints, the flecks of grey, the crow's-feet smiles. My mum is in her eighties – frail but fit, and sharp as a razor. Every week I telephone her at the same time. Every month the family gathers from all parts of the country to share a meal together. We laugh and talk and think and smile, all old harmonies realigned. Middle age is an undervalued prime – a time when we amount to the things we've done, and not simply to the estimations and fashions of others. We are who we seem, crow's feet and all. There's honesty to it.

My son is away at university. My wife and I have spent our first year as 'empty nesters' – watching for signs of lost weight in his posted photographs, and waiting for the odd text or phone call to fill the new space left after decades of close parenthood.

He's thriving – he is funny and kind and talented. We watch him perform in student musicals, and wipe sentimental tears onto our sleeves in the tender moments. There are many tender moments.

I smile into the mirror, and run the fingers of one hand through my hair in an attempt to untangle the grey-flecked mess of sleep. Then I spy that unmistakable genetic watermark. My uneven, rough-hewn nails; crooked veins wriggling over the tendons – the wrinkled, chicken-legged flesh and the coarse hairs. Prematurely old looking, even when I was a child. I have labourer's hands, although I've never laboured on anything more taxing than a tricky theatre script.

They're my dad's hands. They're his dad's hands. And his dad's hands. Backwards through time in a single straight line to the beginnings of me.

Once, in the nineties, I was filming a love scene for a period TV drama in Austria. As the sexual tension rose, the American director suddenly stopped the camera. 'Get those filthy hands away from her!' he shouted. I was confused. He'd just directed me to place my hands on the female co-star's décolletage. I'd simply done what he asked. I realised that he was objecting to my *particular* hands. Their rough appearance was out of keeping with the genteel nature of the seduction. It looked like she was being assaulted by a peasant, rather than wooed by a gentleman. Which, genetically speaking, I suppose she was. We did the scene a different way.

There's always a different way that the things we're born with can be accommodated.

I look at my hands, and feel the echo of that ancient restlessness of the newly arrived. The tyranny of hope without the ease of expectation. My family was only ever a few meals from starvation. Only ever one wrong turn from a lifeboat in the ocean, or the removal of the front teeth by a rifle. And yet there's a thrill to that kind of restlessness. A motivating force that drives my family on and on – the stomach-churning thrill of a trapeze in flight without a safety net to catch us. Every meal is a victory. Every job is our last. We're no longer hungry, but we're always hungry *for* something.

My life is blessed by this focused hunger. It has a motivation. A curiosity. Because I can't keep still, I roll forward. My life is a gift from those who came before me, and a tribute to those who couldn't make it. Their hunger gives me purpose and direction: to endure, so that the ones who follow me might sing a gentler song, so that my son might enjoy the princeling's privilege of not knowing he's born, as my dad would say.

I look up, and catch my face reflected in the mirror again. This time it's Owen's face looking back at me, with Susan and the children at his side. Billy is there – his toothless skeleton smile smirking wide from ear to ear. Iron love smelted in defiance.

'*We are the ones that hunger couldn't kill. The ones that love and blood made immortal. Your life is our reward.*'

I smile back. One of my dry smiles. I leave the bathroom and walk back out into the bedroom where my wife sleeps. I bend down and kiss her forehead. Love in the silence. Running total increasing. Final total unknown. I go to the window. I look down through the leaded glass onto the little graveyard swaddled by bare trees. The crooked gravestones, each with their faded dedications to the people buried there.

Mary Jane Bassett. Died in 1933, aged only three years. A

child so loved and cherished she was carried to her grave by fellow innocents. A story woven by those who still carry her memory.

So who am I, finally? What does my little life mean when measured against the vast ocean swells of life and death that have come before me, and roll on through the centuries after I'm gone?

I am a single beat in the story of the family that bore me. The tiniest of plot twists in a narrative that thrusts the endless drama of our shared flesh and blood through time. I'm that man on the lifeboat, shivering. I'm my father running for dear life up a beach in wartime France. I'm my son, an infant, looking up at me with love in his eyes. I'm action and choice in response to challenge. I am will and decision made in the face of larger things. I'm more than the records that describe me – I'm the response that gives those records meaning. I'm part of a myth that writes itself into form from the chaos of history. The drama in a much larger story. A love poem to my own quiet creators, and a parting song to those who follow me.

The flesh and blood that love makes immortal.

Acknowledgements

My thanks to Iain MacGregor for believing in this book, and for his skill, warmth and good humour; to Annabel Merullo for her endless good advice and support; to Jo Whitford, Sue Stephens, Liz Marvin, Lorraine Jerram and everyone at Simon & Schuster for helping to make it a reality. Thanks also to Ann Tricklebank, Dame Pippa Harris and the production team at *Call the Midwife* for their constant generosity and help with my schedule.

My special thanks to Mary Routledge for her beautiful recollections of husband Billy; to Professor Sharon Peacock CBE for her friendship and invaluable expertise; and to my good friend Jessamy Carlson at the UK National Archives, whose brilliant research and insight have transformed my family tree, and without whom this book could never have been written. I'm particularly grateful for the recollections of my father given by my late aunt and uncle, Mary and Jimmy McGann, and for the living testimony provided by my mother Clare and my wife Heidi, placing essential flesh on the documentary skeleton.

My deepest thanks to my own flesh and blood – McGann, Thomas, Green, Routledge, Walls – for the bonds that endure beyond all maladies. To my wonderful brothers Joe, Paul and Mark, my fellow musketeers, for all their love and courage under the glare of strong lights; to my brilliant sister Clare, my cradle companion and my inspiration, for showing me the right way off the dockside; to Joseph and John, the lost boys, now found; to my brother-in-law Johnny, my lifelong comrade, and my mother-in-law Marie-Louise, whose love for her son David outlasts all wounds; to my dad Joe McGann, who I love so much and miss so often; and to my mother Clare – my friend, my guide, my teacher, my strength, my moral compass – for showing me what it means to grow.

Lastly, endless thanks to my own little family for putting up with me this past year. To my beautiful son Dominic for the light in his eyes, the laughter in our home and the well-timed cups of tea. And to my wife Heidi – my partner in time and the greatest thing that ever happened to me. For her advice, patience, comfort, support, sustenance and strength which made everything possible, and for her love which made me who I am, finally.

INDEX

Page numbers in *italics* refer to illustrations

Thomas, Johnny 215, 241, 244, 245, 246, 251
Tibohine, County Roscommon 11–13, 17
Titanic, RMS 94, 106, 107, 108–20
'tomcat spraying' 237–8, 239–41
Toxteth riots 195
transistors 178, 206, 207
trauma 123–61
  definitions 123
  emotional 123
  immune and inflammatory responses 124–5
  physical 123, 124
  psychological 127–9, 153
  shock response 124
Trench, Dr 54, 56, 57
trimmers *see* black gangs
triple expansion engine 91
Tropic, SS 96–7
tuberculosis 98
typhus 18, 42–3
  death rate 43

'undeserving poor' 17
United Kingdom census 47–8
Upper Frederick Street, Liverpool 130, 131, 141

vaccination 44–5
  cicatrix 55
  mass 45, 46
  smallpox 44–5, 54–5
variolation 45
Velzen, Dick van 249, 250

Wall Street crash 133
Walls, Charlie 132, 134, 135
Walls, Edward 131, 132, 133–4
Walls, Frank 132
The Warp (Ken Campbell) 194
welfarism 69
Whitley Street, Liverpool 89
Withnail & I (film) 236
World Health Organization 45, 124

Yakety Yak (musical) 203–8, 216
Yorkshire Post 110–11